10-07

PUBLIC LIBRARY OF
SELMA & DALLAS CTY
1103 SELMA AVENUE
SELMA, AL 36701

D1222949

101st AIRBORNE

THE SCREAMING EAGLES IN WORLD WAR II

MARK BANDO

ZENITH PRESS

First published in 2007 by Zenith Press, an imprint of MBI Publishing Company, Galtier Plaza, Suite 200, 380 Jackson Street, St. Paul, MN 55101 USA

© Mark Bando, 2007

All rights reserved. With the exception of quoting brief passages for the purposes of review, no part of this publication may be reproduced without prior written permission from the Publisher.

Zenith Press titles are also available at discounts in bulk quantity for industrial or sales-promotional use. For details write to Special Sales Manager at MBI Publishing Company, Galtier Plaza, Suite 200, 380 Jackson Street, St. Paul, MN 55101 USA.

To find out more about our books, join us online at www.zenithpress.com.

Editor: Steve Gansen
Designer: Tom Heffron

Library of Congress Cataloging-in-Publication Data

Bando, Mark, 1949-
  101st Airborne : the Screaming Eagles in World War II / by Mark Bando.
     p. cm.
  Includes bibliographical references and index.
  ISBN-13: 978-0-7603-2984-9 (hbk.)
  ISBN-10: 0-7603-2984-2 (hbk.)
 1. United States. Army. Airborne Division, 101st. 2. World War, 1939-1945—Regimental histories—United States. 3. World War, 1939-1945—Campaigns—Western Front. 4. United States. Army—Parachute troops. I. Title. II. Title: Screaming Eagles in World War II. III. Title: One Hundred First Airborne. IV. Title: One Hundred and First Airborne.
D769.346101st .B374 2007
940.54'1273—dc22
                         2007004471

Printed in China

Front cover: Al Krochka took this classic photo on D-Day morning near Addeville. All troopers shown are members of regimental HQ/501 PIR, except for the glider pilot with bandaged head and Ledbetter of C/326 AEB, kneeling at left. *Albert A. Krochka*

Frontispiece: Although the legend on the gun barrel makes reference to Bastogne, this photo of a 75mm artillery crew with the 321st Glider Field Artillery Battalion (GFAB) was taken later, either in Alsace or in southern Germany in early 1945. *George Wilson*

Title pages: Sand table briefing for 101st Pathfinders at North Witham Airfield. Identified in this photo are Capt. Frank L. Lillyman (center), Lt. Reed Pelfrey (far left), and Capt. Frank Brown (right), who is pointing. *Signal Corps via Tom Mallison*

Back cover, top left: After the battle, the victors of 3/502 display a captured trophy. Standing left to right: Lt. Col. Robert G. Cole, 1st Sgt. Hubert Odom (DSC, G/502), Staff Sgt. Robert P. O'Reilly (HQ, 3/502), and Maj. John P. Stopka (XO, 3/502). *Signal Corps, Ed Wierzbowski collection via Nadine Wierzbowski-Field*; **top right:** December 23, 1944, brought a cause for celebration to the besieged defenders of Bastogne. The skies cleared, and formations of C-47s dropped desperately needed medical supplies, rations, and ammunition. Gliders would bring in surgeons and artillery ammunition. This was one of many examples wherein the troop carrier command's pilots proved their mettle and helped compensate for the many 101st troops who were misdropped back in Normandy. Clear skies also enabled Allied fighter-bombers to destroy columns of German trucks and armor that had collected around the Bastogne perimeter. *Donald Hettrick;* **bottom right:** Two members of regimental HQ/502 in a foxhole on the edge of Drop Zone C. Both have personal weapons close at hand as one writes and another reads a letter from home. The following day, shortly after the duo vacated this hole near a large haystack, a C-47 resupply plane was shot down and crashed at this exact spot. *Len Swartz*

In tribute to Maj. Richard D. Winters, one of many idealistic and brilliant troop leaders of the 101st Airborne in World War II and a man who has become an icon, symbolizing all the courageous warriors of the Screaming Eagle Division.

(Photo taken by Grant Berry, Veterans Day 2004, Media, Pennsylvania)

CONTENTS

ACKNOWLEDGMENTS

Searching long and hard for rare, unpublished photos has long been a significant part of my World War II history research. I've always felt that a book's photo content should be relevant to the written text, should consist largely of images the public hasn't seen before, and should contribute something of unique value to otherwise available historical publications. After my previous photo book for Zenith Press (*101st Airborne: The Screaming Eagles at Normandy*), I was surprised to discover that some readers still expect the oft-published and famous images that can already be found in other books. Not wanting to disappoint expectations, I sought a balance between "classic," previously published 101st Airborne photos and numerous "new," never-before-published images.

Within these pages, you'll find the well-known classics—including the Ike/Strobel airfield photo, the image of Jim Flannigan holding a captured flag at Marmion, and the brick pile surrounded and surmounted by Pathfinders at Bastogne—mixed in with many remarkably clear and obscure photos, printed from the original negatives made by John Reeder (506th), Don Hettrick (377th), Frank Sheehan (101st Division Signal Co.), and many other World War II survivors of the great 101st Airborne Division.

Several personal friends of mine who collect 101st Airborne photos contributed images to this book. Among them: Paul Adamic, Kurt Barickman, Grant Berry, Mike Bigalke, Jim Bigley, Bob Carter, Gary Dettore, Michel deTrez, and Ron Tollison.

Nadine Wierzbowski-Field made a prodigious contribution of Signal Corps photos to this project from her late father's voluminous collection.

As always with my 101st books, I want to acknowledge the official photographers of the division: Albert A. Krochka and Mike Musura, as well as Joe "Gopher" Sloan, who took Krochka's place as 501st photographer during Bastogne until the war's end.

Captain Joseph Pangerl probably took as many 502nd photos as Mike Musura, and his contribution of numerous rare photos to this book is plainly evident. Many other individuals contributed photos and are acknowledged in the credit line of each photo. A number of veterans contributed stories to this work, notably Glen Derber, Don Hettrick, Emmert Parmley, and Lou Truax. Veterans who have mentored me across the decades and continue to do so include Frank Anness, Fred Bahlau, Carl Beck, "Doc" Brinkley, Don Burgett, Albert Hassenzahl, George Koskimaki, Dick Ladd, Jim Martin, Bob Sechrist, and Don Zahn.

The Don F. Pratt Museum's historians and Courtnay Weisberg-Johnson, Chip Cifone, and Dudley Cone also contributed photos, obscure facts, and/or historical documents. Marcel Zwaarts helped provide German unit identification. Most of the maps and diagrams in this book were drawn by former USMC mapmaker Tom Houlihan, while information regarding current landmarks near Best and Sint Oedenrode, Holland, were provided by Dutch historian Jurgen Swinkels.

My wonderful wife, Candace Ann, continues to be *beyond* helpful to me when it comes to photo printing, setting up and transmitting computer files, and proofreading both text and captions. She is a treasure and helps me in many ways. As usual, my friends at the Livonia, Michigan, Kinkos store, Michael C. Kenney and Thomas Malinky, have been helpful with photo duplication throughout this project. Hite Photo in Bloomfield Hills, Michigan, has also done valuable work printing black and white images from vintage negatives.

Many new friends have come into my life in recent years to join ranks with my older friends, each of them inspiring my writing efforts in their own way. People such as Judy Andersen, Ryan Baker, Bill Barksdale, Joe Beyrle II, Tessa deJong, John Fink, Brandon McMorries, Kristina McMorries, Charlie Newsome, Mr. and Mrs. Jim Osborne, Mark Patterson, Bob Pesti, Mark Piszcatowski, Jake Powers, Rich Riley, Jason Walcott, and Terry Webb. All these and many others, including my jump brothers on the World War II ADT, have each touched my life and inspired me in some significant way to keep writing. Thank you all for your support and friendship, which is more valuable than material riches.

During research for this book, I logged my nine hundred eighty-eighth interview with a World War II Screaming Eagle (my first took place in 1968). It is sad to see the ranks of World War II veterans thinning at a rate of nearly a thousand a day. But while we can, it is our privilege to pay tribute to these epic warriors who boldly dropped from the sky into the midst of a formidable enemy. They were indeed the vanguard of freedom in the greatest war of the twentieth century. All the Screaming Eagles, living and dead, are our National Treasure. I hope this pictorial tribute will do them justice.

—Mark Bando
Detroit, Michigan
January 2007

CHAPTER 1

TRAINING AND MANEUVERS

Benjamin Franklin predicted airborne warfare long ago, writing that "ten thousand men descending from the clouds might not in many places do an infinite deal of mischief, before a force could be brought together to repel them." Franklin's eighteenth-century idea envisioned two men each in "five hundred balloons" as a means of deployment long before airplanes or parachutes became a reality. It was perhaps fitting that the first successful airplanes would be tested, invented, and flown by this visionary founding father's countrymen.

The very first use of parachute jumpers as soldiers was slated to involve U.S. infantrymen of the 1st Division as early as 1918, but the armistice ending World War I forestalled that proposed mission. American military parachutists would eventually be deployed in combat when the 509th Parachute Battalion dropped into North Africa in 1942.

In the interim years, parachuting had mostly been confined to amusement rides at world's fairs and stunt descents at air shows. Despite small-scale experiments in the

The 502nd Parachute Infantry Regiment began in 1941 as a battalion. It was not upgraded to regimental size until August 1942. When the 101st Airborne Division was activated, the 502nd became the original parachute infantry regiment (PIR) of the division. In this battalion-era photo, new arrivals, mostly men from Ohio, are being issued jumpsuits on June 20, 1941. Two of them, identified as Rigsby (fifth from right) and John Q. Young (far right), later became members of Company G in the 502nd Regiment. Rigsby was killed on a night patrol in Holland—soon after jumping there—in September 1944. Rigsby's cousin, Gene Baker, was a platoon sergeant in the same company. *Acme Newspictures, Atlanta, GA*

H/502 PIR marching at Ft. Bragg, North Carolina, in 1943. In the right foreground is their company commander, Capt. Cecil L. Simmons, also known as "Big Cec." Simmons had been a uniformed police officer in Grand Rapids, Michigan, and a member of the Michigan National Guard before entering federal service. Also recognizable in the photo are Sgt. Elden Dobbyn and Sgt. J. B. Cooper. The troopers have been issued M42 jumpsuits with white nametapes and are carrying old-style gas masks slung under their left arms. Newer assault-type gas masks were issued for combat jumps into Normandy and Holland. *Signal Corps via C. L. Simmons*

late 1920s, the U.S. military didn't take another serious look at the potential of deploying armed parachute forces until the Russians made mass drops of paratroopers in the late 1930s.

With war clouds gathering in Europe, the German army experimented with paratroop forces prior to their invasion of Poland in late 1939. The Germans demonstrated during their blitzkrieg in the west that airborne forces deployed in small groups could seize key objectives such as bridges and even fortresses. The invasion of Crete further demonstrated to the world—albeit at a costly price to the German invaders—what airborne troops could do. The Americans and British soon copied the German example with experimental, small-scale forces of their own. A U.S. "parachute test platoon" was formed in 1940 and began testing various equipment and parachute types.

Whereas the Germans made paratroopers part of their Luftwaffe, the Americans decided that the primary job of its paratroopers would involve ground combat. After the initial experiments of the test platoon, a number of volunteer parachute battalions were activated and men were accepted into them on a strictly volunteer basis.

In addition to the glamour of belonging to an elite, death-defying unit, volunteers would be paid fifty extra dollars per month as jump pay for enlisted men and one hundred

extra dollars per month for commissioned officers. The earliest battalions were the 501st at Panama and the 502nd at Ft. Benning, Georgia (later at Ft. Bragg, North Carolina). Glider infantry and artillery units were also soon formed and a new tradition of elite warfare had been born in the U.S. Army.

The famous 82nd Infantry Division at Camp Claiborne, Louisiana, was the first large-scale unit marked for airborne status. In World War I, the 82nd had been the home outfit of the legendary Sgt. Alvin York. In 1942, the new division was loaded with a combination of old army regulars and recently conscripted draftees brought into the army by selective service. After Hitler's forces attacked western Europe and then invaded the Soviet Union in June 1941, it seemed only a matter of time before the United States became directly involved. Initially, U.S. Airborne tacticians visualized small-scale deployments of platoons, companies, or battalions of paratroopers with limited objectives. But deployment of entire divisions to open the second front became a more and more appealing idea.

A practice jump at Ft. Bragg, North Carolina, in 1943. The troopers pictured are from I/502 PIR. Their platoon leader (later company commander), Lt. Ivan Ray Hershner, is seated at left near the exit door. Lieutenant Smith is standing at the far end of the aisle near the bulkhead. In this photo, a lot of Airborne equipment is visible, including M2 jump helmets, reserve chest-pack parachutes, padded cases containing weapons (tucked behind the reserve chutes), and a coiled "jump-rope" used to climb down if a trooper landed in a tree or on a rooftop.
Signal Corps via Ivan R. Hershner

Maj. Gen. William Carey Lee, more commonly known as "Bill Lee" or just plain "Bill" to his friends, was the first divisional commander of the 101st Airborne. A World War I veteran and native of Dunn, North Carolina, General Lee was a pioneer in organizing the first U.S. Army parachute formations as well as in writing their doctrine and tables of organization. A strict but well-respected commander, Bill Lee led the division through training and into England for invasion preparation. Sadly, he was forced to relinquish command a few months before D-Day due to a heart ailment. *U.S. Army*

As early as 1942, Allied planners were conceiving and designing ways to penetrate Hitler's Atlantic Wall with test raids on the German-held coast. The Red Army was engaged on a massive scale along a two-thousand-mile front, and Russia was clamoring for the Allies to relieve some of the pressure by advancing on the Nazi homeland from the west. Starting methodically in North Africa to drive Rommel's Afrikakorps from the desert, the western Allies pushed north into Sicily, then staged for multiple landings along the coast of Italy. Brutal fighting in the Mediterranean theatre eventually slowed to a long war of attrition.

The way into Germany obviously lay farther to the north, with a massive crossing of the English Channel into France. For this epic invasion to succeed, division-size airborne units in unprecedented numbers, along with sea-landing forces, would have to secure lodgment. These units, thousands strong, would jump or glide into the areas behind the Nazi-held coastlines to attack the beach defense from behind, paving the way for the seaborne landings. The success of those debarking on the shorelines required weakening and distracting the German defenders to minimize casualties.

Back in the United States, massive drafts of military-age males in 1940 and 1941 had swelled the ranks of the peacetime army, but the picture came clearly into view after Imperial Japan struck the U.S. naval fleet at Pearl Harbor in December 1941.

On December 8, the United States had officially declared war on Japan. Although Germany's ally had been the aggressor, Germany declared war on the United States only a few days later, December 11. Some of the early parachute battalions had already been training for months before America's entry into World War II. Members of the 501st Battalion were dispersed as cadre to train massive numbers of future paratroopers, and the 502nd Battalion would be enlarged into a regiment. The 82nd Infantry Division at Camp Claiborne was divided in half, with part redesignated as the 82nd Airborne Division, and part formed as the new 101st Airborne Division, which was activated on August 15, 1942.

The 101st moved its headquarters to Ft. Bragg, North Carolina, and the 502nd Parachute Infantry Regiment (PIR), sent up from Ft. Benning, became the original parachute infantry regiment in that division. New 101st units that came from the split with the 82nd Division were numbered slightly higher than their sister units in the 82nd. For instance, the 82nd included the 325th Glider Infantry Regiment (GIR), 307th Airborne Engineer Battalion (AEB), and 80th Airborne Antiaircraft/Antitank

Battalion (AA/AT), while the 101st had the 327th GIR, 326th AEB, and 81st Airborne AA/AT. Lieutenant Colonel Benjamin Weisberg conceived, wrote, experimented with, and developed doctrine for the deployment of parachute field artillery with his 377th Parachute Field Artillery Battalion (PFAB). Gliderborne artillery units were also forming, including the 321st Glider Field Artillery Battalion (GFAB), and 907th GFAB.

All glider-borne personnel, whether infantry, medics, engineers, or artillerymen, were not initially "volunteers" as such; the army could order a soldier to enter a glider as surely as any other vehicle, such as a jeep or a truck. And while glider riders suffered a lot of casualties from bad landings and more serious mishaps, they were not entitled to receive hazardous duty pay. To further aggravate the situation, parachutists within the same division treated glider troops with disdain, and many fights erupted from the inevitable resentment. Glider-borne personnel were required to wear old-fashioned ankle gaiters with their low shoes, while paratroopers received tall jump boots with capped toes and high ankles, taking twelve eyelets to lace them up.

The jumpers were also held to more rigorous physical training involving thousands of push-ups, long-distance runs, and speed hikes covering extreme distances in incredibly short times. So, on another level, the daredevil volunteer parachutists felt entitled to scorn all soldiers they considered to be of lesser condition, courage, and motivation. Unfortunately, glider-borne troops also fell into this category. Not until the jumpers saw countless gliders smashed into hedgerows in Normandy, with their fragile human cargoes impaled and mangled, did the paratroopers' disdain for glider troopers stop. The situation was eventually mitigated after hazardous duty pay was approved for these brave soldiers and a special badge was devised to recognize glider training and combat insertion via glider.

Within the newly activated 101st Airborne Division was also a battalion of engineers, the 326th Airborne Engineer Battalion. The battalion's Headquarters and Service (HQ/SVC) Company and companies A and B were glider-borne troops; only Company C was parachute-qualified. After Normandy, only jump-qualified personnel were accepted as replacements into the 101st division. The previously all-glider companies began receiving so many jumping replacements that they began forming a special "jump platoon" in each company. The same happened with replacements arriving into the

Troopers of E/502 PIR lined up at Ft. Bragg in 1943, wearing M42 jumpsuits and overseas caps with the early blue and white Parachute Infantry patches. The patches are on the left side of the cap; until orders came down in 1944, these patches were optionally worn on either side of the flat overseas caps. After the regulations were written in 1944, all enlisted personnel were compelled to wear cap patches on the left side only, while officers wore them on the right side, so that rank insignia could be worn on the left side. Before these regulations came out, many Deuce officers wore the patch on the left side and pinned their rank insignia right through the patch. *Signal Corps, Ray Hoffman collection via R. Campoy*

PROP BLAST PARTY #2   11-14-42   Foster

Prop blast party at Camp Toccoa, Georgia, late 1942. Col. Robert F. Sink, the commander of the 506th PIR, was anxious to have as many of his officers as possible "qualified" as parachutists, which required five jumps. He arranged for an Air Corps plane to drop groups of officers at Toccoa, before the majority of the 506th PIR went to qualify at the Parachute School (TPS) at Ft. Benning, Georgia. Each regiment and its independent battalions had its own uniquely designed prop blast mug, in which assorted alcoholic beverages were mixed for consumption by newly qualified paratroopers. Each individual was required to guzzle from the mug, while the onlookers chanted, "One thousand . . . two thousand . . . three thousand . . . four thousand," just as a jumper would count when leaving the plane and waiting for his parachute to open. Drinking from the mug is Lt. Ed Harrell. The short officer visible over his shoulder is the 3/506 battalion commander, Lt. Col. Robert L. Wolverton (West Point 1938). Capt. Selve Matheson is fully visible, smiling, with a cigarette in his raised hand. Maj. George S. Grant, the XO (second in command) of 3/506, is next, standing with both hands at his side. Capt. Ernest LaFlamme is standing holding the glass, hand in pocket, while Lt. Robert I. Berry stands at far right. Both Lieutenant Colonel Wolverton and Major Grant were KIA immediately upon landing in Drop Zone D on D-Day night. *Robert L. Wolverton collection via Lee Wolverton*

327th GIR after Normandy. Another glider infantry regiment, the 401st, was split into two parts, with half the personnel serving in the 82nd Airborne Division and the other half becoming the 3rd Battalion of the 327th GIR.

The 101st also had a 326th Airborne Medical Company (AMC), consisting of division-level surgeons (all commissioned officers) as well as surgical teams to assist the doctors whenever frontline hospitals could be established. Although the 326th AMC was basically designed as a glider-borne outfit, a third of its personnel were jump-qualified in time for the Normandy Invasion. On D-Day, one-third of the 326th AMC entered Normandy by parachute, with the other two-thirds arriving in equal numbers via sea and glider. This dispersion ensured that at least some of the team members would arrive at the divisional hospital.

Meanwhile, the Parachute School (TPS) at Ft. Benning, Georgia, put volunteers through a four-week parachutist qualification course. These jump-qualified replacements were sent wherever they were needed within the rapidly expanding Airborne Command. In late 1942, many new graduates of TPS were sent to help upgrade the 502nd PIR into full regimental strength. Many others were sent to the various units of the 82nd Airborne Division, which was preparing for overseas movement by early 1943.

During that period, the 101st was completing training and participating in maneuvers and was not yet at full strength. This would be solved by attaching the 501st and 506th PIRs, but only after these independent units completed their separate training. The old 501st Battalion's members had been so thoroughly dispersed that only several former members ever entered the ranks of the newly formed unit of the same number—Colonel Howard R. "Jumpy" Johnson's 501st PIR.

The 501st Regiment existed at a later time, with all different commanders and personnel than the battalion, but it was Johnson's regiment that would establish a combat record during World War II. Ironically, the 501st Battalion's officially approved insignia, a droopy-looking thunderbird, was almost forced on Johnson's later regiment by the Heraldry Office in Washington, D.C. Jumpy Johnson and a team of artists from his new regiment made their own design and wore it throughout World War II despite its nonapproved status.

Like Johnson's 501st PIR, Col. Robert F. Sink's 506th PIR was activated at Camp Toccoa, Georgia, and received special basic training to prepare them for jump school. Unlike basic at other camps, Toccoa basic included familiarization with parachute

Col. Robert F. Sink, with help from Capt. Adam Parsons, designed the infamous obstacle course for basic trainees at Camp Toccoa, Georgia. Parsons later transferred to the Air Corps and became a C-47 pilot; he was Sink's co-pilot on the Normandy jump. The photo shows 506th men negotiating a small section of the course. In November 1942, Col. H. R. Johnson's 501st PIR was activated at Toccoa; they inherited Sink's obstacle course when the 506th departed for jump training at TPS. Johnson's men rarely used the obstacle course. He opted for distance running up and down Currahee Mountain (shown in a period postcard, inset). Donald E. Zahn

equipment, exit training from a mocked-up C-47 aircraft door, and jumps from a thirty-four-foot-tall tower.

The student jumper, wearing a harness attached to a cable, jumped off the tower and dropped fifteen feet before the slack played out. He rode a forty-five-degree angle to the ground, sliding along a slanted cable system. The tower was about the height of a telephone pole, close enough to the ground to make the mortal danger seem all the more real, unlike the false sense of security one gets from gazing out of an airplane window at the seemingly unreal and soft-looking landscape below.

Sink's regiment began training at Camp Toccoa, Georgia, in mid-1942. Using a cadre of regular army training sergeants, Sink's volunteers were a combination of regular army enlistees and selective service draftees who had just entered the service

Spencer O. Phillips from Brownsville, Texas, was a member of H/506 PIR; he was the regimental chin-up champ with fifty-six reps. The 506th had taken pre–jump school basic at Camp Toccoa through summer and fall 1942. In December, the 2nd Battalion departed Toccoa and marched to Atlanta, Georgia, a distance of 118 miles, then rode trains the rest of the way to TPS at Ft. Benning (1st Battalion rode all the way). Spencer Phillips, a member of 3rd Battalion, had to march from Atlanta to Ft. Benning, a distance of 138 miles. Lieutenant Colonel Wolverton led this march, though his feet became bloody and medics had to apply medicine and bandages. After that, Wolverton alternately rode in an ambulance and marched between rest breaks. This was a contrast in command styles to Colonel Sink, who was seen by 2nd Battalion troops riding past their marching columns in a limousine. Spencer Phillips removed his boots on one break and his feet became so drastically swollen that he couldn't get his boots back on. When the troops resumed marching, he continued with them barefoot, walking through mud puddles until his feet became so slippery with mud that he was able to get his boots back on. He completed the grueling march! *Donald E. Zahn*

Members of 3/506 en route to TPS to become paratroopers had to march the 138 miles from Atlanta to Ft. Benning. The successful completion of this march broke the world's marching record, which was previously held by the Japanese army. Individual weapons were carried, including M1919A4 machine guns weighing forty pounds, as well as tripods, mortar tubes, and base plates. This photo shows members of Company H taking a break on the three-day march; many men were sleepwalking toward the end. *Donald E. Zahn*

Student paratrooper jumping from the thirty-four-foot training tower at TPS, Ft. Benning, Georgia. This tower stood about the height of a typical telephone pole with a platform at the top. A student was secured in a harness, where he jumped off, free-falling for fifteen feet, until the lines played out. A slanted cable carried the jumper the rest of the way to the final destination, a sawdust pit. This device gave an opportunity to practice door exit form and landing techniques. It was also a test of courage; more student parachutists washed out of training because they refused to jump from the thirty-four-foot tower than those who later refused to jump from an airplane in flight. The thirty-four-foot tower was just high enough from the ground to provide a sensation of a potentially fatal fall, but the ground was close enough to be perceived as a reality. When parachuting from 800 to 1,500 feet, the ground appears as an unreal abstraction to the jumper. *U.S. Army*

and volunteered for parachutist duties. Sink's "muscle college" included a grueling obstacle course specially created for the 506th, plus frequent runs up the Indian-named mountain known as Mt. Currahee, which rose imposingly above the red mud encampment. A six-mile round trip performed in less than an hour (three miles up and three miles back) was the requirement for all members of this regiment.

Long, punishing runs and endless physical training (PT) were primary features of Toccoa basic training. Like other basic trainees, the new soldiers learned the elementals of weapons handling and firing, marching, drill, and general soldiering. Their rifle range was about a fifty-mile truck ride away in Clemson, South Carolina. When one battalion commander decided to march his troops back to Toccoa from Clemson, a competition started between the battalions to see which could march the farthest and fastest.

In late 1942, the battalions of the 506th departed from Camp Toccoa one at a time to attend parachutist training at the Parachute School in Ft. Benning, Georgia. The 1st Battalion rode there on a train, while Lieutenant Colonel Strayer's 2nd Battalion marched 118 miles from Camp Toccoa to Atlanta, Georgia—about half the total distance—and then boarded a train for the rest of the trip. Colonel Sink himself did not participate in this grueling march. Instead, he breezed past his marching troops in an open limousine. This caused considerable resentment among the troops who witnessed it.

Lieutenant Colonel Robert L. Wolverton's 3rd Battalion rode trains from Camp Toccoa to Atlanta, then completed the trip to Ft. Benning by marching the last 138 miles. Private First Class Donald E. Zahn from Minnesota was a member of the 60mm mortar squad of 1st Platoon H/506 and had been captain of the track team at his high school. Before the march from Atlanta to Ft. Benning, Zahn convinced all the members of his squad to paint the soles of their feet with Merthiolate, a trick he had learned from his old track coach. This toughened the skin on the soles of the men's feet and helped prevent blistering.

Lieutenant Colonel Wolverton (West Point 1938), the 3rd Battalion commander, suffered terribly on this march but insisted on making the long walk with his troops. At each rest break, medics attended Wolverton's bloody feet, applying salve and bandages as best they could. The intrepid officer alternated walking and riding for a stretch in an ambulance, but he earned great admiration from his men for his gutsy determination in completing the march with them.

As Sink's battalions departed for Ft. Benning in late 1942, Col. Howard R. Johnson's 501st PIR, composed of a similar mix of regular army and draftee volunteers and with a training cadre of old army regulars, was activated and embarked on basic training at Toccoa. Jumpy Johnson's training requirements

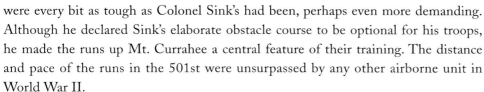

were every bit as tough as Colonel Sink's had been, perhaps even more demanding. Although he declared Sink's elaborate obstacle course to be optional for his troops, he made the runs up Mt. Currahee a central feature of their training. The distance and pace of the runs in the 501st were unsurpassed by any other airborne unit in World War II.

Johnson had served in the regular army for more than twenty years, and he was a consummate runner. He was also a ruthless taskmaster who drove everyone, including himself, to accomplish the impossible. Captain Lawrence Critchell, the official chronicler of the 501st PIR wrote, "Colonel Johnson was the friend of anyone who could bite his teeth and go on, until he was blind. The utmost, the impossible . . . those were his goals."

Jumpy Johnson was a dramatic motivator and master of group dynamics who staged adrenaline-pumping pep rallies, inciting his roaring troops to destroy the evil minions of the Axis by meeting force with greater force. Interestingly, he had only recently completed the jump course himself at TPS. Because he was afraid of parachuting, he drove himself to jump as much as possible, sometimes making three or four jumps in a single day. His obsession to defeat the inner coward caused him to log more than 130 parachute jumps before the 501st actually went into combat.

Jumpy Johnson personally led his regiment in calisthenics each morning. He would shout into his megaphone, "Who's the best?"

"*We* are!" came the refrain.

"What are we here for?"

"To fight!"

"Who are we going to kill?"

"Those slant-eyed bastards and Nazi sonsabitches!"

These responses were repeated daily until they were ingrained and automatic.

At C Stage (the 250-foot tower stage) of jump training, students encountered the so-called "shock harness." Many later agreed this was the single most terrifying aspect of paratrooper training. Fastened in a harness, the student was hauled up to a minimum of ninety feet, facing the ground as shown. Upon hearing a signal from an instructor (shouted by megaphone), the student pulled a ripcord handle, then while free-falling, he moved the handle from one hand to the other (without dropping it) and counted, as one would on a parachute jump. The instructors didn't really know if an individual student remembered to count or not, but dropping the handle while falling required a student to repeat the procedure—something that nobody wanted to do. The purpose of this device was to teach students to think and function while under the stress of falling at altitude. When the device broke in mid-1943, killing a former catcher from the Baltimore Orioles baseball team, the shock harness was discontinued. *Ivan R. Hershner*

A paratrooper descending in a T-5 parachute with camouflaged canopy, twenty-eight feet in diameter. Most parachutes used in training had white canopies made of nylon (silk was abandoned early in the war as it was too expensive and not plentiful enough). By D-Day, 60 percent of the parachutes used by the 101st Airborne had camouflage canopies (three shades of green), as shown here. The smoke over the drop zone was used to guide descending troopers as close as possible to the assembly area. On actual combat jumps, color-coded smoke was used to enable members of 1st (red), 2nd (white), or 3rd (blue) battalions to gravitate to their respective assembly areas after landing. The term *rally point,* as used in recent Hollywood movies, was *not* used by World War II paratroopers. *Donald Hettrick*

Johnson then exhorted his troops to "growl!" In the second battalion area, Jumpy would tell Company F that Company D was growling louder. Then the Fox Company guys would really turn up the volume. But Dog Company became officially known as the "company that growls" because they consistently produced the loudest racket. Johnson told his troopers, "I'm the pappy of every mother's son in this regiment," and in addition to his nicknames of "Jumpy" and "Skeets," Johnson was also referred to by some of the enlisted men as "Pappy Johnson."

QUALIFYING THE 506TH AND 501ST AS PARATROOPERS

As mentioned previously, the two PIRs destined for attachment to the 101st Airborne had taken special pre–jump school basic training at Camp Toccoa. When both regiments arrived at TPS, they were allowed to skip the usual first week of physical conditioning, the A Stage. The troops learned parachute packing and had to make their first five jumps with parachutes they had packed themselves. When packing one's own parachute for the initial jumps, it was done "like porcupines make love . . . very carefully," in the words of Dick "Farmer" Turner of B/506.

Lengthy calisthenics, long morning runs, and sessions of hand-to-hand combat training in the judo pit took up the rest of their training schedule the second week. Week three at TPS was "tower week" with individuals fastened into a parachute harness and hauled up to the top of the 250-foot-tall "free towers" to be released to practice proper chute control and landing techniques. Another feature of the towers was the so-called "shock harness," which most former TPS students agree was one of the scariest aspects of parachutist training. Glen Derber of HQ 2/501 PIR described his experience on the shock harness eloquently in his diary:

[This] exercise wasn't so pleasant nor easy. You were strapped into a parachute harness and then while lying face down on a mattress, were hooked up to a couple of rubber shock cords. In this face down position they hoisted you to the top of the tower from where the mattress took on the dimensions of a postage stamp. At a signal from the instructor standing below, you were required to pull a rip cord handle on your chest, thrust both arms out fully to each side, bring them back together, and transfer the rip cord from your right to your left hand. The problem was that pulling the rip cord released your body into a free fall, which at the end of 20 feet, was interrupted by the shock cords. This jerked you from a horizontal to vertical position and if you hadn't passed the rip cord to the other hand before this shock you were liable to drop it. This meant another trip to the top and no one looked forward to doing it more than once, besides the embarrassment! At the top, the thought crossed my mind as to whether I would be able to land on that mattress down there if the cords broke. In fact, this very thing happened, killing a man, and the exercise was stopped.

That man was a former catcher for the Baltimore Orioles named Jim Donovan. Sometime in mid-1943, he was killed on the shock harness when the supporting straps broke at the intended end of his free fall. This incident caused the shock harness to be eliminated as a training phase in future classes at TPS.

After the tower stage, all student parachutists faced the ultimate test in week four of jump training. Five jumps were made from various altitudes, ranging from 1,200 to 1,500 feet, using static line parachute systems that opened the chute automatically about four seconds after the jumper exited the door of his plane. The first four jumps at Ft. Benning were daylight jumps, and the fifth and qualifying jump was made at night in darkness.

Jumping at relatively low altitudes from a C-47 in World War II was a rather unpleasant experience. Airborne doctrine at the time called for exits a fraction of a second apart, so jumpers exited the plane practically on one another's backs, making proper body position nearly impossible. This was done to cause the jumpers to land in relative close proximity to one another on the ground. Because planes would be traveling at 110 to 125 miles per hour, even a one- or two-second interval between exits could cause two consecutive jumpers to come to ground hundreds of yards apart.

Jumping from a C-47, parachutists experienced a loud, roaring blast of cold wind generated by the left wing's propeller. (The parachutists would conduct a verbal four-second count before taking corrective action if a parachute hadn't opened in the elapsed time.) At the moment the parachute was deployed, the falling parachutist experienced a sudden jerk to the body, which would be amplified by poor body position.

Often the World War II jumpers exited the plane falling in an inverted (head first) body position, causing their entire body to whiplash into a correct vertical (head at top) position in a split second upon the opening shock. Glen Derber said that on one practice jump, he looked down at his feet before his chute opened. Instead of seeing the ground beyond his toes, he saw the plane he had jumped from. He had unintentionally gotten himself into an inverted body position. A substantial opening shock soon followed.

After making the first five qualifying jumps and getting their "jump wings," World War II paratroopers disdained any concern about maintaining proper body position upon leaving the plane. they expressed the attitude, "who cares?" The chute was going to open, and that's all that counted to them. Although careless exit positions could result in varying degrees of parachute malfunction, most of those problems were correctable while descending.

Steering and control of the World War II–era T-5 parachutes was extremely limited, and those men lucky enough to avoid power lines, highways, fences, and trees hit the ground with a considerable bone-jarring impact. This could vary depending on atmospheric conditions, ground currents of wind, and other weather factors. But

Members of the 81mm mortar platoon, 2/506 at Camp Mackall, North Carolina, early 1943. John D. Halls (third row, second from left, standing and wearing a helmet) was killed in the D-Day morning battle to take the 105mm battery at Brecourt Manor, near Le Grand Chemin, France. He was the trooper shown killed in the HBO film *Band of Brothers,* though he was mistakenly described as a member of Company A and referred to as *Hall,* not *Halls.* The 506th PIR did have a John D. Hall, who belonged to Service Company, but Hall was killed along with an entire stick from Charlie Company when their C-47 crashed near Picauville, France, before reaching the Drop Zone C area.
Jack Barickman via Kurt Barickman

jumping with round-canopy parachutes of only twenty-eight feet in diameter usually resulted in hard landings.

Parachutes also had a tendency to oscillate, which to the observer looked like the jumper was swaying back and forth like a pendulum. The oscillation was really more like swinging in circles, making the moment of landing even more unpredictable and hazardous. Seeing jumpers wearing casts and hobbling on crutches, doing the "Ft. Benning Hop," afterward reinforced the belief among nonjumpers that parachuting was a death wish for the insane. The paratroopers themselves, with their "who gives a damn" attitude, embraced views such as these that added to their macho mystique.

Each student who graduated after completing the five requisite parachute descents was then qualified to blouse his trousers around the top of his shiny brown jump boots and to wear the parachute cap patch and silver jump wings of a U.S. Army paratrooper. This accomplishment engendered a tremendous amount of pride. Members of this elite branch were now part of a tight-knit brotherhood, scorning what they viewed as "lesser" branches of the military. Woe to any glider-borne or straight-leg soldier who dared go to town wearing jump boots with bloused trousers; not even aspiring student parachutists were allowed to blouse their trousers until they had graduated TPS and received their wings.

Violations usually resulted in brawls, wherein the jumpers would forcibly remove the boots from the feet of unqualified wearers. More often than not, the targets of this wrath ended up unconscious with the boots cut from their feet with a sharp knife. Even a female U.S.O. performer who appeared in North Africa to entertain the troops wearing jump boots learned this the hard way when resentful paratroopers detonated a small explosive charge in her dressing room to express their displeasure.

The term *airborne* described an entire branch, which at the time included both jumpers and glider troopers. The paratroopers initially disliked being called *airborne troops* because it did not specify which part of an airborne division they were members of. They preferred the more proper *parachute infantry, parachute engineers,* or *parachute field artillery,* with the word *parachute* emphasizing their elite status. This would change after World War II, when even the Parachute School was renamed the Airborne School.

The 2nd Battalion of the 503rd PIR had sailed to the United Kingdom. After training at Chilton-Foliat England (future home of the 502nd PIR), the battalion was redesignated the 509th Parachute Infantry Battalion (PIB) and flown to North Africa, where they made the first combat jump in U.S. Army history. The remainder of the 503rd would be deployed to the Pacific theatre of operations, where they would eventually make the famous jump on "the Rock"—Corregidor—to liberate that island from the Imperial Japanese Army. The 82nd Airborne also sailed to North Africa, debarking in 1943, to prepare for jumps in Sicily and Italy.

Back in the states, the 506th moved on from TPS to Camp Mackall, North Carolina, the home of Airborne Command that conducted plans and training and wrote airborne warfare doctrine. That camp was named for John T. Mackall, a private in the 509th PIB who was killed on the first combat jump in North Africa. Camp Mackall became the training base for the 506th PIR as well as the 541st and later the 542nd. In spring 1942, the 501st PIR completed jump training at TPS and migrated to Camp Mackall as well. A small airstrip had been built there, and small-scale maneuvers and some parachute jumping was done there. Practice firing of weapons on the range also continued.

Glen A. Derber from Oshkosh, Wisconsin, was brighter than most of his fellow troopers. As a result, he couldn't help making sarcastic remarks about training and his superior officers. When his remarks were overheard, it caused problems for him. About one day at the light machine gun firing range in his diary, Glen penned the following:

> We were firing the light machine gun (LMG) at field targets set at varying distances, to give practice in quickly adjusting fire. Each member of [my] platoon got to fire about half a belt or so at the targets. When all had a chance at it, the platoon walked out, to examine the results.
>
> The near targets, set at 200 and 300 yards, had quite a few holes in them, but as we walked out to the 400 and 600 yard target especially, only a few holes were found. Back at the firing line, I jokingly said, "I could stand out there all day and be fairly safe!" This angered the lieutenant and he ordered me to go out there and [to] be a target. Undaunted [but] by now feeling foolish [I] took off on the double and hoped I could find something to hide behind when I got out to 600 yards. It turned out to be a test of who would turn "chicken," and the lieutenant gave in and called me back after I had run out a ways. Guess he was pondering how he would explain a dead or wounded member of his platoon.

Despite his frequent sarcasm, Glen was not a problem for his superiors, because he did not go to town, chase girls, drink too much, or cause problems with the local civilian populace. The same could not be said for many of his fellow troopers.

Lieutenant William J. Russo, a strict disciplinarian in Glen's company, decided the troops were getting lax and undisciplined. While the HQ 2/501 was on a maneuver in the woods, he led them in calisthenics and had the group sound off loudly, shouting the rep number of each exercise. A superior officer forced Russo to stop this. He stated that the shouting could be heard for miles away and to stop because they were supposed to be simulating war conditions. The men laughed about it. Derber wrote, "Lieutenant Russo was irked and gave us all a lecture, telling us this wasn't funny, there was a war on and people were getting killed in combat every day in Italy."

That evening at chow, Glen Derber's sarcasm got him in trouble again:

That same day as chow was being served in a woods, we were all lined up, waiting our turn to eat, and I started . . . repeating Lieutenant Russo's lecture. Unknown to me, Lieutenant Russo was sitting a little ways off eating his meal and overheard me. My little joke was interrupted by a harsh call from Lieutenant Russo "Come over here!" [I] quickly left the chow line and reported to the lieutenant, where I was dressed down severely and told to go back to my tent and stay there and was "under company arrest" and would be properly dealt with later, probably a court martial. I returned to my tent a very scared and worried trooper! Later, my own platoon leader, Lieutenant Mullins came to my tent . . . and asked why I, with the highest IQ in the company, was always getting into trouble this way. Lieutenant Russo had asked me a similar question, which I answered with "It was probably due to the way I was raised," whereupon Lieutenant Russo asked if I was raised on a squirrel farm and grinned at his own humor. I stood stone faced at this remark, which only infuriated Russo more. In due time, I was informed that instead of a court martial, I would be put on company punishment and be required to pull a week of KP duty. After that stint, I'd had enough of KP duty for a while. Thereafter, I was extremely careful who I made wisecracks about and made sure no one in the immediate area overheard me.

Lieutenant Corey Shepard was a platoon leader in Item Company of the 502nd PIR, also known as the "Five-Oh-Deuce," or simply the "Deuce." His wife, Edwina, was pregnant at the same time as his battalion commander's wife, Allie Mae Cole. Baby Robert Bruce Cole arrived a few months earlier than Mrs. Shepard's Robbie.

Mrs. Shepard attended a party at Ft. Bragg, North Carolina, in 1943, before the 101st Airborne sailed to the United Kingdom to prepare for D-Day. While at the party, she observed a pile of potato salad on the floor, and only found out afterward that the regimental commander's wife had been sliding through it in her bare feet an hour before.

A forty-foot-high wooden training structure at Camp Toccoa, erected by the 506th to enable trainees to practice climbing and descending on assault nets. This would have been better suited for training regular infantry units, who would debark troop ships on this type of net to board landing craft for beach landings. In actual combat, this had no relevance to what paratroopers did, but it was another means of getting men accustomed to heights. Harry Mole (left) and Joseph Mero (right) became friends; both had arrived from Camp Upton, New York, and both were residents of Long Island. Mero was fatally wounded in action in September 1944 and would die while in the hospital. *H. Mole*

Mrs. Shepard later wrote some of her reflections about that party:

> I remember going to the prop blast (big, splashy dance party the paratroopers had—the last one before going over seas). There were all those big, strapping, handsome young men oozing energy and testosterone, just passionately ready to get over there and do what they had been training for.
>
> I remember after they [the regular army] had gotten there and done the build up and finally gone in—it was what war is—this terrible reality and instant death all around, as they waded and trudged in those beaches after our guys had dropped into trees and wherever, and a lot never made it, even for a few minutes. I just never could forget how they looked at that prop blast, and there was one I remembered particularly, just because I had heard him talking so confidently and bravely, and he died in the first day or two.

Early in 1943, the 502nd was stationed at Evansville, Indiana, living at the airfield in pup tents. From there, they could be flown and parachuted into maneuvers in nearby Kentucky or Tennessee. Some maneuvers pitted airborne units against one another, such as the time the 508th PIR (home station Camp Blanding, Florida, and later to be attached to the 82nd Airborne Division) parachuted at night onto waiting troops from Colonel Johnson's 501st (not yet a part of the 101st Airborne Division.

Eventually, troops of the 506th PIR also spent time at Evansville, and in July 1943, the 506th became members, by attachment, of the 101st Airborne Division. This entailed leaving Camp Mackall and joining the division at Ft. Bragg.

At this time, the 506th began wearing the Screaming Eagle divisional insignia on their left shoulders in lieu of the red Airborne Command shoulder patch, which the 501st would continue to wear through December 1943. Although the 101st Airborne had long ago been christened the "Eagle Division," it is believed that the Deuce's boxing and football coach Lt. Bob Burns coined the term *Screaming Eagles* when he gave that title to the Deuce's football team. It was soon adopted as the unofficial title of the entire division.

General William C. "Bill" Lee had been among the earliest paratrooper officers in the U.S. Army and had been instrumental in writing doctrine and organizing and forming this new branch. General Lee was a rugged outdoorsman and a combat veteran of World War I who hailed from Dunn, North Carolina. He became known as the father of the Airborne because of his instrumental role in forming the new units. Bill Lee was the original commanding general of the 101st Airborne and would be joined by Brig. Gen. Don F. Pratt, the assistant divisional commander, and Gen. Anthony C. McAuliffe (West Point 1918), who was the divisional artillery commander and twice served as acting divisional commander.

Soon after attachment of the 506th to the division, the 101st Airborne boarded trains to the port of embarkation at Camp Shanks, New York. The ultimate destination of "somewhere in Europe" became obvious to the troops. An advanced party of 101st officers had already sailed over to the United Kingdom to plan billeting locations and arrange other logistical details for the division's deployment. Among those

The 501st PIR followed the 506th to Toccoa, TPS, and Camp Mackall. Johnson's regiment completed jump training in spring 1943 and took up residence at Camp Mackall, North Carolina, until December. The photo shows two squads of H/501 PIR at Mackall in 1943. Note the simulated elastic effect, in which the bottoms of pant legs are bunched around the top of the jump boots. This involved using a rubber parachute retaining band or a condom, stretched around the outer top of the boot to blouse the bottom of each pant leg around the top of the boot rather than tucking it inside the boot. Odel Cassada, second from left in the center row, and Staff Sgt. Robert J. Houston, top left, standing above Cassada, were both awarded the Distinguished Service Cross for their heroic actions in taking Hill 30 below Carentan, France, on June 12, 1944. *John P. McMullen*

in the advance detail were Maj. Thomas H. Sutliffe and Capt. Evans C. Thornton, both members of the 502nd PIR.

In August 1943, the 101st Airborne Division (such as it was constituted at the time) was transported to the British Isles aboard two troopships, the SS *Strathnaver* and the SS *Samaria*. The arrival of the *Strathnaver* group would be delayed for weeks due to mechanical problems that forced that ship and its occupants to dock in Newfoundland and ultimately transfer all passengers to the SS *John Ericcson* for completion of the voyage.

All but one unit of the division were in England by the fall of 1943. The exception was the 501st PIR, which was participating in 2nd Army maneuvers in Tennessee in fall 1943 while still stationed at Camp Mackall, North Carolina. The 501st would sail to the United Kingdom aboard the SS *George W. Goethalls*, arriving at the end of January 1944. At that time, the 501st was attached to the 101st for the duration of the war in Europe.

(GPA 41-44-49) (4-6-44) ALL SET

CHAPTER 2

ENGLAND BEFORE D-DAY

In late August 1943, the 101st Airborne Division boarded trains near Ft. Bragg, North Carolina, and headed northeast to ports of embarkation. Until arriving in the New York area, the troops had no clue whether they were being deployed to Europe or the Pacific. Early in September, several thousand members of the division departed New York, bound for England on the SS *Strathnaver*. Elements aboard included the 502nd PIR, the 326th AEB, the 377th PFAB, the 907th GFAB, and the division's signal, quartermaster, and ordinance companies. Sailing on another ship, the SS *Samaria,* was the 506th PIR, the 321st GFAB, and the 327th GIR.

When these ships departed, they were part of a massive convoy consisting of vessels as far as the eye could see. But soon after departure, the *Strathnaver* developed mechanical problems and had to drop out of the convoy. This was rather unsettling to the troops aboard because of the threat of German U-boats, but soon an American bomber with British markings appeared, circling overhead, followed by Canadian warships that escorted the *Strathnaver* into a narrow channel leading to the port at St. Johns, Newfoundland.

A view looking down the aisle of a plane bearing members of 2nd Platoon F/506 PIR. A series of similar photos were taken before takeoff from Upottery, but Al Krochka's 501st photos are believed to be the only 101st photos actually shot in the air on the way to Normandy.
Tom Young collection via T. Poyser and Bill Brown

Gen. Maxwell Davenport Taylor arrived in spring 1944 to replace the ailing Bill Lee, who was sent back to the states. Erudite, educated, and multilingual, Taylor was a West Point graduate who served as division artillery commander for the 82nd Airborne Division in the Mediterranean theatre before assuming command of the 101st. Taylor led the division into Normandy as a brigadier general but received his second star in summer 1944, before leading the division into Holland. *U.S. Army*

Tug boats pulled antisubmarine nets aside, then replaced them as the ship passed through, circled a mountain, and entered the hidden harbor. Scores of military vessels were docked there. In the ensuing weeks, the troops aboard were marched, two companies per day, several miles uphill to Fort Pepperell where they could eat in the mess hall, play ball, and exercise.

When the *Strathnaver* was repaired, the troops reboarded, and the ship tried to negotiate the narrow channel leading to the open sea. However, the *Strathnaver* scraped bottom, which caused the lower portions of the ship to flood faster than the water could be pumped out. The ship with all troops aboard returned to St. Johns and docked again.

Meanwhile, as the *Samaria* reached the United Kingdom with the other half of the division aboard, a new ship had to be found to transport the passengers of the *Strathnaver* the rest of the way to England. So the SS *John Ericsson*, which had been part of the original convoy, was diverted from its return voyage to the United States and sent to pick them up. This made the crew members aboard the *Ericsson* very unhappy. Their families had been expecting them, and their return was now delayed.

It proved to be more of a problem than simply transferring the troops and their equipment from one ship to the other because shipboard provisions were nearly depleted. This required a side trip to Halifax to pick up more food before completing the voyage to the United Kingdom. As a result, the *Ericsson* did not dock at Liverpool until October 18. The journey had lasted six weeks.

The 327th, 506th, and 321st had arrived weeks earlier and settled into various billets, ranging from Nissen

Capt. George Buker commanded the regimental S-2 section of the 502nd PIR. Here he is seen on a bridge in the United Kingdom wearing an A2 leather flight jacket bearing the unauthorized bat wings and skull pocket patch of the 502nd PIR. This insignia consisted of a decal on a leather disc, which gave the appearance of being painted on the jacket. Fully embroidered cotton versions were more common. *Mike Musura*

Col. Howard R. Johnson was the original commander of the 501st PIR. A native of Washington, D.C., Colonel Johnson was born June 18, 1903, and spent many years in the army prior to World War II. He was the most colorful troop motivator of any of the regimental commanders in the 101st Airborne. *Eugene Amburgey*

Following a demonstration jump in spring 1944, Lt. George Eberle (West Point 1943) posed with a trooper who parachuted through the roof of an English greenhouse. Wind caught the trooper's canopy and pulled him through the glass a second time. *Lage Photo via Alan and Brenda Mitchell*

huts, with their long corrugated buildings and humped roofs, to newly constructed barracks. Other troops were housed in former horse stables. All the 101st Division billets were in Berkshire and Hampshire counties, about eighty miles west of London. The 506th troopers lived mainly in Aldbourne, Ramsbury, and Little-cote. The 502nd would be situated near Hungerford in the Den-ford/Chilton-Foliat areas, former home of the 2nd Battalion of the 503rd Parachute Infantry Regiment (2/503 PIR), who had departed after being redesignated the 509th PIB to make the first American combat jump of the war into North Africa.

Other divisional units were stationed between Newbury and Reading, with the independent 501st PIR arriving in late January 1944 and being billeted south of Newbury (regimental HQ and 2nd Battalion in M34 tents) and at Lambourne (1st and 3rd battalions in Nissen huts and stables). Divisional head-quarters were located at Greenham Lodge and Newbury, and various subunits were billeted at Camp Ranikhet, Basildon Park, Whatcombe Farm, Donnington Castle, Benham Valence, and Brock Barracks in Reading.

Throughout the months preceding D-Day, the 101st troop-ers would make numerous practice parachute jumps and partici-pate in a number of maneuvers that simulated the missions they would perform in the actual invasion.

Most exercises were night problems, the first inkling the troopers had that their entry to the continent would take place

Practice jumps were common in the months preceding D-Day; this night jump was made on May 13, 1944. The troopers pictured are members of HQ 3/502 PIR. From left to right, on the left side of aisle: Capt. Edward "Poop" Barrett (S-3 of 3/502), Dell Winslow, Sgt. 1st Class Harwell Cooper, two unknown, Joe Lofthouse, and Bill Cady. Standing at the end of the aisle: unknown and George J. Schwaderer. On the right side of aisle, from right to left: Lt. Corey Shepard, Fitzgerald, "Eddie" Edwards, Virgil Thornton, two unknown, Kenneth Cordry, and unknown. *Signal Corps via Joseph Pangerl*

in darkness. "In England, everything happened at night," said Lt. Raymond Clark of Company H of the 502nd (H/502). Many insertions were simulated by the troops being dropped off in darkness from trucks rather than planes. They then had to either locate an objective by using maps, compasses, and landmarks or assemble and attack simulated objectives, such as bridges, artillery bunkers, or coastal exits.

Exercises codenamed Beaver and Tiger took place in the early spring. During Exercise Tiger, German torpedo boats sank maneuvering ships carrying a follow-up force of engineers and chemical and quartermaster troops in what became known as the Slapton Sands tragedy, taking its name from the stretch of beach along the south coast of England where the rehearsals for the invasion took place.

A mass demonstration parachute jump was made in daylight for British Prime Minister Winston Churchill and other VIPs on March 23, 1944. This jump was performed by the 506th PIR, minus 1st Battalion, and the 377th PFA Battalion.

Early in 1944, a divisional Pathfinder school was established at Nottingham under command of Capt. Frank L. Lillyman. The mission of the Pathfinders would be to jump into combat ahead of the rest of the parachute echelon. Using color-coded

lights and radar, these trained Pathfinders would guide the main serials of planes to their drop zones in darkness.

Prior to his assignment as head of the 101st Pathfinder school, Lillyman had been company commander of Item Company of the 502nd PIR (I/502). The outspoken Lillyman had a caustic, critical sense of humor like Lieutenant Colonel Ewell of the 501st. This trait did not endear him to many other officers, including his regimental commander, Col. George van Horn Moseley. Captain Robert Clements of Company G overheard "Old Moe" refer to Lillyman as an "arrogant smartass," adding, "I don't want that SOB in my regiment." Thus Capt. Ivan "Ray" Hershner assumed command of I/502 as Lillyman departed for Pathfinder duty.

Likewise, many of the men who ended up in Lillyman's new unit were not the elite of the division, but rather, were individuals whose companies could "spare" them. This is not to take anything away from the courage and dedication of the Pathfinders, but there are some misconceptions about how those who ended up in this unit did so and how much of their heroic mystique came out of preceding everyone else into the battle zone.

Another view taken in the same plane, same jump, with Dell Winslow (3/502 Battalion clerk) standing in foreground. This night exercise resulted in many jump-landing injuries that cost the 101st Airborne more than one hundred troopers who would have dropped into Normandy but had to be put out of the lineup. H/502 jumped over the town of Ramsbury, England, and some troopers landed on rooftops or on the hard cobblestone streets. _Joseph Pangerl_

Elaborate sand tables were constructed by the S-2 sections of various subunits showing all-terrain features in the macro grid area where each unit was to land. Although the troops learned these details, landing even slightly off target in a contiguous, nearby area rendered this knowledge useless in France. The sand table shown was used to brief members of Company C, 326th Airborne Engineer Battalion (AEB). *Joseph Crilley*

Attendance at religious services accelerated as D-Day drew closer. In this photo, Father Francis L. Sampson, the Catholic chaplain of the 501st PIR, administers Holy Communion at the marshalling area adjacent to Merryfield Airfield from which the 501st, minus 3rd Battalion, would depart. *Edward Hughes*

Many of the volunteers were busted former noncommissioned officers, while others did not really volunteer. They were individuals such as Austrian-born T-5 Joe Haller and his two buddies, Joe Dejanovich and David Hadley, known in the communications (commo) platoon of HQ 1/501 as "the three kings." Their company commander, Capt. John Simmons, had said he heard Haller making sarcastic "pro-Hitler, master race" jokes, and Simmons considered all three of these men to be undesirables. He therefore put their names forth as volunteers for Pathfinder duty, of which they were informed after the fact. They still could have refused, but they chose not to, making them volunteers of a sort.

Men who already had training in communications, like the three kings, were also given preference for this assignment because they were familiar with radio equipment and had learned Morse code. Each rifle company in the three PIRs was requested to ask for Pathfinder volunteers. In F/501, a batch of volunteers from 1st Platoon and one from 2nd filled the available slots before any 3rd Platoon men even heard about Pathfinder duty; likewise in I/506, where the entire 2nd Squad of the 2nd Platoon jumped at the chance and filled the quota of Pathfinder volunteers for that company before the others had a chance.

Col. Howard R. Johnson made a final motivational speech to his troops at Merryfield before they walked out to board their planes. He raised his large bowie knife overhead and shouted, "Ere another dawn . . . I hope this knife is buried in the back of the foulest, black-hearted Nazi bastard in France!" Following the speech, Johnson shook hands with every man present as they filed out to the runways to don their equipment and parachutes. *Albert A. Krochka, Herb Moore collection via Jim Bigley*

This famous photo of 506th Regimental Demolitions Saboteurs, who were members of Jake McNiece's "Filthy Thirteen," was taken at Exeter Airfield. This particular group of demolitions men was assigned to 3/506 for a special mission at the Douve River bridges. Clarence Ware and Chuck Plauda applied war paint, using the same black and white paint that appeared as "invasion stripes" on the C-47 fuselages. *Signal Corps*

Shortly before D-Day, additional personnel were sent from each company to jump in with the Pathfinders and provide security for them during their signaling duties. The men who volunteered for security duty were not regarded as "true" Pathfinders by the men who had trained for months at Nottingham and had learned to operate the Eureka radar sets and Halophane lights. However, the security personnel were entitled to wear the Pathfinders' winged torch insignia on their left sleeve and are generally considered to be true Pathfinders.

Even the security personnel weren't always volunteers, such as Lt. Reed Pelfrey, who had gotten on the wrong side of his battalion commander, Lt. Col. Robert G. Cole (West Point 1939). Cole volunteered him for Pathfinder security duty (in much the same way Captain Simmons volunteered the three kings) shortly before D-Day. He was sent to Nottingham with a private who had recently been busted from the grade of sergeant and had not really *volunteered* in the normal sense of the term.

E/501 troopers Robert Mileski and John Bouska talked over their chances of surviving the D-Day night jump and

At Greenham Common Airfield, 2/502 troopers posed while waiting for orders to march out and board their planes. Left to right: Guy Whidden, Schmolinger, Len Langford, and Grodowski of the light machine-gun platoon. *Reginald Davies*

Another light machine-gun group, with Reg Davies at upper left wearing a cricket signaling device tied around his neck. *Phil Rohaty via Adamic and Davies*

decided the odds would be better if they arrived in the combat zone ahead of the main serials at a time when the Germans were not yet alerted. This theory convinced them to volunteer to serve as Pathfinder security personnel, although in reality, their plan would be negated by a strong and alert response from the German troops positioned near Drop Zone D. Bouska and Mileski received plenty of enemy fire as they descended near the German hornet's nest at St. Come du Mont.

Regardless of how and why they ended up in this role, the Pathfinders of D-Day have become folk heroes by virtue of their first-in status. Several sticks of Pathfinder personnel, drawn from each parachute regiment, would jump into France between 0015 and 0045 hours on D-Day to mark Drop Zones A, C, and D with amber, green, and red lights.

About two months before D-Day, certain officers and noncoms received a high security clearance status known as "BIGOT," and these "BIGOT-ed" personnel were informed that the target area for the upcoming airborne invasion was a portion of Normandy, France, behind the east coast of the Cotentin Peninsula. This section of coast, codenamed "Utah Beach," would be assaulted by sea-landing infantry from the 4th Division at H hour (0630) on D-Day. The 82nd and 101st Airborne divisions would land by parachute beginning more than six hours before the first wave of regular infantry hit the beach.

PATHFINDERS LEAD THE WAY

Captain Lillyman's 101st Airborne Division Pathfinders would begin landing soon after midnight on the morning of June 6, 1944, to mark Drop Zones A (amber lights), C (green lights), and D (red lights). The Pathfinders consisted of ten sticks of men, with three sticks from each regiment and one composed of miscellaneous personnel, mostly from the 326th AEB and 377th PFAB.

Servicemen from every unit in the U.S. military have claimed to be in this photo—one of the most famous of World War II. The paratroopers in this series taken at Greenham Common on June 5, 1944, are all members of the 502nd PIR. Anyone saying they are in it who was not a member of that organization is making a fraudulent claim. Left to right: Hans Sannes D/502, Bill Bowser E/502, General Eisenhower, Ralph Pombano E/502, Schuyler Jackson HQ/502, Bill Hayes E/502, Carl Vickers D/502, Lieutenant Wallace Strobel ("23" sign around neck) E/502, Henry Fuller E/502, Bill Boyle E/502, William Noll E/502. *U.S. Army*

Lillyman's stick landed first, shortly after 0015 hours, at St. Germain de Varreville, to mark Drop Zone A. They jumped a couple of miles northeast of the originally designated location but decided to set up their signals behind the St. Germain church. There was not sufficient time to run to the Loutres area carrying the lights and radar through German territory. The first serials would begin arriving about a half hour after Lillyman's group touched French soil.

The Pathfinders of the 101st Airborne Division were indeed the first men in on D-Day. In fact, the first

A rare pre-invasion shot of Brig. Gen. Anthony C. McAuliffe, the division artillery commander, with Brig. Gen. Don F. Pratt, the assistant division commander. Both officers are wearing Air Corps A2 flight jackets. It is interesting to note McAuliffe wearing the paraglide cap patch, designed by the 505th PIR before their departure to North Africa in 1943. This patch was introduced to the 101st Airborne when Gen. Maxwell D. Taylor joined the division in spring 1944. This is the earliest-known example of the patch being worn by anyone in the 101st (other than Taylor) before D-Day. After the return from Normandy, this patch was widely introduced in the 101st to replace the earlier patches that displayed only a parachute or a glider in various color combinations. *Pratt Museum, Ft.*

The original Waco glider known as the "Fighting Falcon" was built with money collected by the Greenville, Michigan, public schools. Just before D-Day, the original Falcon was replaced by a newer one with a steel plate on the floor and a Griswold nose on the front end. This new glider became "Glider No. 1" of the fifty-two craft "Chicago mission." The original Falcon moved back to "No. 45." Pictured are Lt. John May (Pratt's aide), Gen. Don F. Pratt (KIA), Lt. Col. Mike Murphy (pilot), and Lt. John M. Butler (co-pilot) also KIA when landing in France. *Pratt Museum, Ft. Campbell, KY*

Sand table briefing for 101st Pathfinders at North Witham Airfield. Identified in this photo are Capt. Frank L. Lillyman (center), Lt. Reed Pelfrey (far left), and Capt. Frank Brown (right), who is pointing. *Signal Corps via Tom Mallison*

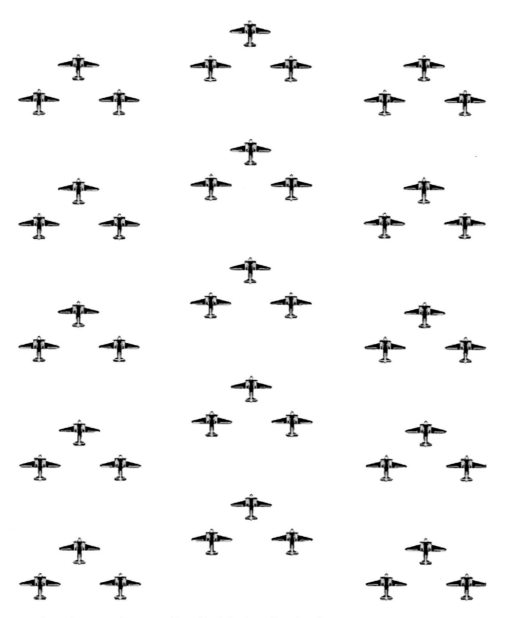

This diagram shows a typical serial formation of forty-five C-47s echeloned in fifteen Vs, with three aircraft in each V. This is how they flew to a combat mission.
Tom Houlihan

two Americans to die were 501st Pathfinders. Stanley Suwarsky, a 3/501 man, jumped five minutes earlier than Harold "Gene" Sellers of 2/501. It is impossible to know which of them died first. Sellers jumped at 0043 and Suwarsky came to ground a few minutes earlier. Both men were killed almost immediately upon landing.

Back in England, the main serials started taking off near 2300, a time when total darkness had just about settled in. From Greenham Common and Membury came the 502nd PIR and the 377th PFAB. Their destination was Drop Zone A. From Merryfield, the 501st PIR departed, minus their 3rd Battalion, headed for Drop Zone D near Angoville au Plein. From Welford, 3/501 would jump in the same serial as 101st Division HQ personnel. Like the 506th PIR (minus 3rd Battalion), the Welford serial was bound for Drop Zone C near St Marie du Mont. Most of the 506th departed Upottery Airfield in search of Drop Zone C, while 3/506 departed Exeter bound for Drop Zone D. The 502nd and 377th jumpers would begin their

"Suiting up"—two members of the 502nd PIR donning equipment on the evening of June 5, 1944, in preparation for boarding a C-47. *Rosenfield collection via J. Beyrle II*

descents about 0050, while the 3/506 would jump last, about fifty minutes later.

The 6,670 paratroopers of the 101st Airborne would be delivered in 432 C-47s, with most troopers jumping between 0100 and 0200 hours. The Air Corps called this the "Albany mission." The 82nd Airborne would begin jumping after the 101st was on the ground, with most of their personnel landing between 0200 and 0300. The 82nd was delivered in 369 C-47s. This was known as the "Boston mission."

The drop zones for both divisions were all located in the Cotentin Peninsula, behind Utah Beach and south of the port city of Cherbourg. Although Commonwealth forces deployed their own paratroopers of the British 6th Airborne Division closer to Caen, no American paratroopers were dropped behind Omaha Beach.

It is possible that if the 101st Airborne had landed behind Utah and the 82nd behind Omaha that the Cotentin mission (i.e., opening and securing the beach exits at Utah and blocking German reinforcements) could still have been accomplished. In retrospect, we know that German reaction in the Cotentin was delayed and piecemeal. Their counterattacks against the beachhead were too little, too late.

Inserting American paratroopers behind Omaha might have averted the slaughter that took place there when sea-landing forces came ashore at dawn, but Airborne losses would have been high. In reality, Utah Beach received priority treatment due to the importance of capturing the port town of Cherbourg as soon as possible.

THE BEST LAID PLANS

The 3rd Battalion of the 501st PIR would be "in reserve," landing on Drop Zone C to provide security for 101st Division Headquarters. As such, elements of division HQ would be jumping in the same serial. However, on the actual drop, some sticks would receive the green light

Two members of F/506 PIR at Upottery Airfield adjusting equipment, identified as Pvt. Robert Janes and Cpl. George R. Martin. *Col. Tom Young 440th TCG*

Sgt. Harry Clawson, a member of H/506, posed from four angles, displaying main and reserve parachutes, plus much miscellaneous equipment including binoculars, a musette bag crammed full of sundries, and ankle armament (an M3 trench knife on the left ankle and a British-made Webley revolver in a web holster on the right ankle). An M1 Garand rifle, fully assembled, is angled behind his chest parachute, and his helmet bears markings for an NCO, as well as 506th spades, with the battalion tic mark at three o'clock instead of the correct nine o'clock. The entire 3rd Battalion entered Normandy bearing 1st Battalion helmet tics—a mistake that was not corrected until July 1944, after returning to England. Sergeant Clawson, a former Eagle Scout who was awarded the Silver Star in France, would be KIA at Opheusden, Holland, in October 1944. *Donald E. Zahn*

Two commanders became casualties upon landing. Right, Col. George van Horn Moseley, the original regimental commander of the 502nd PIR, broke his leg severely when landing near Hiesville, which ended his reign as commanding officer of the Deuce. Below, Lt. Col. Robert L. Wolverton, commander of 3/506, landed in a tree near St. Come du Mont and was killed while still hanging in his harness. *Pratt Museum, Ft. Campbell, KY*

LT COL
ROBERT L WOLVERTON

too early. The reasons why this happened are not known, but it caused some HQ sticks as well as many 3/501 sticks to drop in the area south and mainly west of Drop Zone C. These unfortunates would come to ground in the St. Jores/Pretot/Appeville areas, as well as Baupte/Raffeville. Two G/501 planes would be shot down near Pont le Abbe with only three jumpers surviving from one of the two planes.

On June 2, 1944, Lt. Col. Julian J. Ewell, the CO of 3/501, issued a memo listing some of the procedures that were planned for the D-Day drop of his battalion. Some excerpts follow:

To: All Personnel in the Unit
General Information

Forty-five (45) planes of 435th (Group) will carry us and detachments from Division Headquarters to War. It will be a night flight and jump. Take-off time approximately 2350 hours—DZ time 0126 hours—last leg of flight an azimuth of 93 degrees—speed on jump not over 110 miles per hour—total time out (to DZ) one hour thirty-six minutes—total time over France, twelve minutes.

The flight will be preceded by a formation of British bombers, neutralizing fire from ships or from ground. Flight

will be adequately covered by night fighters all the way, with increased numbers of such while actually over France.

Numerous diversionary activities are now being carried out and will be carried out on actual jump. For example, even though our planes are now not flying daily, trucks with radio equipment are roaming over England, calling the control tower here (Welford), to deceive the enemy into believing that planes are carrying out regular daily flying missions, while actually never leaving the parking area.

Every pilot knows the flight in detail and is capable of taking his plane to the DZ. The lead plane is equipped with the latest Pathfinder and radio location equipment, also two (2) navigators.

[After listing "Check Points for Loading," "Check Points for Jump Master Before Takeoff," and "Check Points During Takeoff," the memo concludes:]

Colonel Johnson (standing at left), was commanding officer of the 501st Regiment. His plane was piloted to Drop Zone D by Colonel Kershaw, the commanding officer of the 441st TCG. This serial (carrying the 99th and 100th troop carrier squadrons), had mixed results in accuracy, dropping some first battalion members on the wrong side of Carentan. Johnson landed a mile north of his objective, the La Barquette Lock. Also in this photo are Leo F. Runge, Maj. Francis Carrel (regimental surgeon), and Waylen "Pete" Lamb. *U.S. Army*

Lt. Rodney Parsons of D/502 was photographed in front of his plane by Capt. George Lage, the 2/502 surgeon at Greenham Common Airfield on June 5, 1944. In this interesting study of equipment, we can see a map case, Air Corps ammo pouches, leg scabbard for M1A1 carbine, assault gas mask carrier, binoculars in case, compass in pouch, wrist watch, M3 trench knife worn in M6 scabbard in front of belt, and white unit identification rag for 2/502 PIR around left shoulder. *Lage Photo, Alan and Brenda Mitchell*

CHECK POINTS DURING FLIGHT

1. Men keep chutes on, ready to jump if need be—all straps buckled.

2. If attacked, remain seated. Do nothing until you are given the word.

3. Utilize buckets and cups in plane for their purpose.

4. All lights will be turned out on order from pilot's compartment—black out curtains remain drawn.

5. Wounded men will be placed in center aisle next to pilot compartment door.

6. In case of emergency, order to "Bail Out" will be by bell and also by verbal orders from pilot's compartment. It will be a static line jump. If over water, you will remain with plane . . . Channel craft for pick-up purposes are present.

7. Signals from pilot will be given orally, relayed by crew chief by use of inter-plane communications with pilot and by use of lights. This includes warning ten (10) minutes from DZ, red light four (4) minutes out, and jump signal—green light.

Col. William Parkhill was the deputy commander of the 441st TCG, flying the lead plane of a serial of 301st and 302nd Squadron C-47s. Aboard were Lt. Col. Robert A. Ballard's men of 2/501 PIR. Parkhill saw the thick cloudbanks at the west coast of the Cotentin Peninsula, and unlike those who had preceded him, he made a command decision—against orders—to fly under the clouds, at three hundred feet. His entire serial followed him under and past the cloudbanks, remaining in perfect formation, then climbing to 750 feet for the drop as they approached Drop Zone D. Months later, Colonel Parkhill received the Distinguished Flying Cross for his initiative, as well as a promotion to a higher command. *William Parkhill*

8. Move number three or four man up to manual salvo release catch when jump time draws near. He will PULL when given green light. THIS IS IMPORTANT.

9. During flight, door bundles will be placed with end against right wall. On red light, it will be moved into position in door.

10. Crew chief will assist in pushing out door bundles by sitting with back to right wall and pushing with feet on signal of jump master.

JUMP—GREEN LIGHT ON

Stick jumps in SOP manner. If for any reason stick does not jump on DZ C, it will make 180 degree turn to right and when over DZ D will drop there.

NOTE: It is essential that every man jump. If plane is shot up, move wounded men out of the way and jump. We need every man. Do NOT hang up bundles in door; take them out with a rush.

J. J. Ewell
Lt. Col. Inf. Commanding

Maj. Lloyd Neblett was flying a C-47 on Parkhill's left wing, and while over Drop Zone D, an equipment bundle from Parkhill's plane struck the right wingtip of Neblett's plane. Prior to that impact, Neblett's plane had dropped to an altitude below three hundred feet. The photo shown here was taken in England the following day; it demonstrates how six feet of wing and seven feet of aileron were torn off. Despite this damage, Neblett was able to fly the plane back to England and land safely. The happy results of Colonel Parkhill's serial were a notable exception to other troop carrier drops that night, which ranged from mixed to disastrous results. *Lloyd Neblett*

CHAPTER 3

NORMANDY, PART I: THE INVASION

That night of nights, June 5, 1944, spelled a one-way journey to destiny for the 6,670 paratroopers of the 101st Airborne Division who boarded more than four hundred C-47 transport aircraft at various air bases in England. The troopers were superbly conditioned and well trained, but they were totally inexperienced in combat and could not have known what was in store for them.

Private First Class Donald R. Burgett of A/506 was one of them. Burgett took training and qualified as an airplane pilot after World War II. Having the knowledge of a pilot in retrospect, he wrote impressions more than sixty years later of his takeoff for Normandy. The airfield was Uppottery, with pilots and crews of the 439th Troop Carrier Group. Burgett wrote:

> Once in the plane . . . it was beginning to get dark . . .
>
> I can hear the pilots cranking the engines—the cough and firing as they caught and revved up. The pilots pushed the throttles to proper RPMs, checked their maps and gauges. The C-47 shook and vibrated as though eager, and we were silent to the man.
>
> The ship farthest to our left added throttle, moved forward toward the runway, did a right ninety, and paraded left to right before us as vanguard, moving between us and the runway [as it headed] to the right end of the runway and takeoff point.
>
> We watched the flames of exhaust in the growing dark, as the ship filled with 101st Eagle men loaded with tools of war, shadowed past.

This trooper has been identified as a seriously wounded 508th Pathfinder of the 82nd Airborne. He ended up in a position occupied by strays from the 502nd PIR, dug in southwest of St. Mere Eglise. He reportedly died a day or two after this photo was taken. *Eddie Sapinsky*

It became our turn; the ship shuddered and moved, turned right, and followed the ships in line before us. Our pilot firewalled the throttles and we went as over a bumpy country road, heading toward the skies and Normandy. When the gear cleared the ground, we were airborne, we cheered as one, breaking the silence.

We were going to war.

After circling and assembling above England for many minutes, the C-47s headed out across the Channel, turning near the Channel Islands of Jersey and Guernsey for a west-to-east run across the Cotentin Peninsula, a distance of about twenty-two miles. The drop zones were located behind Utah Beach on the east coast of the peninsula, so the green light signal to jump would be given shortly before flying over water again. This is why some troopers who got the signal too late were dropped into the Channel east of Utah Beach.

Certain apologists for the troop carrier (TC) pilots have claimed that with the extraordinary weight load carried on D-Day, the C-47s would have stalled had they slowed to less than one hundred miles per hour. They also say that any paratroopers who claim their pilots were going well over 150 mph when they received the green light are also making impossible claims. However, TC pilot Fred Trenck of the 301st TC Squadron stated that he reached speeds as high as 180 while flying across the Channel. He claims to have achieved this speed with twenty-one fully loaded paratroopers aboard his plane.

Many troopers knew their plane was going faster than normal when they jumped. Much of their equipment was violently ripped off when their chutes opened—something they had not previously experienced on practice jumps. The pilots flew these speeds as part of the necessary evasive action. On the other extreme, Trenck said that speeds as low as 80 mph would not have stalled a C-47, even with the D-Day weight load.

Some 6,670 parachutists of 101st Division HQ, the 377th PFAB, the 502nd, 501st, and 506th PIRs began jumping just before 0100, having been preceded by the small Pathfinder echelon. Despite heavy ground fire, mostly from machine guns and 20mm antiaircraft guns, about one-third of the pilots managed to drop their passengers in the correct locations. The remainder landed anywhere from a half mile to more than fifteen miles from their intended drop zones.

Significant weight loads on each individual jumper caused the pilots to feel a slight bounce as each jumper went out the exit door. Some troopers complained of sudden changes in altitude and direction. This, combined with a dispersal of the neat formations when entering unexpected cloudbanks on the western edge of the Cotentin Peninsula, resulted

Paratroopers near the church at St. Marcouf, France, were dropped about five miles north of Drop Zone A and shouldn't have been there. The man in the foreground of this photo was a stray from the 508th PIR, 82nd Airborne Division. *U.S. Army*

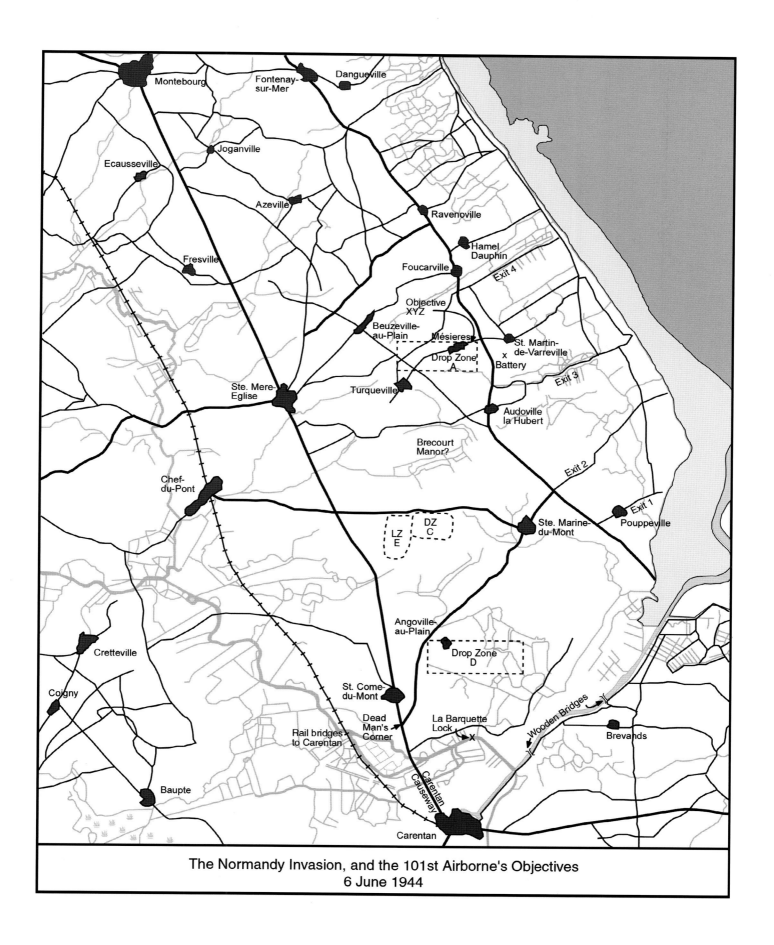

The Normandy Invasion, and the 101st Airborne's Objectives
6 June 1944

The Marmion Farm at the south edge of Ravenoville consisted of a number of rectangular stone buildings, where paratroopers of many different units gathered because they were misdropped miles above Drop Zone A. Troopers from A and D Batteries of the 377th PFAB; Companies B, C, and HQ 3/502 PIR; Companies A, D, and E of the 506th PIR; as well as 508th strays have been confirmed among those who drifted in to this assembly area. Maj. John P. Stopka of 3/502 was the ranking officer present, and he took command of this mixed force. *U.S. Army*

in scattered drops. But the pilots at the controls were simply taking what they believed to be necessary evasive actions to bring their aircraft through the fire. These decisions, although contrary to preflight instructions, undoubtedly saved planes from certain destruction and, more importantly, saved the lives of paratroopers and aircrews.

The 502nd PIR, slated for landing farthest north on Drop Zone A, was the first regiment to jump. While much of their 1st and 3rd battalions landed in the general vicinity of their objectives, the entire 2nd Battalion homed in on the wrong pathfinder signal and dropped 2/502 on Drop Zone C, far south of their target, the coastal guns near St. Martin de Varreville. The bulk misdrop of 2/502 personnel proved to be of little consequence as their objective at St. Martin de Varreville had already been abandoned by German forces after a May 26 bombing had informed them that the gun battery was pinpointed by the Allies.

Conversely, many planes carrying 2/506 (intended for Drop Zone C), homed on the Drop Zone A signal and dropped that battalion between Foucarville and

The famous image of Jim Flanagan of C/502 holding a captured flag was also taken at Marmion, while the photo below is a frame from 16mm movie footage showing troopers milling about in the courtyard. *U.S. Army*

Lt. Col. Patrick Cassidy was commander of 1/502 PIR. This unit landed in the Drop Zone A area and fought in the Fourcarville–St. German and St. Martin de Varreville sectors on D-Day. Cassidy's command post at Objective W was taken over by the new regimental commander, Lt. Col. John H. "Mike" Michaelis. *Pratt Museum, Ft. Campbell, KY*

Audoville la Hubert. Many other troopers of that serial received the green light too early and landed near St. Mere Eglise. The 439th TCG carried regimental HQ 1st and 2nd battalions of the 506th with widely varied results in landing. Although a good number of sticks from this serial did land in the vicinity of predesignated Drop Zone C, one stick from regimental headquarters (RHQ) landed way up near Montebourg, while numerous 1st Battalion sticks were dropped miles north of Drop Zone A, in the Dodainville/Ravenoville area.

One serial of forty-five planes of the 301st and 302nd squadrons (441st TCG) bearing Lt. Col. Robert A. Ballard's 2/501 PIR had the best drop of any 101st Airborne unit that night. Landing correctly in a concentrated area on Drop Zone D, this group was second from last of the 101st serials to jump, landing between 0134 and 0137.

There is a reason why this serial managed to retain formation when approaching the DZ. The pilot, Lt. Col. William Parkhill, was deputy commander of the 441st TCG and he was leading this serial. As they approached the cloudbanks at the west edge of the peninsula, he went against orders and made a spontaneous decision to drop in altitude to 300 feet. All the other planes in that serial followed his example. In this way, those forty-five planes flew under the cloudbanks and maintained perfect formation. After clearing the cloudy area, they rose in altitude to the requisite 750 feet for the green light, slowed to 105 mph, and made a textbook drop.

Staff Sergeant Joe Kenney of E/501 was aboard a plane named "Pee Wee," piloted by Lt. Fred Trenck of the 301st TCS. Kenney wrote in 1972, "Just before the green light, I heard [another trooper] screaming at me. I had not hooked my static line to the steel cable in the plane and would've gone out the door without realizing it. On the green light, our pilot, Lieutenant Trenck, slowed the plane down and lifted the tail as we exited."

Few paratroopers have been able to remember the name of their D-Day pilot, but Lieutenant Trenck's exemplary performance made quite an impression on Kenney. While over the drop zone, Trenck saw a lone C-47 that had strayed from another serial, flying head-on through the 301st serial in the opposite direction.

Drop Zone D proved to be the hottest of the 101st drop zones. The Germans fired a lot of machine guns, rifles, and a few 20mms. Despite a great volume of small-caliber fire, there was an absence of larger antiaircraft fire. They also sent up white flares over the drop zone, which lit the area almost like daylight as the troopers were exiting their planes.

Troopers looking up from the ground could clearly see the dramatic sight of subsequent jumpers coming out the doors of the troop transports. This was unique to Drop Zone D.

RHQ and 1st Battalion of Colonel Johnson's 501st PIR were delivered by the 99th and 100th TCS, with mixed results. Although some of the planes managed to find Drop Zone D, others strayed south, dropping several sticks at St. Georges de Bohon and near Graignes where they would team up with more than 150 misdropped 82nd troopers from 3/507. The 440th TCG delivered the 506th's 3rd Battalion to the area just short of Drop Zone D. This area was heavily occupied and defended by German troops, and Lieutenant Colonel Wolverton's 3rd Battalion was scattered all over the area below St. Come du Mont. Not exactly a concentrated landing pattern, but better than most others that night. Those jumpers who were not killed or captured hiked to their objective, the wooden bridges on the Douve River.

Fewer than 150 troopers found their way to that objective on D-Day. Wolverton and his executive officer, Maj. George Grant, were both killed upon landing. Of the 3/506's company commanders, Captain van Antwerp of Company G was killed and Captain Harwick (H) and Captain McKnight (I) were both captured. This was the last of the 101st Airborne serials to jump (at about 0145).

After all 101st units were on the ground in France, Pathfinders of the 82nd Airborne jumped to mark their drop zones. The serials carrying the 505th, 507th, and 508th Parachute Infantry Regiments followed behind them.

On D-Day, a requisitioned French farm cart paused at Capt. George Lage's 2/502 aid station in Holdy. Joe Pistone of F/502 stands at right, holding the bridle, while Carl Robare of D/502 is seated on the cart holding his M1 rifle in a vertical position. *Lage via Alan Mitchell*

The 377th PFA Battalion experienced the most catastrophic misdrops of any unit that parachuted into Normandy on D-Day. Only three of their twelve 75mm pack howitzers were even located. One of those was bogged down in the mud of a swamp and could not be dragged out. Another was assembled and loaded on a road near Valognes, but after firing one round, had to be abandoned because the crew faced being surrounded by superior enemy forces. Only one of the twelve howitzers came to ground close enough to the consolidated 101st bridgehead to be recovered and utilized.

The scattered artillerymen, most of whom had been deposited on the wrong map six to fifteen miles north of Drop Zone A, would have to fight for survival as infantrymen. Many would be killed or captured before reaching friendly lines, and the 377th suffered more casualties in Normandy as a result of the misdrops than they sustained in the rest of World War II.

Despite well-documented Normandy misdrops by some of the 9th Air Force pilots, the troop carrier command would redeem itself many times over on the missions that followed. Many of those pilots were decorated for incredible acts of individual initiative and courage. Their motto was "valor without arms."

UNUSUAL JUMP EXPERIENCES

Richard "Farmer" Turner of B/506 was taller than average and was loaded down with a British made leg-bag containing one hundred pounds of equipment, including a one-mile reel of communications wire, gas mask, grenades, and other items. He was second from the exit door, but the pilot of his plane never turned on the red light as the plane approached the drop zone. As a result, the men aboard that plane did not have time to perform the customary check of equipment. The jumpmaster, Lt. Rennie Tye, suddenly saw the green light appear near the door. He shouted for the men to

Capt. Francis Liberatori and "Red" Randle taking a break at the base of a hedgerow in France. Libby would be wounded in the spine a few days later, causing lower body paralysis that he endured until his death in the early 1970s. Liberatori was company commander of C/326 AEB, and following World War II, he became a prominent architect in the Springfield, Massachusetts, area. *Joseph Crilley*

Tech Sgt. "Pinky" Walsh and Mike Milenczenko of F/502 PIR on a chow break in Normandy. They have shed their jump jackets in the warm weather. This photo demonstrates the wool olive drab (OD) clothing worn under the M42 suits as well as the early elastic suspenders with inverted U leather fasteners and the rigger-modified jump trousers with canvas reinforcement to the knees and cargo pockets. *Joe Pistone*

simply "stand up, hook up, and go!" The plane was flying extremely fast when Turner went out the door, and his equipment bag was lost when it was ripped from his leg during the opening shock of the parachute. The drop was made from an altitude of less than five hundred feet. After only one oscillation, Turner's feet hit the ground, but he somehow landed without injury.

Private Robert L. Garrett of Dog Company 506th was the last man of his nineteen-man stick. As a result, he was standing just in back of the radio operator's compartment when ground fire hit the nose of his plane and smoke and fire belched out of the bulkhead doorway. The plane was over St. Mere Eglise, and it went into a forty-five degree nose dive as the paratroopers began struggling uphill to the exit door. Garrett felt the plane bank to one side, and he was forced to climb the ribs of the interior of the fuselage, as if on a ladder, to reach the exit door. He then rolled out the door, fearing that the tail of the plane would strike him in midair.

The opening shock was a pleasant surprise to Garrett, but something didn't feel right. He looked up and couldn't clearly see his canopy, so he pulled his reserve chute. He was oscillating when he heard his plane crash nearby. Just as his reserve blossomed open, he hit the ground in the middle of an oscillation, landing hard on his side against his entrenching shovel. This caused debilitating pain and, as he later discovered, a ghastly bruise. Garrett got out of his chute and rolled into a drainage ditch. He could hear many Germans running around and yelling nearby, and he was afraid that the noise of assembling and loading his M1 rifle would be heard. He placed the blade of his M3 knife in his teeth and held a grenade ready to throw, thinking, *If they find me, I'm gonna take a few of them with me.*

After awhile, he saw another serial fly over, and many troopers of the 82nd Airborne began landing in the same area. One trooper came to ground very close to Garrett and helped him to get his parachutes off and organize his equipment. Garrett recalled that the 505th guys were equipped with those "snappin' bugs" (aka "crickets," signaling devices that snap when pressed), although they didn't dare use them after the first day: "We'd heard rumors that the Germans had captured some and had figured out how to use them."

In great pain from his jump injury, Garrett improvised a cane from a tree branch. He limped painfully through eight days of fighting until finally being evacuated for recuperation in a British hospital.

Although many 506th troopers lost most of their equipment, attempting to descend with British-made leg-bags, the members of the "Forty Thieves" (1st Platoon H/506) under Lt. Ivan Mehoskey were given different orders that also proved to be unfortunate miscalculations. These troopers were ordered to put their main weapon, along with ammo, grenades, and other equipment in a parachute "kit bag" with zippers and handles of web material. A jump rope was used to wrap through both handles, then tied to the D-loop on the right front of the T-5 parachute harness. Each trooper would exit with the filled kit bag in his arms and would lower the rope after the opening shock to allow the bag to dangle beneath him.

Most troopers had the bag ripped from their grasp by the prop blast, breaking when it hit the end of the rope and sailing off in the dark air space above France. Men such as Pfc. Don Zahn came to ground with no more formidable armament than a trench knife and perhaps a hand grenade or two.

Al Krochka took this classic photo on D-Day morning near Addeville. All troopers shown are members of regimental HQ/501 PIR, except for the glider pilot with bandaged head and Ledbetter of C/326 AEB, kneeling at left. *Albert A. Krochka*

The Chateau Colombieres at the north edge of Hiesville was the predesignated location for the 101st Airborne's divisional hospital. Here, a wounded German receives first aid from a medic of the 326th Airborne Medic Company (AMC). Note the white cross stencil on the trooper's helmet as well as the arm brassard with an unusually small Red Geneva Cross. Brassards with small crosses were characteristic of the 326th AMC. *Still from Lillyman 16mm film*

Stan Clever of 3/506 exited his plane over Drop Zone D with a forty-pound light machine gun in a British leg-bag. Rather than the bag ripping from his leg with the opening shock, Clever experienced the opposite problem. He couldn't get the release to work and realized with dismay that he was going to have to land with all that weight on his leg, which almost guaranteed a broken foot. Clever was pleasantly surprised to land in chest-deep water that cushioned the impact and saved him from injury. "The Krauts actually done me a favor by flooding those fields," Clever said. Others were not so fortunate, and many troopers would drown in relatively shallow water that night while struggling to free themselves from their ponderous equipment loads.

Not long after daylight, Clever was among the first dozen troopers to arrive at the wooden footbridge across from Brevands, France. He had two cans of machine-gun ammo, as well as the LMG, but his assistant gunner had not arrived yet with the

Another still from the D-Day film shot at Colombieres shows two wounded 101st troopers standing in the courtyard of Columbieres with many German prisoners. *Still from Lillyman 16mm film via SMR*

tripod. Clever began moving the weapon back and forth on a berm parallel to the river, firing at likely targets on the enemy side of the Douve River, including tracers at a large haystack in front of a barn. But the recent heavy rains had soaked the hay and it would not flame up as he had hoped.

At mid-day, Clever's assistant, Robert Secor, arrived with the tripod and more ammo. The crew set up their LMG position on the extreme right flank of the foot-bridge force. But there was a considerable gap of almost five hundred yards between their force and a Company H group that was holding the road bridge closer to Carentan. Captain Charles Shettle, the 3/506's operations staff officer, was the senior ranking officer of that battalion to make it to the objective, so he assumed command.

The Germans had only recently installed the two bridges for tactical military reasons. The local French did not want the bridges because they blocked seaborne commerce to the marina in Carentan. Shettle's force would hold the bridges for several days to ensure that no German reinforcements crossed them en route to repelling the beach landings.

Lieutenant Joe Doughty of Company G and several of his men made a minor incursion across the footbridge on D-Day to briefly reconnoiter enemy positions on the south bank. At the road bridge, several five-man groups followed scout Pfc. Don Zahn of 1st Platoon H/506 in a recon-in-force that resulted in a brief but brisk fire-fight before the intruders returned to the north bank. On D-plus-1, without reliable information from Shettle's force, two Allied fighter-bombers attacked both the road and footbridges and bombed the center out of each of them. After the war passed this area, the local French civilians would do a thorough job of removing the remainder of the bridges, leaving almost no trace of them.

CHICAGO MISSION: THE FIRST GLIDERS ARRIVE

Landing Zone E near Hiesville was the designated spot for the fifty-two CG-4A gliders bearing mostly 101st medical and communications personnel, along with two antitank gun batteries of the 81st Airborne AA/AT Battalion. These 81st glider artillerymen were armed with British-made "six-pounder" antitank guns. The gliders arrived just before 0400 over the landing zone, but one bearing a crucial radio set capable of carrying radio traffic from France to England had been lost when it cut loose prematurely while still in English air space. Yet another glider had strayed far southeast and landed near Graignes, about seven miles southeast of Carentan.

Glider No. 1 of this so-called "Chicago mission," piloted by Col. Mike Murphy and bearing the assistant divisional commander of the 101st Airborne, Brig. Gen. Don F. Pratt, was loaded with a jeep and four occupants. The Fighting Falcon II came to ground south of Hiesville but could not be stopped on the wet, dewy grass. It finally collided with a large tree and fallen log that were situated in a hedgerow. The impact from this collision pinned Murphy in the wreckage and broke both his legs. General Pratt was killed when his neck broke, and the co-pilot was also killed when a tree branch penetrated the dome of his skull. Only Pratt's aide, Lt. John May, escaped uninjured.

Most of the gliders landed between St. Marie du Mont and the N13 highway, with more finding Landing Zone W (south of St. Mere Eglise) than the intended

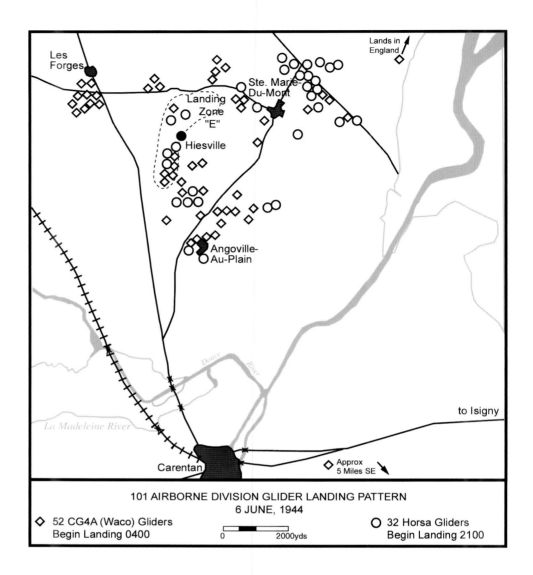

Les Forges

Ste. Marie-Du-Mont

Landing Zone "E"

Hiesville

Angoville-Au-Plain

Lands in England

Douve River

La Madeleine River

Carentan

to Isigny

Approx 5 Miles SE

101 AIRBORNE DIVISION GLIDER LANDING PATTERN
6 JUNE, 1944

◇ 52 CG4A (Waco) Gliders
Begin Landing 0400

0   2000yds

○ 32 Horsa Gliders
Begin Landing 2100

Landing Zone E. However, the casualties in all fifty gliders were relatively low: five killed, seventeen injured, and seven missing. But the loss of the SCR 499 radio set would prove significant when trying to contact scattered subunits in various parts of the peninsula as well as on June 10–11, when the 502nd could have received air support had their plight been communicated to air bases via headquarters in England.

MEANWHILE, UP IN DROP ZONE A

Captain Joseph Pangerl headed IPW (Interrogation Prisoner of War) Team 1, who would be interrogating any prisoners taken by the 502nd PIR. After landing east of St. Mere Eglise, Pangerl joined a large column of marching paratroopers led by Lt. Col. Robert Cole. Turning south toward his predesignated regimental command post at Loutres, Pangerl arrived near dawn to discover that Colonel Moseley was missing and had not arrived to establish a command post.

Lieutenant Colonel John "Mike" Michaelis was the regimental executive officer and was second in command. He made the decision to abandon the predesignated

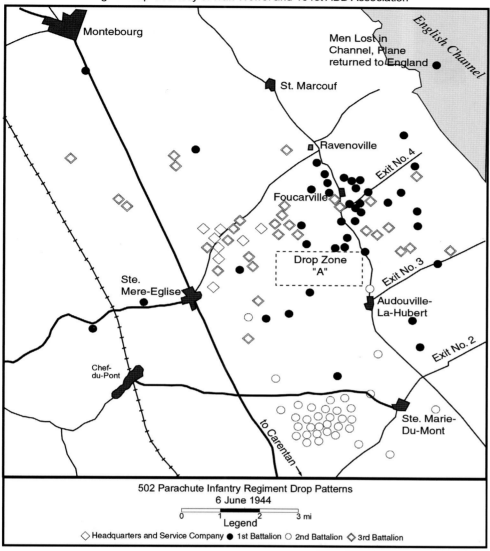

502 Parachute Infantry Regiment Drop Patterns
6 June 1944

Legend

◇ Headquarters and Service Company   ● 1st Battalion   ○ 2nd Battalion   ◇ 3rd Battalion

location and march with all available troops that had assembled at Loutres to unite with Lieutenant Colonel Cassidy's 1st Battalion at Objective W, which was situated much closer to the 502nd's primary objective at St. Martin de Varreville.

Near first light, Michaelis' group would walk down the Mezieres road, traversing the famous XYZ complex backward, in the opposite direction that Sgt. Harrison Summers would travel in clearing the various buildings later on D-Day. Pangerl's journal describes some of the action during the move of Michaelis' group on the approach to and fight through les Mezieres:

> By about dawn, [I] was with a small group including Lt. Col. Michaelis. We moved up deserted roads 'til about dawn, when we [saw] a group of houses across a field in the semi-darkness. A patrol found signs of German troops, so they formed a skirmish line across the field toward the houses. Rifle fire broke out on both sides and Col. Mike set up a C.P. in the woods at the edge

Recently captured Fallschirmjagers from the German 6th Parachute Regiment are herded down the road and into a field south of the Chateau Colombieres to dig graves for the many German soldiers killed in the vicinity. *Still from Lillyman 16mm film*

Wreckage of General Pratt's glider, the Fighting Falcon, south of Hiesville. In previous publications, this photo has been erroneously identified as a craft carrying 82nd Airborne personnel due to the oilcloth arm brassard worn by the dead man in the wreckage. This is actually Murphy's co-pilot. The long piece of horizontal wreckage and the flag painted on the right side of the glider nose were crucial elements in identifying the wreckage. On the left side of this glider's nose was a large painted Screaming Eagle, which was salvaged from the wreckage and is now displayed in the Pratt Museum. *U.S. Army via Pratt Museum, Ft. Campbell, KY*

of the field, just as the sun was coming up over the trees. I was standing next to him, with a Sgt. from the 82nd, who was on his far side, talking, when a German mortar round landed on the far side of the Sgt. We were all knocked to the ground by the force of the explosion, probably a 50mm light mortar shell. Only the Sgt. was badly wounded. We called a medic and the fighting continued a short time and the Germans withdrew.

On going through the field toward the houses, I came across my first German, a young lieutenant, shot through the head, lying about 100 feet from our C.P. His Luger pistol [was] covered with blood from his wound.

One of our men came up, saw us and asked me, "Do you want the gun, sir?" I said, "No." He took it out of the hand of the dead German officer and wiping the already congealing blood off on the grey uniform and wet grass, [he] stuck it casually into his jump suit pocket and continued on across the field. I took the Soldbuch from [the officer's] jacket and saw that he was from a service company.

Going back to the C.P., the medics were doing their best to help the wounded [82nd] Sgt., but he was unable to walk . . . we had to move on because the firefight was bound to attract larger German units. We left the Sgt. and did not hear from him again.

As we continued to move . . . we came across more Germans and another firefight ensued. When things quieted down, we had the

Lt. Clifford Carrier of the 506th PIR driving a captured German tracked motorcycle, known as the *Kettenkraftrad*, at a farm north of Carentan. These vehicles were designed for power, not speed, and could be used as a *schlepper* to tow and carry equipment. *John Reeder*

report of a few Germans around the bend at a crossroad. I went forward with a few soldiers and, sure enough, there were several dead Germans lying in the road. They had been searched by our troops and [their] identifications were lying scattered around in the road.

The hedgerows along the road were 3–4 feet high and [they] cut you off, as if you were in a separate room. As I knelt down and started making notes of unit identification, I looked up and saw that my former companions had left and [I] was all alone.

As I continued taking notes, suddenly out of the corner of my eye, I saw a German infantryman jumping down from one of the hedgerows with a rifle in his hand. As I dived into the nearest ditch along the road, I saw him do the same thing, on the opposite side of the road. There was no movement to be seen or heard, so I began to crawl backwards in the ditch, back to the cross-roads. As soon as I got to the corner, I saw our men still standing around waiting to move out. I told them what happened and we ran back around the bend, but the German soldier had apparently done the same thing I did and backed the other way in his ditch to get back to his comrades. [Since] we now knew that the Germans had seen us and knew our location, we wasted no time and headed SE to our assembly area. This was on the morning of "D-Day" and it was a beautiful, warm, sunny day.

We were now coming into a more inhabited area, which I think was what we called on our maps the XYZ buildings. We took a break along the road [beside] the small, low wall surrounding a group of buildings. Several troopers went forward into the buildings and immediately rifle fire started.

We all scattered, taking cover. There was a small stream across the road, and I took cover in the shallow riverbed under the little stone bridge. Later, I was to remember one of the principles of close combat. Never look into the sun with the enemy in the shade. These troops must have been in previous combat, because they retreated into the houses, opened the windows, but stayed back in the darkness of the rooms. They could see us clearly in the

D-Day at Holdy, southwest of St. Marie du Mont. Right, Doc Lage's 2/502 aid station and below, a Horsa glider, which crashed at 2130 hours on June 6 while carrying members of 82nd Airborne's division HQ personnel.

bright morning sun. I foolishly joined in the firefight and [I] fired several shots into the windows. The next thing I knew, there was this loud crash and I thought somebody had hit me on the helmet with a heavy hammer and dust and smoke flew in front of me. I ducked down out of sight and took off my helmet. There was a slight crease directly in the center of the top of it. Three inches lower and it would've been right between my eyes. I later thought that he had set his sights too high and we were so close that his shot [went] over my head. So much for close combat . . . By now, the paratroopers had formed a semi-circle around the buildings and opened up with everything they had—rifles, Tommy guns, LMG, and even bazookas. It didn't last long, and with all the firing, explosions, etc., the houses caught fire and a white flag was waved by the Germans.

Slowly [they] came out and were herded onto the road. One of the soldiers was a little apart from the others, and this young trooper looked at him and said, "That's the SOB who shot my buddy!" He whipped out his (trench) knife, and started for the [German] who had his hands over his head. I called out to [him] in German and he ran over to me with the trooper and knife after him. For a few moments, they ran around me in a circle, until I called to the trooper and said, "Let me question him first."

With that, he stopped, with a wild look on his face, but [then he] put the knife back in his boot and walked away. In the meantime, all these other troopers stood watching as if in a movie.

A captured 105mm German howitzer taken at the Audoville ghost battery by a small scratch force of troopers from F/502 and the 82nd Airborne Division. This 105mm is identical to those captured at Holdy and Brecourt, batteries assigned to cover Exits 1 and 2 at Utah Beach. This battery was responsible for laying fire on Exit 3. Pfc. Benjamin Shaub of F/502 was primarily responsible for taking this position and was awarded the Silver Star in recognition of his single-handed charge of the gun crews. *Joe Pistone*

Needless to say, the German was on his knees at my feet, with his arms around my legs, sobbing. I tried to talk to him, but he was so unnerved [that] it was a few minutes before I could even understand him. [He belonged to] a unit which was supplying the German [artillery] battery, which we were supposed to take, but which had been destroyed several days before by our bombers.

Fearing that we were attracting too much attention from nearby German units, we took off again. We lined up the PWs, but one young soldier had a thigh wound and said he couldn't walk. I tried to convince him he could walk, but he said he couldn't. Several of his comrades offered to carry him, but that would've slowed us up too much. A tough Sgt. said they would leave a guard with him and the rest of the unit would go on. We had gotten a few hundred yards out of sight when there was a shot and the guard came trotting up saying that he had tried to escape.

Officers of the 502nd PIR on D-plus-1 near Hiesville, France. Left to right: Maj. Allen "Pinky" Ginder, regimental S-3; Mike Michaelis, who became regimental commander as a result of Moseley's broken leg; Lt. Glen C. Crawford with an unknown private; and David S. Newbury, who was Michaelis' enlisted jeep driver. Newbury would be killed in a glider crash on the Holland Invasion in September 1944. Michaelis' next jeep driver, Garland Mills, was also killed a few days after Newbury by an artillery shell at Sint Oedenrode. Note the remains of a damaged Horsa glider that blocked the road at this spot. *Joseph Pangerl*

ELSEWHERE IN DROP ZONE A

The northernmost consolidated group was above the intended north limits for the 101st Airborne bridgehead on D-Day. This group had assembled at the Marmion farm, at the south edge of Ravenoville, France. The men who collected there were mostly members of 1st Battalion of the 506th PIR, and 1st Battalion of the 502nd PIR, with strays from 3/502, 2/506, A Battery 377th PFAB, and some 82nd Airborne men of the 508th PIR.

Lieutenant Fred Culpepper of D Battery 377th had been captured after landing and was taken to the Marmion farm, where he was soon liberated when the fortress fell to attacking American paratroopers. Seeing that the area was under heavy artillery fire, both from the cruiser *Quincy II* off the coast as well as a German artillery battery to the north, Culpepper led a D-Day patrol three miles north through enemy territory until they were in visual range of the Crisbec gun battery. Realizing that taking that source of enemy fire was well beyond their abilities, the patrol withdrew to Marmion.

Charles Eckert of A Battery, 377th PFAB. This captured German artillery piece exploded on the high ground south of St. Come du Mont, above Carentan. Troopers from the 101st were firing it toward Carentan when an empty casing stuck in the breech. An American fragmentation grenade was used to dislodge the casing, but grenade fragments stuck in the bore of the weapon, causing the next shell fired to explode before clearing the muzzle. *Ed Benecke*

Also on D-Day afternoon, a sizable herd of German POWs was driven west along the D15 road in front of a group of American paratroopers who were trying to push them toward St. Mere Eglise. When a German MG42 opened fire on the prisoners, they scattered, forcing the Americans behind them to fire at them to prevent their escape. As a result, the entire group of prisoners was wiped out.

Major John P. Stokpa had assumed command of the Marmion force, and his force fought skirmishes nearby through the night of June 6–7 before abandoning the place to rejoin their units of origin. Next along the D14 road heading south was an isolated group of mostly A/502 troopers under Lt. Wallace Swanson. These men had lost their original company commander, Capt. R. L. Davidson, who had been misdropped in the Channel and drowned. They accomplished their mission of setting up roadblocks to prevent German reinforcements from reaching the coast. They also took a fortified hill on the west side of the D14 north of the turnoff to Haut Fournel. Elements of the 1st Battalion of the Deuce would take that hamlet, stopping German vehicles and infantry in the late afternoon.

Lieutenant Mort Smit; his CO Capt. Fred Hancock; and Lt. Bernard Bucior, who was seriously wounded and evacuated to Utah Beach, were in the vicinity. Bucior and many other wounded men would die when the hospital ship evacuating them to England was sunk by a mine in the Channel.

Captain Hancock had been sent to Haut Fornel by Lt. Col. Pat Cassidy simply to see what was going on there. In the pastures north of Haut Fornel, Hancock was captivated by the bravery of Lt. Rance Cotton, who was in charge of the 1st Battalion's 81mm mortar platoon. He watched as this large officer advanced, paused, and "pointed like a bird dog," before attacking groups of Germans single-handedly. Cotton routed a number of Germans while tossing grenades, rushing, and firing his M1 at the Germans, laughing maniacally the entire time.

Advancing rapidly ahead of his men, Cotton captured eleven enemy soldiers and herded them to a house where a temporary POW compound had been established. Cotton picked up two more prisoners en route to the compound. Hancock could see that one of them had been wounded in the back, his tunic bearing a bloody hole above the kidney area. Another prisoner had the first joint of his middle finger blown off by a bullet. Hancock would write Cotton up for a Silver Star for his bold, inspiring D-Day actions.

A German short-barreled infantry howitzer, captured near St. Marie du Mont by 101st troopers. Note the unusual camouflage scheme painted on the frontal shield, reminiscent of camo patterns used by the Germans in World War I. *Ed Benecke*

The La Barquette Lock on the Douve River in June 1944. The camera was facing southwest, and the barn and house of the lock keeper's family are visible. The town of Carentan lies about a mile behind those buildings. *Albert A. Krochka, Herb Moore collection via Jim Bigley*

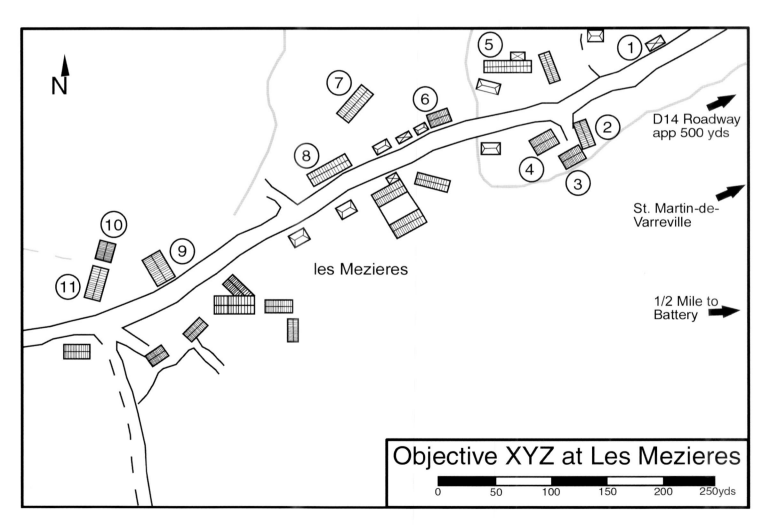

N

⑤ ①
⑦
⑥
⑧ ②
④ ③
⑩
⑨
⑪

les Mezieres

D14 Roadway app 500 yds

St. Martin-de-Varreville

1/2 Mile to Battery

Objective XYZ at Les Mezieres

0   50   100   150   200   250yds

In front of the Chateau bearing Lieutenant Smit's legendary pond, a German truck had been knocked out by bazooka fire and was burning on the road. Several hundred yards to the west was a field where the remains of a crashed C-47 troop carrier aircraft had come to ground. This was the plane bearing company HQ E/506 under Lt. Thomas Meehan.

By evening, elements of the 4th Infantry Division would consolidate with 1/502 and form a front line near Beuzeville au Plain. South of Foucarville was St. Germain de Varreville, a hamlet consisting of no more than some farms clustered around a small church. This was where Capt. Frank L. Lillyman and his Drop Zone A Pathfinders had set up their radar signals for Drop Zone A.

Along the D14 road southward on its west side there sat a long, rectangular building known on D-Day as Objective W. It was later burned down by an angry paratrooper whose buddy had been killed there upon landing that night. The trooper declared the original building to be cursed.

Objective W was the predesignated command post for Lieutenant Colonel Cassidy's 1st Battalion of the 502nd. However, Lieutenant Colonel Michaelis' group arrived in the morning and declared it to be the new regimental command post. From there, assaults would be launched on the group of houses to the southwest known as les Mezieres to the French and as the XYZ complex to the Americans.

The tail section of a crashed British-made Horsa glider. This is the detachable tail section, with the vertical stabilizer visible. This glider did suffer considerable damage upon landing and crashing through a hedgerow. One of the wings broke off and is lying atop the tail section. On June 7, many gliders (both WACO and Horsa) bearing 82nd Airborne personnel landed in the 101st area west of St. Marie du Mont and south of St. Mere Eglise. To describe the sound of a glider crashing into a hedgerow, one trooper said, "Imagine one hundred guys standing on chairs with a wooden orange crate in front of them on the ground. At a given signal, they all jump down on their crate simultaneously. That was what a glider crash sounded like." George Koskimaki collection

On June 7, the U.S. Navy played a significant role in 101st history. The USS *Susan B. Anthony* was one of two troop ships carrying seaborne elements of the 101st Airborne Division to France. The *Susan B. Anthony* hit two floating mines and began to sink. All personnel aboard transferred to two nearby destroyers without loss of life, but personal weapons and equipment were abandoned and went down with the ship. Fortunately, artillery ammunition and howitzers for the 321st and 907th GFA battalions were aboard another ship and reached shore safely. *Bob Salley*

In that hamlet of les Mezieres, a series of French houses on both sides of the road were being used to billet German artilleryman. Their gun positions in a field southwest of St. Martin de Varreville had been heavily bombed by the RAF on May 26. As a result, three of their artillery pieces had been removed from the site and only one destroyed piece remained in position. Thus, the primary objective of the 502nd PIR had been neutralized even before the invasion began.

Locals testify that on the night before the parachute landings, Allied bombers flew along the entire east coastline of the Cotentin, seemingly bombing in a random fashion, but not concentrating on the St. Martin de Varreville gun battery as they had on May 26.

On D-Day morning, despite abandonment of the gun battery positions, the crews remained in their billets in the les Mezieres/XYZ complex. Three brave individuals from Baker Company of the 502nd led the way in assaulting and clearing those French houses of German troops. Staff Sergeant Harrison Summers was joined by

Late morning of June 7, Lieutenant Colonel Ballard's 2/501 troopers were awaiting naval artillery support from the USS *Quincy II,* a heavy cruiser with 8-inch guns sitting out in the channel. This fire was to open the way for an assault on St. Come du Mont. The first four rounds landed on target and obliterated a house containing a German headquarters. The next four-round concentration fell short, however, killing a half dozen of Ballard's men and wounding many others. St. Come du Mont would not be liberated until June 8. The original *Quincy* was a World War I cruiser, but it was sunk in the battle of "Ironbottom Sound" near Guadalcanal in 1942. *Gary Porter*

Pfc. John Camien in rushing the houses, smashing in the doors, and mowing down the occupants with a Tommy gun. Covering fire was provided by William Burt, a machine gunner who would later be killed at Bastogne. Although Camien would be evacuated with wounds, he was never to receive the accolades that Sergeant Summers received for his part in this action. Summers would be awarded the Distinguished Service Cross, along with the reputation of being the "Sergeant York" of World War II's 101st Airborne Division.

South of les Mezieres, Lt. Col. Robert Cole led elements of his 3/502, mostly Item company members, out toward the coast along Exit 3 from Utah Beach. Positioning his troops behind the large concrete fortifications that protected Exit 3, Cole's men ambushed the German occupants as they abandoned the bunkers and tried to run farther south. These Germans had panicked when they were confronted by the beach landings and realized that they also had American paratroopers in position behind them.

As D-Day progressed, the units in the Drop Zone A area completed their assignments, with elements of A/502 attacking the fortified hill at Foucarville and liberating some buddies who had been captured upon landing the night before.

OTHER SIGNIFICANT D-DAY ACTIONS

At least two 105mm artillery batteries were knocked out on D-Day morning. One was situated near the Brecourt manor between St. Marie du Mont and the hamlet of le Grand Chemin. Elements of 2/506 assaulted these four gun positions, capturing and destroying the artillery pieces one at a time. Although Lt. Richard D. Winters of

The German artillery garrison at "Objective XYZ" in Mezieres, France, was cleaned out, primarily through the efforts of these three troopers, clockwise from top left: Staff Sgt. Harrison Summers, Pfc. John Camien, and Pfc. William Burt, all members of B/502. Burt, a machine gunner, was later KIA at Bastogne. *Hank Bauer, Marcy Camien, and Pratt Museum, Ft. Campbell, KY*

Captured German sergeants inventory newly arriving prisoners at Utah Beach before shipping them to POW reception centers near Southampton, England. Most of the prisoners appear happy to be out of the fighting. More than ten thousand Germans surrendered in Normandy during the first ten days of the Invasion. *Acme War Photos*

Lt. Col. Benjamin Weisberg was the original commanding officer of the 377th Parachute Field Artillery Battalion (PFAB). He jumped as artillery liaison to the 502nd PIR from Colonel Moseley's plane. Weisberg's battalion was badly misdropped in France by troop carrier pilots who deposited most of the 377th on the wrong map, north of the Montebourg-Valognes area. Due to the resulting casualties, Weisberg's enmity toward the troop carrier pilots reached a potentially dangerous level. Weisberg was relieved of command shortly before the Holland mission and replaced by Lt. Col. Hank Elkins. The original members of the 377th loved Colonel Weisberg and credited him for the later war successes of that battalion. *U.S. Army, Pratt Museum, Ft. Campbell, KY*

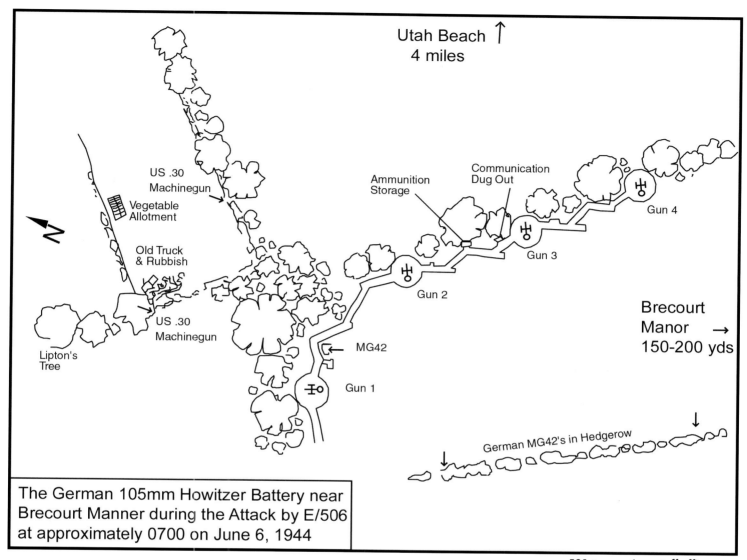

Utah Beach ↑
4 miles

US .30
Machinegun

Vegetable
Allotment

Old Truck
& Rubbish

US .30
Machinegun

Lipton's
Tree

Ammunition
Storage

Communication
Dug Out

Gun 4

Gun 3

Gun 2

MG42

Gun 1

Brecourt
Manor →
150-200 yds

German MG42's in Hedgerow

The German 105mm Howitzer Battery near Brecourt Manner during the Attack by E/506 at approximately 0700 on June 6, 1944

501st operations staff officer map

Company E led the assault on the battery, members of every company in 2/506 have been identified in this action—notably John D. Halls of the 81mm mortar platoon and Rusty Houck of Fox Company, both of whom were killed in the action. Pfc. Gerald Loraine, who received the Silver Star for his part in the action, was a member of Service Company of the 506th.

A few miles south of the Brecourt guns that covered Exit 2 were four additional guns near the hamlet of Holdy. These guns covered Exit 1 at Pouppeville. On the night jump, a number of unfortunate paratroopers had landed right in the positions of the Holdy battery and were killed in a terrifying and bloody slaughter. The unfortunates who landed there and died in that field were Sgt. Clifford Halsted, Jimmy Campos, George J. Rigaux, Lawrence R. "Dicky" Doyle, and George R. Bailey. All of these men were members of HQ 1/506 PIR.

Their fate had been determined by the position they occupied in their planes. The troopers who jumped before them landed safely in Holdy, and those jumping after landed beyond the field, toward St. Marie du Mont. Among those who jumped later

Steve Mihok and a fellow trooper from HQ 2/506, dug in near the typical entrance to a hedgerow-bordered Norman field. Mihok was misdropped and was considered MIA for the first several days after D-Day. *Steve Mihok*

and survived were Richard "Doc" Brinkley, Barney Becker, Ralph Campoy, Angelo Dukelis, and Stanley "Stash" Branowski.

Brinkley and Becker were members of the mortar platoon. They discarded their ineffectual M1 carbines and acquired a Thompson submachine gun and a Browning automatic rifle from U.S. casualties. With those automatic weapons, they helped a bazooka gunner knock out the Holdy gun battery. Being separated from their company, over the next two days they hunted Germans to avenge the victims of Holdy.

A third gun battery covering Utah Exit 3 is believed to have been situated in the vicinity of Audoville la Hubert. There is photo evidence that this battery existed and was knocked out by strays from F/502, mainly Pfc. Ben Shaub, but other details, including its precise location, have never been verified.

Fifty-two WACO gliders carrying AT guns of the 81st Airborne AA/AT Battalion, plus miscellaneous support, medical, and communications personnel, had landed in Normandy in the predawn darkness of D-Day morning. On D-Day evening, at about 2130, a single platoon of the 327th GIR arrived in British-made Horsa gliders. This was the 327th's regimental AT platoon, equipped with small 37mm AT guns. Except for this one platoon, the entire 327th Glider Regiment would enter Normandy by ships, along with most of the 326th AEB, the 907th GFAB, and the 321st GFAB. Only about half of the total membership of the 101st Airborne Division were parachutists on jump status who had parachuted into Normandy.

Early on June 7, the SS *Susan B. Anthony* hit a mine in the Channel and sank. Its passengers, consisting of much of the two glider field artillery battalions and the 326th Engineer Battalion, evacuated to two destroyers without any loss of life. The artillery pieces and heavy equipment, along with some of the personnel of those battalions, were aboard another ship, the SS *John Mosby*.

The troops who evacuated the sinking *Susan B. Anthony* were forced to leave their individual weapons and equipment on the sinking ship when transferring to the rescue ships. After coming ashore and rejoining the 101st Division near Hiesville, these troops had to be reissued all personal equipment, from weapons to toiletries and rations.

One of the many Germans who were killed while attempting to escape to the far side of Carentan. *John Reeder*

501ST PIR ACTIONS ON AND BELOW DROP ZONE D

Lieutenant Colonel Robert A. Ballard's 2/501 had been accurately dropped in the correct place on Drop Zone D, but early morning probes from the assembly area toward the objective (St. Come du Mont) had been halted after several 501st troopers lost their lives above les Droueries and at le Haute Addeville. Lieutenant George Schmidt of Company E was killed while leading an attack on the large stone farm buildings above les Droueries, while Robert Huston, Don Schinkoeth, and James J. Luce were killed at le Haute Addeville.

Near a sizeable stone-washing trough, Leo Gillis of Company F shot several Germans who were responsible for killing Luce and Huston. The Germans began forming a main line of resistance along the hedgerow behind the trough, and Lt. Quincy M. Couger and Gillis fought them there all day on D-Day. Gillis' total for the day was sixteen Germans shot. Lieutenant Couger was killed that evening, and now the area above the trough is known as "Gillis corner."

Later on D-Day, Ballard maneuvered his battalion around the edge of the drop zone and was in position above les Haute Addeville, coming from a different angle that night. The following morning, many troopers who had jumped farther north came flowing into Ballard's area. Their attack on St. Come du Mont

Lt. Charles Moore, a platoon leader in C/326 AEB, reading a map near Angoville au Plein. *Joe Crilley*

D-Day positions in hedgerows south of Drop Zone D below Angoville au Plein. This was in Lieutenant Colonel Ballard's assembly area, where 2/501 troopers were surrounded by enemy forces and unable to reach their D-Day objective of St. Come du Mont. *I. Jack Schaffer*

that night. The following morning, many troopers who had jumped farther north came flowing into Ballard's area. Their attack on St. Come du Mont was preceded by 8-inch artillery support from the cruiser USS *Quincy II* from off the coast.

The first salvo of four shells from the *Quincy* made a direct hit on a French farmhouse believed to be a German command post and blew it off the map. As Ballard's troops rose up to attack following the second salvo, the next four shells landed short, killing about six friendly troops and wounding many others. Although the survivors reorganized, it was a demoralizing blow and St. Come du Mont would not fall into U.S. hands until June 8.

The wounded from this and other actions in the area south of Angoville au Plein were evacuated to the church of that community where first aid was administered to more than eighty patients in the first two days by 2/501 medics Ken Moore and Robert Wright. Both of those medics would receive the Silver Star for their lifesaving work. The church with bloodstained pews at Angoville au Plein has since become a famous historical landmark of the Normandy Invasion.

Down at the Douve River, Col. Howard R. Johnson's members of RHQ and 1st Battalion of the 501st PIR, were holding the la Barquette Lock. After withdrawing in the face of heavy fire near Vierville, the first battalion of the German 6th Parachute Regiment would blunder into Colonel Johnson's positions on June 7, resulting in the total destruction of that battalion. The German paratrooper battalion moved laboriously across country through flooded fields; the church steeple in Carentan was the landmark that would lead them back to their regiment.

Leo F. Runge and Lieutenant Owens faded back, giving the Germans harassing fire for hundreds of yards and leading them into a deadly U-shaped ambush set up by Johnson's concealed force. The German paratroopers walked right into this trap, not realizing that a strong American force was dug in directly in their path. The Germans sought cover by lying in the ankle-deep water caused by deliberate, pre-invasion overflowing of the nearby lock. They managed to return fire and succeeded in killing a few Americans, but some Germans could eventually be seen flinging their rifles up into the air as a signal of intent to surrender. Some of those who attempted to surrender were reportedly killed by their own leaders.

Leo Runge, one of Colonel Johnson's bodyguards, had rejoined the main force. Runge could speak German, and he placed a small recognition panel on the muzzle of his rifle and waved it, until firing tapered off on both sides. After an initial failed attempt in which heavy firing resumed, preventing a parley, Runge walked into the open a second time, accompanied by Colonel Johnson and George "Birdlegs" Dickson of C/326 Airborne Engineer Battalion.

The German officer commanding the pinned-down battalion was persuaded to walk into U.S. lines, and the survivors of his force eventually followed him into captivity. A total accounting later revealed about one hundred fifty Germans had been killed and another three hundred fifty taken prisoner. This action was the biggest conventional fixed battle fought by any 101st Airborne unit in the Normandy Invasion.

A mile closer to the Channel on the Douve Canal, fewer than 150 members of 3/506 under Capt. Charles Shettle had assembled at their battalion objective, the two wooden bridges recently installed by the Germans. After initial American incursions to the south shore on D-Day, this sector settled into a holding action, accomplishing the mission of preventing German troops from crossing the bridges to reinforce the Utah Beach defenses.

Shettle's troops would be relieved in the area by elements of the 327th GIR on June 8, but Allied planes dispatched from the United Kingdom bombed the center out of each bridge on June 7. This happened because 3/506 had no radio communications with any Allied forces outside their sector and the high command was uncertain which side owned

One of the first U.S. tanks to reach Colonel Johnson's isolated force near Peneme was this M4 Sherman tank of Company A 70th Tank Battalion. The tank's name, "All American," was inspired by its company letter designation and was also, ironically, the nickname of the 101st's counterpart 82nd Airborne—the "All American" division. *Albert A. Krochka, Herb Moore collection via Jim Bigley*

The chateau Le Bel Enault lies just west of the hamlet of Addeville and was built a century before World War II by a wealthy French botanist. On D-Day, the stately chateau was being used as a German command post. Col. Howard R. Johnson of the 501st PIR parachuted into the field just across the road from the front entrance of Bel Enault and was fired on by a German soldier while removing his parachute harness. Johnson returned fire with his oft-practiced .45 pistol quick draw, dropping the German in his tracks. Several days later, when the area had been secured, Colonel Johnson returned to the location with his driver and bodyguards to prove the story was true. The body of his victim was still there. In this photo, Colonel Johnson stands second from right. Leo F. Runge, his interpreter, stands at far left. In the rear, the facade of the chateau is visible. *Albert A. Krochka, Herb Moore via Jim Bigley*

those bridges. Many commanders had already written off 3/506 as a fighting force, assuming they had been wiped out in the initial landings.

On D-plus-1, the 502nd PIR moved inland from the Utah Beach exits, with some heading west from Audoville la Hubert, then south from Turqueville, while others passed through St. Marie du Mont and headed west from there. These troops would stage and regroup at les Forges, la Croix Pan, and Blosville. The 3rd Battalion would liberate Houesville, where sizable enemy counterattacks from the west were halted.

Lieutenant Ralph Gehauf led a recon and intelligence patrol from 3/502 in the Houesville area, and when that group was late in returning, an H/502 patrol went to search for them. This resulted in a deadly ambush that cost the lives of Sgt. Norwood Cumming and Staff Sgt. David Vaughan, and the wounding of others. Lieutenant Gehauf's group did eventually return safely and went on many subsequent patrols near Carentan.

Divisional operations centered on the village of Hiesville, where the predesignated divisional hospital was established in the Chateau Colombieres. General Maxwell D. Taylor's headquarters was situated in the Lecaudey farm, about a mile west of Col. Robert F. Sink's 506th CP at Culoville. Taylor, at the time still a brigadier general in Normandy, had assumed command of the 101st Airborne Division in spring 1944 when General Lee relinquished command due to a heart condition.

The 3rd Battalion of the 501st PIR, in divisional reserve, had accompanied 101st Division headquarters from Welford Airfield on D-Day to provide security. Many of their sticks, as well as some division HQ sticks, however, had been misdropped west of Carentan.

Colombieres became a collecting point for German POWs as well, and many were recruited to dig graves for their fallen comrades when a temporary cemetery was established nearby. The hospital was bombed on the night of June 9–10, 1944, and the damage was so severe that the Chateau had to be razed and rebuilt after the war.

In the Drop Zone C area, St. Marie du Mont had been liberated and tanks and self-propelled (SP) artillery of the 70th Tank Battalion and 65th Armored Field Artillery Battalion had linked up with elements of the 506th PIR. Together, on the morning of June 7, they would drive south along the D913 that became known to the 506th as "the death road." They liberated Vierville, Angoville au Plein, and Beaumont before reaching Dead Man's Corner above the Carentan Causeway, and then being recalled to Beaumont for the night.

Pursuit of the withdrawing Germans through the many fields along the D913 road typified the nature of hedgerow fighting. Individual enemy targets were seldom seen, and firing was mostly done at places where the Germans were thought to be. Enemy bodies were discovered when attacking and capturing a hedgerow, but it was impossible to know whose fire had killed them.

The junglelike nature of fighting in the Normandy Bocage country sometimes resulted in unexpected close encounters. In his book *Happy Landings,* Richard "Farmer" Turner of B/506 wrote:

> I was leaning up against a tree in the hedgerow country. Another man in B Company came up and said to me in effect "get out of the way." He shoved me somewhat and I moved out of the way quickly. He pointed his rifle straight up, perpendicular to the ground and fired. Lo and behold, a sniper came tumbling down out of the tree, as an animal would when shot during a hunt in the United States.

We had one less enemy to contend with. I should note that in the Normandy hedgerow country, one could observe many wooden platforms and paths, built in some of the taller trees, to make it easier for snipers to move about.

A captured photo showing members of the German 6th Parachute Regiment posing in their camouflaged jump smocks before D-Day. *Donald E. Zahn*

A similar account comes from John Kliever, who was lying in a ditch at the base of a hedgerow during a break in the fighting. Sitting beside him was Johnny Granados, who had a bayonet affixed to his M1 rifle. Suddenly, a German came over the top of the hedgerow and dropped down directly onto Granados, who simply held his bayonet upright and impaled the enemy soldier. The German died almost immediately, but Granados had difficulty removing his bayonet from the dead man's body. Kliever suggested he fire the weapon, which proved useful in facilitating that removal.

Around the same area, Art "Jumbo" DiMarzio, another Dog Company man, was resting on his back with his head on his helmet, eating a K ration. A German with fixed bayonet rushed up from out of nowhere and started jabbing at Jumbo as he rolled away on the ground. But the German's bayonet went into Jumbo's leg. He grabbed the barrel of the German's rifle to prevent him from withdrawing the edged weapon and lunging again. As he held the rifle immobilized, another Dog Company trooper fired and killed the German.

The only sizeable group of U.S. paratroopers south of the Douve River was an isolated force at the town of Graignes, seven miles southeast of Carentan. Here, more than one hundred fifty members of the 82nd Airborne's 3/507 PIR had been

Another captured photo of German 6th Parachute Regiment personnel, posed at the jump school near Dreux, France, and equipped with Panzerschreck antitank rocket launchers. *Bruce M. Beyer*

significantly misdropped, along with two planeloads of 501st troopers from HQ 1/501 and Company B.

One of the fifty-two CG4-A gliders of the 0400 D-Day "Chicago mission" had strayed to the Graignes area as well. Pilot Irwin J. Morales and co-pilot Thomas Amad thus wound up as part of the Graignes battle force. Ahmad would be killed in action at the church, but Morales escaped. Why this particular glider strayed so far off course remains a mystery. Virtually all the other gliders of that serial landed in a relatively concentrated area, near Landing Zone E and Landing Zone W, in the vicinity of Hiesville and St. Marie du Mont.

Numerically powerful German forces overran the Graignes garrison on Sunday, June 11, 1944, but most of the American force melted away into the swamps between Graignes and Carentan and made good their escape. Before withdrawing, however, these troopers had inflicted grievous losses on the German attackers. Deprived of victory, the vengeful Germans murdered all the wounded Americans who were left behind in the retreat. Their victims included the town priest, Father LeBlastier, the B/501 commander, Capt. Loyal Bogart, and others who were receiving first aid in the town church.

Two views of Utah Beach. Above: Even days after D-Day, German heavy artillery batteries situated west of St. Mere Eglise could lay fire on the shoreline. Left: Regular infantry troops that debarked at Utah Beach moving inland along Exit 3, near Audoville la Hubert. *Signal Corps via R. Margittay*

Many local houses were burned and the American walking-wounded prisoners were taken to le Mesnil Angot, several miles south of Graignes, where they were bayoneted into a ditch in a lonely farm field and barely covered with loose dirt. Among the nine troopers murdered there were Richard Hoffman, William Love, and Roy Callahan of the 501st PIR, and Medical Captain Abraham Sophian of 3/507. Their bodies were discovered by a French farmer named Louis Lescalier the day after the atrocity. The perpetrators are believed to have been from the 17th SS Panzergrenadier Division, although they were never identified or charged after the fact.

CHAPTER 4

NORMANDY, PART II: THE PUSH INLAND

Although General Taylor had promised the 101st troopers that they would be relieved after "three hard days of fighting," this was not to be the reality. After June 9, a new and urgent mission presented itself. With most of the troops coming across Utah Beach either being diverted north, toward the port prize of Cherbourg, or west, to cut the escape route of Germans stationed in the Cotentin Peninsula, survivors of the 101st Airborne would get the assignment of capturing the city of Carentan, France.

While elements of the 506th held an east–west line above the Douve River, the 501st and 327th worked their way around the east side of Carentan, mostly encircling it, after crossing the Douve closer to the Channel. After the 502nd secured a bridgehead to the north outskirts of Carentan, the 506th would circle to enter the town from the west.

Carentan lies at the base of the peninsula, and taking it as soon as possible was essential to linking up with the beach-landed troops from Omaha Beach. Also, there was concern that German reinforcements gravitating toward Utah Beach would push through Carentan to the coast, driving a significant wedge between the two American beachheads.

Michaelis' 502nd PIR drew the assignment with Lieutenant Colonel Cole's 3rd Battalion leading the way down the main road into Carentan from the north. The most direct route into Carentan from the high ground below St. Come du Mont was down the N13 road, which traverses several miles of pastureland before entering Carentan from the north.

While 1st and 3rd battalions of the 502nd were fighting beyond Bridge No. 4, Lieutenant Colonel Chappuis' 2nd Battalion was in reserve between St. Come du Mont and Dead Man's Corner. This photo shows John Cucinotta, Franklin Ray Blasingame, and William S. Goebel (later KIA) in an orchard near St. Come du Mont, France. *Ed Sapinsky*

A 75mm howitzer, used by German forces in Carentan, that was destroyed by naval artillery fire from the 14-inch guns of the battleship *Texas*. Mike Musura, the 502nd regimental photographer, shot this photo on June 12, 1944. *Musura Photo*

Because those pastures were flooded in 1944, this road comprised a causeway under which four rivers crossed at right angles. The three northernmost bridges came in close succession: over the Jordan River (1), the Douve River (2), and Le Groult (3). Finally, after a longer interval, came the last bridge before Carentan, over the Madeleine River (4). By June 10, the second bridge had been blown out by engineers of Fallschirmjager (FJR) 6, and the 502nd troops who crossed the Douve did so on an improvised bridge made of planks and wire scavenged from a nearby fence.

Moving south along the N13 causeway single file, Cole's troops were virtually without cover. Crawling along the road or its shoulder made the troopers perfect targets for enemy soldiers positioned at varying distances to the west of the causeway. The Screaming Eagles who drew this assignment could only wonder what cruel vagaries of fate conspired to place them in such a hellish predicament. As most of them edged down the right side of the causeway, flat on their bellies, many slid down into the cold water at the edge of the inundated pastureland to avoid being silhouetted.

The urgency to take Carentan as soon as possible was aggravated by the primitive state of communications between fighter aircraft bases in the United Kingdom and the front line below St. Come du Mont. The result was that the Air Corps could not be given an accurate assignment to provide air support to the advance of Cole's battalion. The American armor that had come ashore was diverted elsewhere and artillery support was minimal.

Occasional screams were heard as bullets found Cole's men one by one. Many were wounded and some killed, but the survivors kept edging forward. The fortunate ones who made it to the end of this gauntlet fanned out and dug in just north of Bridge No. 4.

For troopers still strung out along the causeway, the long day dragged on, with German sharpshooters aiming for their heads. Lieutenants Bennie Klemantovich and George Larish of Company I were killed, while Ted Benkowski of Company G survived with one eye shot out. Lieutenant John Painshaub was seriously wounded and would be wounded again, this time mortally, during the night. A litany of the dead and wounded from Cole's battalion would run into dozens of names.

During the long night of June 10–11, a few bold individuals squeezed past the Belgian gate that had been placed by the Germans on Bridge No. 4 to slow down the

St COME du MONT   No. 1   No. 2   No. 3 FARMHOUSE   BRIDGE No. 4

DOUVE RIVER

MADELEINE RIVER

Aerial view of the Carentan Causeway with its four bridges over the Jordan (1), Douve (2), Le Groult (3), and Madeleine (4) rivers, along which the 502nd PIR advanced on June 10–11, 1944, to attack Carentan. *Signal Corps*

attackers. Those who reconnoitered below the Madeleine River during darkness moved south along the east side of the N13, advancing several hundred yards. At the same time, Frederick von der Heydte's Fallschirmjager Regiment was taking up positions in the hedgerows on the west side of the road.

Before daylight, two German planes flew over the causeway, one dropping a bright parachute flare, illuminating the area like daylight. Another JU-87 came north up the N13 from Carentan, first strafing with its machine guns and then dropping antipersonnel bombs on the troops near the elevated road. This caused more casualties, although the strafing plane was shot down and reportedly crashed into one of the rivers.

Near first light on June 11, swarms of German machine-gun bullets were periodically sweeping across the surface of the causeway, but Lieutenant Colonel Cole was walking up and down it as if he were invincible with a .45 pistol in his hand. Miraculously, the enemy fire did not hit him. He stood on the road above three of his Item Company troopers who were taking cover in the roadside ditch.

"What's wrong, fellows?" Cole asked.

"We're pinned down, sir!"

"Aw," Cole replied, "we're not pinned down. C'mon, let's go get that sonofabitch!"

Official U.S. Army portrait of Lt. Col. Robert G. Cole, commander of 3/502, who led his battalion in the assault on Carentan, receiving a posthumous Congressional Medal of Honor for his fearless and inspiring leadership. *U.S. Army, Pratt Museum, Ft. Campbell, KY*

Chester "Bob" Elliott of I/502 stood up, grasping his forty-pound LMG and carrying a partial belt of ammunition. "Where do you think you're going?" asked one of his companions. "Hell, if he's brave enough to lead us, I'm going to follow him!"

Elliot crossed the fourth bridge accompanied by Cornelius Owens and Leroy Gravelle. They ran several hundred yards south on the east side of the road and met some bold 1st Battalion troopers who had already leapfrogged Cole's advance, as well as Capt. Cecil "Big Cec" Simmons, the Company H commander.

Simmons greeted Elliot, saying, "Let me hold that machine gun for you while you catch your breath." Big Cec then sprayed about one hundred fifty rounds from it into the German-occupied hedgerow in a field across the west side of the N13 road. Shortly after Simmons handed the weapon back to Elliot, a German bullet struck Owens in the upper chest and, as he lay dying, the 1st Battalion troopers began to fade back to the bridge. German troops were beginning to come around the left end of the hedge in front of Elliot. He fired his LMG from the hip, mowing down a batch of them "like bowling pins."

When Owens was confirmed dead, Elliot and Gravelle joined the retreat back to Bridge No. 4, which was being hit by German small arms and mortar fire. Elliot went down into the water and attempted to walk across the bottom of the Madeleine River with the LMG on his shoulder. He started to drown and was forced to abandon the weapon in the river. He barely reached the opposite bank.

"You damn near drowned!" Lieutenant Colonel Cole said.

Elliot was flat on his back, coughing up water. He couldn't talk, so he simply waved his hand from side to side, letting Cole know he would survive.

By now, Item Company numbered less than thirty men. Cole ordered the remaining members of I/502 to go up the causeway and remain in reserve. Lieutenant Robert Burns was the only Item Company officer still standing, but he and his survivors would circumvent Cole's order and managed to remain in the fight by mingling with 1st Battalion troops later that day.

As the sun began to appear on the east horizon, several hundred members of Cole's battalion squeezed past the Belgian gate obstacle on Bridge No. 4, one man at a time. German machine-gun bullets made sparks as they impacted the gate, and some of the paratroopers fell dead or wounded. But eventually, Cole assembled a group of survivors from G, H, and HQ Company, 3rd Battalion, south of the last bridge.

A farmhouse several hundred yards to the right-front (west) was being used as von der Heydte's command post. The V-shaped hedgerow in between was filled with German paratroopers. Beyond the farm, known as the Ingouf farm, was an apple orchard also manned by German parachutists. Cole sent the 3rd Platoon of Company H in an advance across the open field to the first hedgerow south of the bridge. The Germans concealed therein allowed the Americans to advance to a range of seventy-five yards before opening fire on them. Some men were hit, and all of them went to ground except for Pvt. Albert Dieter, whose arm had been shredded by a burst of German machine-gun fire. Dieter about-faced and walked upright back to the bridge as more bullets followed him. He reported in to Captain Simmons, sustaining more wounds before being evacuated.

Meanwhile, Lt. Reed Pelfrey and Lt. Raymond Clark were pinned down on the open ground with the survivors of 3rd Platoon. Both wounded and unwounded feigned death and lay still. After what seemed like four hours to Pelfrey, but was actually closer to an hour and a half, the survivors of 3rd Platoon would finally be released by Cole's bayonet charge. Although the Germans knew that some of the Screaming Eagles on the ground seventy-five yards in front of their positions were still alive, they were short of ammunition and so stopped firing into them.

In the meantime, mortar and artillery rounds were landing in the area, then exploding smoke shells preceded a bayonet rush. During the unfolding drama, Lieutenant Pelfrey was wondering how he had gotten himself into such a predicament. Although it was hard to imagine getting away, he never really believed that he was going to be killed that day. As shells from both sides exploded around the prone men, Pelfrey heard one trooper talking out loud, even as he feigned death, "When is this sonofabitch going to do something?" Then another, "Oh Lord, if you get me out of here alive, I swear I'll come to church every Sunday for the rest of my days. . . . Why don't they do something?" Despite the gravity of the situation, Pelfrey couldn't help but smile at what he was hearing.

The primary opponent of the 502nd at the north edge of Carentan was the German 6th Parachute Regiment, commanded by Col. Friedrich August von der Heydte (pictured above right). This highly educated and combat-experienced officer happened to be a cousin of Klaus von Stauffenberg, leader of the attempt by renegade Wehrmacht officers to assassinate Hitler with a bomb in his conference room on July 20, 1944. Heydte narrowly escaped being implicated as one of the conspirators. *E. Janssen*

Back closer to the bridge, Cole was striding up and down his line of survivors, saying:

These goose-stepping Heinies think they know how to fight a war! We're about to learn 'em a lesson! There's several thousand Krauts in front of us and only a few hundred left of us, but we are well able to take this thing. We can't even think about taking prisoners. I'm gonna put such an artillery barrage on them that we hope they'll be addled. I want you to put your bayonets on your rifles. We'll call for smoke. When you hear me blow the whistle, get up and charge to the orchard behind that farmhouse. If your buddy gets hit, keep going, you can't afford to stop! Go ahead and smoke a cigarette. For some of you it will be your last cigarette, because some of you won't make it. When I blow the whistle, I want every one of you goddamn jayhawks right on my ass!

A smoke barrage followed, and there is some debate among survivors about how much artillery was directed into the German positions. Some swear only the three small pieces being fired from St. Come du Mont by the 377th PFAB were employed. Others say that some naval artillery shells sent from the Channel by the USS *Quincy II* also landed in the area. Joe Lofthouse, one of Cole's radio operators, had long since discarded his entrenching shovel. During the seemingly endless wait for the signal to charge, he used his bayonet to dig a small hole, then lowered his head into it. Lofthouse felt that while he might survive a bullet in the butt, he did not want to get shot in the head.

When the whistle blew, the charge got off to a rather ragged start. Some men hadn't heard the instructions; others did not hear the whistle. But Lieutenant Colonel Cole led by example, running across the bullet-swept fields brandishing his .45 automatic, which he fired in the general direction of the enemy. He could see only a fraction of his men at first and some of those went to ground, but he worked on them and got them up and running again.

Gradually, more and more troops followed, with First Sergeant Sprecher leading Company H in the temporary absence of Captain Simmons, who had been knocked unconscious by a close mortar shell explosion. Sprecher was first to reach the Ingouf farm house, and he shot the lock off the door.

Cole and Major Stopka moved in to establish their command post inside as survivors of the charge continued west, engaging more German paratroopers in an apple orchard, where mail clerk Bob Brune and Lt. Edward Provost employed cold steel on several Germans to conserve ammunition (Brune was later killed in action, while

A view (facing west) of the field where Lt. Col. Robert G. Cole's 3/502 made their bayonet charge on June 11, 1944. This photo was taken more than ten years later, but at a time when the terrain still remained in the same configuration as it was in 1944. The cameraman stood just west of Bridge No. 4 facing the Ingouf Farm, visible in the distance.
Paul Woodage

Provost would suffer a bloody face wound). The lieutenant, still feeling the adrenaline, walked to the rear for first aid shouting, "They *squeal* when you stick 'em!"

Cole's men fanned out to provide protection for their new battalion command post. Some, like Joe Lofthouse, ascended the stairs and began firing out the second floor windows toward the orchard. The field behind them was littered with the bodies of fallen comrades, both wounded and dead. Here, 3rd Battalion fought a touch-and-go battle all day.

Meanwhile, 1st Battalion of the Deuce had joined the fight, with companies A and C continuing south on the main road and fighting at the cabbage patch along the west side of the N13. After crossing Bridge No. 4, part of Baker Company under Lt. Homer Combs went west, past the Ingouf farm, to hold the right flank for Cole. Fighting in a small complex of farm buildings known as the Pommenaque farm, they held off German attacks from the west for much of that day. Lieutenant Combs himself would be killed, as was Lt. Melvin M. Spruiell, a forward observer from the 377th artillery, who had assigned himself the job of infantry troop leader when his radio failed to function.

The Army Historical Section took this photo of the road that ran north to south, situated behind (west of) the Ingouf Farm. Although two of the original farm buildings still stand in 2007, postwar industrial construction has totally obliterated this road. *SLA Marshall collection, Carlisle War College via Jim Bigley*

Losses on both sides were so heavy that by the afternoon a ceasefire was necessary to pick up and evacuate the wounded. The extremely tall Maj. Doug Davidson, regimental surgeon of the 502nd PIR, began his walk southward way up near the house at Dead Man's Corner, waving a white flag on a pole, an enlisted medic on either side of him. After crossing Bridge No. 4, the intrepid trio never missed a step even with Germans firing into the road beside their feet. Eventually, they entered the German lines and proposed a German surrender. This was declined, but Davidson and the medics managed to achieve the necessary, albeit brief, ceasefire.

The fighting resumed in earnest after Major Davidson recrossed the front line. It ended in late afternoon when the last German counterattack was dispersed by friendly artillery fire and the concentrated small arms fire of Cole's intrepid battalion. This bloody and historic day-long fight would open the way for other elements of the 101st Airborne Division to take and occupy the city of Carentan the following day. Cole was cited to receive the Congressional Medal of Honor but would not live long enough to wear it.

CARENTAN FALLS ON JUNE 12, 1944

Colonel von der Heydte made the decision on June 12 to withdraw his remaining troops from Carentan, leaving only a small, token rear guard behind that scarcely delayed the 101st in occupying the town. This crucial prize would enable the Americans to link up forces that had landed at Utah and Omaha beaches. The 6th Para

This was the approach to the Pomenaque settlement, facing north, between the Ingouf Farm and the railroad tracks that run from Carentan to Cherbourg. During the fighting that followed Cole's charge on June 11, 1944, Lt. Homer Combs led a B/502 force that protected Cole's right flank by waging an intense private battle in this area. *SLA Marshall collection, Carlisle War College via Jim Bigley*

Regiment commander later claimed he would have held Carentan just a while longer had he known that the 17th SS Panzergrenadier Division would arrive on the scene as soon as it did. Other elements within the German high command allege that von der Heydte did in fact know the proximity of that division. If this is true, then his decision to withdraw likely was made to prevent the certain extinction of his regiment.

According to General Pemsel, von der Heydte suffered "a temporary physical and mental breakdown" around that time. He also had to face a formal inquiry convened by the 17th SS Division's judge, Major Schorn, to explain why and how Carentan had been abandoned to the U.S. Army. Due partly to his friends, who were influential and high-ranking commanders, von der Heydte was allowed to resume command of his regiment, which would fight all through the retreat across France. The commander of the 6th Para Regiment would also narrowly escape implication in the July 20, 1944, assassination attempt on Hitler due to an involved relative.

While troopers of the 401st Glider Infantry, along with companies E, F, and H of the 506th were entering Carentan, Lieutenant Colonel Ewell's 3rd Battalion of the 501st PIR assaulted and captured Hill 30, due south of Carentan. This involved crossing a large swampy area west of St. Hilaire Petit Ville, and then charging up the east face of the thirty-meter-high hill against small arms and 20mm cannon fire. Two members of 3/501 received the Distinguished Service Cross for their part in that fight: Sgt. Odel Cassda of H/501 and Staff Sgt. Robert Houston of HQ 3. The hill had been manned by Ost volunteers from the 795th Georgian Battalion.

Following up on this fight, the entire 501st Regiment continued south to la Billonnerie, where Company F and part of the HQ 2/501 ran headlong into an attack by the 6th Company of the 37th SS Panzergrenadier Regiment, a part of the 17th SS Division. After an intense half-hour engagement, Company F fell back two hedgerows and dug in to form a main line of resistance for the night. Their withdrawal was supported by artillery of the 907th Glider Field Artillery Battalion.

Fox Company lost one enlisted man, John J. Penta, and an officer, Lt. Raymond Oehler, killed in the engagement, as well as numerous wounded. Staff Sergeant Leon F. "Country" Evans was mortally wounded during the withdrawal, and Leroy Prahm was killed by mortar fire at the new line. However, against these losses the Americans counted forty dead SS troopers who fell in the initial engagement. Leo

Gillis testified that most of them were killed by a thirty-three-year-old machine gunner named Stanley "Pappy" Green, of 3rd Platoon F/501.

As 2/501 dug in near la Billonnerie, 3rd Battalion outposted the D171 at the turnoff for Baupte, while elements of the 506th faced west in the vicinity of Douville (now called Donville), France. A U.S. attack was planned for the morning of June 13.

After the battle, the victors of 3/502 display a captured trophy. Standing left to right: Lt. Col. Robert G. Cole, 1st Sgt. Hubert Odom (DSC, G/502), Staff Sgt. Robert P. O'Reilly (HQ, 3/502), and Maj. John P. Stopka (XO, 3/502). *Signal Corps, Ed Wierzbowski collection via Nadine Wierzbowski-Field*

THE GERMAN ATTEMPT TO RETAKE CARENTAN: THE JUNE 13 COUNTERATTACK

Early on June 13, elements of the newly arrived 17th SS Panzergrenadier Division, bolstered by survivors of the 6th Parachute Regiment, attacked Carentan from the south and west. Elements of the Gotz von Berlichngen Division in the attack included the 37th SS Panzergrenadier Regiment, the 17th SS Panzer Battalion, and a pla-

Maj. John P. Stopka of Sheridan, Wyoming, displaying a favorite item of captured German equipment, an MP40 burp gun, taken in the Normandy fighting. Stopka would assume command of 3/502 PIR after Cole's death in Holland. Stopka was also KIA on January 14, 1945, in the woods west of Bourcy, Belgium. *Signal Corps, Ed Wierzbowski collection via Nadine Wierzbowski-Field*

toon of the 17th SS Panzerjager Battalion (tank-hunting battalion), consisting of modified Mk III and Mk IV self-propelled 75mm artillery. The Germans also employed a regular, outdated Mk III command tank, which was knocked out on the road between Carentan and Cantepie.

Attacking elements ranged east to Montmartin en Graignes (hitting 327th GIR lines) and west to the D171 highway, where German armor drove north toward the Baupte road. At the junction known as la Fourchette, elements of the 501st PIR, supported by a British-made six-pounder antitank gun manned by the 81st Airborne AA/AT Battalion, held the line. The strongest German attempt came along the road between Auvers and Douville, and past the fields north of Douville along a parallel east-to-west road.

Most of the German armor, by necessity, remained road-bound due to the hilly terrain, hedgerows, ditches, and fences in the area. The 1st and 2nd battalions of the 506th PIR defended the terrain on both sides of the east-to-west highway between Carentan and Cantepie, with 3rd Battalion situated south of that highway in a sunken road later called "Bloody Gully." A wider, more open valley farther west and having the railroad embankment as its right flank, became known as "Bloody Gulch." Colonel von der Heydte, commanding the German 6th Parachute Regiment, held his 3rd Battalion in reserve, sending his 2nd Battalion west along both sides of that railroad line, which connected Carentan to la Haye du Puits.

Early that morning, before the fighting began, a G/506 trooper named Robert Parks walked out in front of his company positions near Bloody Gully. He observed the deceased body of a German soldier who had been hit in the back of the head by a bullet. Lying near the fallen enemy, Parks observed an American paratrooper helmet painted with the spade stencils of his regiment. Curious, Parks knelt and retrieved the helmet, examining the liner. This helmet also had a bullet hole through the back and written in it was the name "Malcolm Reece."

Parks was both surprised and stunned by this discovery. He was surprised, because Reece was his first cousin. They had enlisted together from Tennessee, went through training together, and ended up in the same company, but jumped into France from different planes. Seeing the bullet hole in the helmet shocked Parks, and he immediately assumed that his cousin had been killed. They had not met on the ground since the D-Day drops. But seeing a possible relation between the location of the hole in the helmet and the hole in the back of the dead German's head, Parks placed the helmet on the dead German and confirmed that the holes matched up. The German had been wearing an American helmet at the time he was shot. Perhaps he was snooping around U.S. lines at the time and had figured this ruse would prevent him from being shot at by American troops.

Ironically, a German sniper hundreds of yards west of his location had probably killed him, mistaking him for an American. After all, snipers usually aimed for the head; this one had evidently recognized the U.S. helmet through his telescopic sight and acted accordingly. Parks really wanted to retain this helmet as a souvenir, but had no way to carry it with him during the fighting. After World War II ended, Malcolm Reece returned from captivity. He had been taken prisoner on D-Day and his discarded helmet had evidently been picked up by this ill-fated German.

Liberated horse cart used by 501st PIR troops near Addeville, France, to haul weapons and ammunition. *Albert A. Krochka, Herb Moore collection via Jim Bigley*

American units jumped off in an attack about 0700 hours on June 13, heading west into German-held territory. They were stunned to see German infantry and armor passing them in the opposite direction in an attack of their own. Out of this chaos began the battles of Bloody Gulch and Bloody Gully.

Fred Loutensock, a T-4 (technical rank equivalent to sergeant) radioman in D/506, saw three German "tanks" pass his position traveling single file, but well spaced, on a narrow road near Bloody Gulch. These were actually self-propelled (SP) artillery cannons with light armor, which might be loosely classified as tanks. Although he did not see what happened to them, none of them returned to their point of origin, and he presumed they were all knocked out.

Lieutenant Joe McMillan had assumed command of Dog Company 506th after the June 8 death of Capt. Jerre Gross near Dead Man's Corner. On the morning of June 13, McMillan observed a lone StuG IV coming along a narrow road, which was flanked on both sides by hedgerows. More importantly, the Panzergrenadiers assigned to protect the vehicle had been picked off by sharp shooting Screaming Eagles. McMillan instructed Pfc. John Kliever to leap onto the top of the tank from a hedgerow and to "just rattle around up there."

As the tank was passing the spot where Kliever had mounted the hedgerow, he leaped onto the left front of the vehicle, then began jumping up and down on the front track

A view of Utah Beach taken by Al Krochka, the 501st photographer. *Albert A. Krochka*

Hettrick's War: An Artillery Observer's Baptism of Fire

Lt. Donald Hettrick, England, 1945

Lieutenant Donald Hettrick was a forward observer (FO) for the 75mm pack howitzers that comprised the Airborne artillery of the 377th Parachute Field Artillery Battalion (PFAB). He started in D Battery, which was primarily an anti-aircraft unit equipped with .50 caliber machine guns. Hettrick's talents as a forward observer were more urgently needed in Holland and Bastogne, so he spent a lot of time with the 327th GIR in Holland and with parachute infantrymen of 1/502 PIR, calling in fire missions at Bastogne. Lieutenant Hettrick can claim credit for taking out many enemy troops in the various campaigns of the 101st Airborne.

Although trained as an FO, Hettrick injured his shoulder in England before D-Day and was not allowed to parachute into Normandy. He would come ashore in France shortly after D-Day with seaborne elements and make his way inland to rejoin his battalion. Hettrick's D Battery was designated for antiaircraft duties in Normandy and dropped .50 caliber machine guns instead of disassembled pack howitzers in Normandy equipment bundles.

Being held back from the jump by his commander Lt. Col. Ben Weisberg probably saved Hettrick from death or capture. Most sticks of the 377th PFAB were misdropped on the wrong map by Troop Carrier Command on D-Day, and many 377th troopers perished as a result. As combat days progressed, Hettrick found himself attached to various parachute infantry companies of the 502nd PIR, for which the 377th was customarily designated to provide artillery support.

Out on the main line of resistance (MLR or front line), as well as out on the outpost line of resistance (OPLR) at times, or even in front of the main line, Hettrick was forced to keep a low profile and to never allow the Germans to spot him while using his binoculars. All GIs who were observed using binoculars attracted concentrated German attempts to eradicate them with extreme prejudice. Both sides realized what terrible damage accurately observed artillery fire could do, and FOs came to view themselves as wanted men with a price on their heads. As FO George Walker of the 463rd PFAB said, "It was an unwritten law on both sides. When you locate an enemy FO, it's the same as with snipers. You don't take them prisoner, you *kill* them!"

Lieutenant Hettrick was a gun fancier, and he loved to fire small arms with precision accuracy. It wasn't his fault that he was put in the artillery instead of the infantry. Hettrick had equipped himself with an M1 .30-06 caliber Garand eight-shot semi-automatic rifle fitted with a scope because he also wanted to take a personal toll of the enemy with rifle fire. His first opportunity to do so would come after being attached to a parachute infantry company of the 502nd on the MLR outside Carentan, France. Lieutenant Hettrick writes:

When we finally got to report to our battalion commander, Lt. Col. Ben Weisberg, we were sent out to a nearby unit to serve as forward observers. Luckily, it was a very quiet, static position and we set up radio communications with our fire direction center (FDC). Then we waited to see what developed. We did not have too long to get a little bit of German activity. Five enemy soldiers appeared from an underground bunker. They crawled up a short knoll and disappeared. It was our first sight of the enemy and we watched to see what developed. Some four hours later, we saw a repeat of the movement.

I remembered all the good buddies who were killed a few days before. Most of them were misdropped in their parachute jump into Normandy. They were shot while landing as they landed amidst the whole German army. Not too much chance to defend themselves. But that is warfare, and the GIs had to make the best of it. The 377th Parachute Battalion lost eleven of their twelve howitzers. Ours was the worst drop of the Airborne Invasion of Normandy . . . not many were anywhere near their drop zone.

I was able to obtain an M1 Garand rifle with scope. When I saw the five enemy soldiers the second time, I decided to put a stop to their brazen activities. Sure enough, they repeated their bunker exit for me to put the crosshairs on the middle of the top man's back and to touch off a shot. Then the next, then the next, until all five were hit dead center and all had dropped. I have not told very many people about this incident because it appears to be a cruel way to fight. Actually, are there any nicer ways to kill an enemy?

Immediately after my vengeful shooting, an infantry lieutenant raced over and chewed my butt for disturbing the quiet interlude. He said that the last man that did something similar, the Germans fired mortars and wounded some of his men. I learned quickly that you cannot pop off a couple shots to satisfy an urge and place bystanders in harm's way. By the way, the previous shooter was killed in the mortar attack. Enough said about that.

A day or so later, my team was shifted to a different area, where some artillery observation was needed. Another quiet area seemed to be in store for us, but not for long. Luckily, we were at a hedgerow with some extra large foxholes nearby. We had about five [parachute] infantrymen right next to us, sitting on the edge, writing letters, washing, and whatever. Soon we heard shells landing down the line from our position. I asked a GI what they were shooting at, and he replied, "Lieutenant, there's nothing there to shoot at." So I continued to look over the area with binoculars, trying not to get drowsy in the warm sun. Here's where my sixth sense came to life. On an instantaneous impulse, I yelled. "Duck!" It took perhaps one second for all of us to drop into our foxholes. Just as we did, a brace of four mortar shells landed amongst us. We were covered with falling leaves, twigs, and dirt. No one was touched, but the field bags the guys were using were riddled with steel fragments. One soldier asked how I knew to duck, because he had not heard any incoming mail. I had no answer to that question.

My sixth sense was to save people quite a few times in the many battles to come. In this case, it hit me by one or two seconds, and later it would warn me by just enough minutes to leave an outpost before German shells destroyed it. When we were at a site, the guys all knew that when Lieutenant Hettrick said to get the hell out of here, you did not ask questions or dillydally. You just grabbed radios and equipment and left the premises.

I did learn something about the German shelling. In artillery, you need to adjust for range and deflection from a previously fired check point or a concentration. All this firing data is filed with FDC. for future fire missions. On many future shoots, it sure has been a life saver. The krauts were shooting at the hedgerow to set the range, then when they were ready to zap us, they moved so many yards to the right and they hit right on target. It was just that simple a way to get on target: an easy and deadly solution. This was my team's baptism of fire.

housing. He wanted to toss a pineapple grenade in the barrel of the main battery but was discouraged by the muzzle brake. Lieutenant McMillan, who happened to be taller than average, ran alongside the vehicle until he saw the turret open slightly. He activated a thermite grenade, lifted the hatch higher, and tossed it in as Kliever hopped off. The vehicle soon came to a stop. The entire crew burned to death inside. This was one of the self-propelled guns knocked out by the 506th that day (the other having been knocked out by bazooka fire from E/506).

Over at the junction of the D171 highway with the Baupte road, a lone six-pounder manned by members of A Battery 81st Airborne, AA/AT Battalion, succeeded in knocking out another StuG IV right near the road junction and disabling another that had reached a tree line on the east side of the highway about two hundred meters southeast of their gun position. They later complained that the parachute infantrymen they were supporting had abandoned their positions in the face of the German armor. However, the 81st AT gunners held their ground and halted the German armor. Members of this crew included Cpl. Charles Marden, Pfc. Joe Trenge, Pfc. Vincent Fiersuk, and Lt. Thomas Kiernan (1st Squad, 1st Platoon, A/81). Sergeant Clarence Tyrell of H/501 was killed in this battle, evidence that not all of the infantry personnel had fled the scene.

It has been written elsewhere that the 17th SS Division was already experienced when they attacked on June 13. This is basically untrue. Except for a small percentage of cadre personnel, the vast majority of men in Gotz von Berlichingen were experiencing their very first combat on June 13, 1944. In a statement after the war, Colonel von der Heydte, the commander of the 6th Para Regiment wrote:

In an orchard near Drop Zone D at St. Come du Mont, C. B. Williams posed amid discarded equipment from 3/506. Lieutenant Colonel Wolverton's battalion had landed here on D-Day. *Ed Sapinsky*

The 17th SS Panzer Grenadier Division . . . was well armed and well equipped [but] surprisingly poorly trained. The majority of the officers had neither the training nor the combat experience to enable them to fill their positions adequately. The artillery of the 17th SS . . . was not able to concentrate its fire flexibly . . . to fire ahead of attacking infantry, from sector to sector (or in Normandy, from hedge to hedge). The artillery of the 17th SS . . . usually fought a "private war" without paying any attention to the infantry.

However, after furious seesaw fighting, some elements of the 506th were forced to give ground in the face of superior numbers of SS grenadiers and armor. Parachute infantrymen in that area were short of ammunition and had few bazookas available to deal with armor. Although the U.S. 2nd Armored Division was en route from stations near Omaha Beach to support the 101st Airborne, they would not arrive in the area southwest of Carentan until early afternoon. Prior to their arrival, the 2nd Battalion of the 502nd PIR was committed to help the 506th contain the German onslaught.

Private First Class Emmert O. Parmley was a member of 2nd Platoon of the F/502, which had launched a brisk counterattack through the fields north of the railroad embankment. Parmley and a corporal by the name of Brown were ordered by

Lt. Nick Schlitz to be rear guard and to round up any stragglers. Brown soon opted to vanish, a decision that would cost him his stripes.

Each of the Company F men who were counterattacking that day wore red ribbons looped around their left shoulders and under their armpits as a recognition sign. They had been ordered to fix bayonets to their rifles. As Parmley trudged westward alone, following his platoon, he decided to climb up on a hedgerow to observe. His assignment the previous day had involved policing U.S. weapons from the cabbage patch north of Carentan and near the field where Lieutenant Colonel Cole's bayonet charge had transpired. While doing this, he also looted numerous fallen German parachutists. Among the souvenirs he had "liberated" that day and now wore was a pair of elbow-length German paratrooper gloves (gauntlets).

Parmley was surprised when he observed a lone German paratrooper who was trotting straight toward his hedgerow from behind. Evidently, this was one of the men who had reached the Carentan rail station before receiving instructions to withdraw and infiltrate back to rejoin the rest of Fallschirmjager 6 near Cantepie. Parmley had the man in his sights, but when he aimed and pulled the trigger repeatedly, nothing happened. He later discovered that his rifle's bolt was not fully seated forward, preventing the weapon from firing.

The approaching German was closing fast, but he merely smiled and waved to Parmley. All the German could see was a figure aiming a rifle at him but not firing, wearing a camouflaged helmet and German paratrooper gloves. He evidently assumed that Parmley was one of his comrades. Parmley slid down the back side of the hedge bank and moved about ten feet to the left. He was fumbling in his pockets for a hand grenade when the German climbed over the hedgerow, right where Parmley had just been, and hopped down, smiling and walking toward him.

The friendly German was a clean-shaven, handsome twenty-year-old, and he approached to a range of ten feet before realizing that Parmley might not be a comrade. The German, who was grasping his Mauser rifle at his side with one hand, was startled yet fascinated at the sight of a grimy, unshaven American wearing Fallschirmjager gauntlets and a red ribbon tied in a bow around his shoulder. His jaw dropped open in wonder as he puzzled over which army Parmley belonged to. Like the dead Germans who Parmley had examined the day before, this tidy soldier had on a necktie and a blue flier's blouse under his camouflaged combat smock.

After leaving their initial objective, the wooden bridges on the Douve Canal northeast of Carentan, survivors of H Company 3/506 regrouped north of St. Come du Mont. Pictured standing here are: unknown 3/506 trooper, Ferdinand Wilczek, William W. Willis. On ground: Bruce Paxton, unknown 3/506 trooper, and Johnny Hahn (later KIA). *Fred Bahlau*

On June 13, 1944, elements of the 17th SS Panzergrenadier Battalion attacked toward Carentan from the southwest, assisted by the 6th Parachute Regiment. Some self-propelled guns of the Panzerjager battalion, like the one shown above, joined the assault. This one was disabled by antitank fire, and the commander was shot as he tried to escape the vehicle. *Lage Photo via Alan and Brenda Mitchell*

Parmley raised his M1 rifle and began jabbing toward him with his bayonet in a threatening manner, demanding that he drop his weapon and surrender. Suddenly, the German dropped to the ground as if he had fainted. Parmley would learn that John W. Sissel, a member of his 2nd Platoon Mortar Squad, had watched this incident from across a perpendicular hedgerow and had shot the German with his M1 carbine. For some reason, Parmley had not heard the report of that shot. The bullet took the German in the spine, causing him to immediately collapse.

Colonel von der Heydte later claimed that elements of his regiment had reached the Carentan railroad station that day by following the railroad tracks into town. These troops were the only German attackers to actually get into Carentan on June 13. That some of them managed to extricate themselves during the German withdrawal without being killed or captured is no small miracle.

American paratroopers had managed with furious small arms fighting to hold the 17th SS at bay until arrival of the 2nd Armored Division. After Parmley saw the

Right: A generic photo of Waffen SS grenadiers on the Normandy front, exhibiting the same appearance as the troops who attacked Carentan on June 13, 1944, resulting in the famous battles of Bloody Gulch and Bloody Gully. *German Press*

In mid-June 1944, Lt. William Russo's 2/501 81mm mortar platoon set up beyond Hill 30, near La Billonnerie, France. Using binoculars, Lieutenant Russo observed a German dispatch rider approach the suspected command post of the 37th SS Panzergrenadier Regiment. He laid four mortars on the approach road. The next day, a motorcyclist again approached the same way, from the same direction. Russo ordered all of his zeroed-in mortars to fire. The shells landed and exploded at the intended location just as the cyclist arrived on that spot. He and his bike were blown sky high, and the two photos shown on this page depict the results. *Mike deTrez collection*

German paratrooper mysteriously collapse, a Sherman tank from F/66th Armored Regiment of the U.S. 2nd Armored Division crashed through his hedgerow, almost running over the body of the recently fallen Fallschirmjager. The tank proceeded through a manmade gap in the next hedgerow to the west and arrived in time to extricate elements of F/502 from a bad situation. Some of them had gotten too far forward and were surrounded by SS troopers.

While charging across an open field later that evening, Parmley was hit through the rear base of his neck by a rifle round. The shooter only missed his head because daylight was fading and Parmley was running at the time he was shot. Parmley believes he was shot on a downward angle by a sniper in a tree. "There were lots of bigger guys to shoot at, so why he chose me, I don't know—maybe he liked the challenge of hitting a smaller target." He was evacuated from Normandy after receiving this wound, but he would never forget his close encounter with the German parachutist.

Elements of the 2nd Armored Division launched a furious assault on the Germans beyond Bloody Gulch. The D/66 Armored Regiment after-action report indicates how the 2nd Armored earned its nickname "Hell on Wheels":

A Mark III German tank, already obsolete in 1944, was used by the 17th SS as a command vehicle in their attack of June 13, 1944. After the tank was knocked out and abandoned, Lt. Joe Pangerl and Lt. Larry Hughes of HQ/502 posed in it. *Joseph Pangerl*

> D Company attacked at 1400 along the route running west between Carentan and la Campagne. . . . It was a rainy and dismal afternoon. The terrain was evenly divided into small squares by ditches and hedges. The Germans . . . were well entrenched. D Company charged the hedgerows and ditches, traversing each hedgerow with machine guns and firing into occasional tree tops for snipers. The total results were scores of dead, three 75mm antitank guns, one Mk IV tank, and no prisoners.
>
> D Company reached a line running north and south through the village of Douville where it was relieved by Company F 66th Armored Regt. . . .
>
> The company had expended some 75,000 rounds of .30 caliber ammunition, 225 rounds of 75mm H.E., 750 rounds of .45 caliber ammunition, and 25 hand grenades. Our losses were one M4 tank, one officer wounded, one enlisted man injured. This hard-hitting initial assault against an entrenched and determined SS Panzergrenadier Regiment cracked their line and broke their will to resist further in this sector.

Thanks to a violent attack by the 66th Armored Regiment, 14th AFA Battalion, 3/41 Armored Infantry Regiment, and other 2nd AD units, the German intruders were driven back past their original start line with heavy losses. Cantepie, and soon after Auvers, France, were liberated and occupied by members of the 502nd PIR.

The second half of June 1944 was spent holding defensive positions to the south and west of Carentan. Some of the positions faced the swampy Prairies Marecaguses beyond Meautis. The survivors of Cole's 3rd Battalion 502nd PIR were still in the line, with Company G first occupying Cantepie, then moving to establish a line southwest of there, near la Godillerie. Lieutenant Colonel Steve Chappuis' second battalion faced west near Auvers, and 1st Battalion was in reserve on the north flank along the Carentan–la Haye du Puits railroad line. Lieutenant Colonel Cassidy's 1st

Reflections on Combat Survival and Life on the Battlefield, by Sgt. Louis Truax D/506

Now this is a very critical point: since a gun barrel is straight, one end must be higher than the other. The higher a man's shoulder, the lower the front end of the barrel. The sound of rounds overhead automatically tells him how high he can raise his shoulder and still live. Some men's shoulders automatically go higher than others. Sounds complicated, but it's really very simple. The higher his shoulder, the more [endangered] he becomes. The better his ears are, the longer he lives. In training, a machine gun or M1 rifle has a frightening effect at over three thousand yards. Schmeissers, Thompsons, Stens, *et cetera,* maybe one thousand yards. When a man is in a hole, he hears these rounds overhead first . . . then the guns that fire them. His ears must tell him how high those rounds are over his head . . . three hundred feet, two hundred feet, one hundred feet, ten feet, five feet, or six inches. Hence the famous words *pinned down.* When he has heard enough of them, he becomes acclimated. He seems to automatically know how high he can raise his head.

On the subject of mess gear, I never used anything but a canteen cup in combat. We didn't have any food except K rations most of the time, occasionally C rations. Once in awhile, I'd shave in my canteen cup, [and I] carried K ration toilet paper in my helmet.

We never crowded around a slit trench toilet. Good way to gather a barrage of eight-eights; always watched for krauts bunching around a toilet, too. When light or smoke was not a problem, I'd fill my helmet half full of dirt and pour Kraut tank gasoline in it. Then I'd cook me up bullion or chopped pork and egg yolks. K rations always had "Camels," "Luckys," or the much-hated "Wings" in them. Since I only smoked a pipe, I've been known to scrounge tobacco off dead Limeys or even the Kraut "ersatz" tobacco. Foul smoking stuff compared to "Prince Albert," but when you're hungry, you can even "eat" smoke or think about eating the bark off the trees. I always carried Halazone tablets to purify water or melted snow.

I was never squeamish about taking things off dead Yanks, if I needed them—boots, sleeping bags, weapons, *et cetera* . . . anything I needed . . . only way to survive . . . GI field glasses, .45 Colt automatics, *et cetera.*

Battalion later sent patrols south into the swampy areas, as did elements of regimental HQ/502.

The 501st had established HQ at le Sapin, a stately chateau on the Carentan–Periers highway, a few hundred meters north of the road junction where antitank gunners of A Battery, 81st Airborne, AA/AT Battalion, had stopped the two German SP guns on June 13. The 506th PIR was still on their right flank, tying in with the lines of the 502nd. To the left of the 501st were elements of the 327th GIR, whose lines extended as far east as St. Pellerin, east of the highway to St. Lo. The 30th Infantry Division would eventually occupy that sector, between Graignes and St. Jean de Daye, to begin their drive into France.

The 175th regiment of the 29th Infantry Division had liberated Isigny and tied in with the 327th to unite the Omaha and Utah beachheads. The stage was being set for the eventual liberation of St. Lo followed by the breakout of late July 1944, six weeks after D-Day. The breakout would signal the end of the battle of the hedgerows, and only then would Gen. George S. Patton's mighty Third Army begin their brisk drive across France, through Paris, and on to the German border.

The various regiments of the 101st would spend the second half of June patrolling and sweating out incoming mortar and artillery barrages. Captain Cecil L. Simmons was still commander of H/502 PIR, one of Lieutenant Colonel Cole's rifle companies that had played a crucial role in the famous bayonet charge of June 11, 1944, north of Carentan. Captain Simmons found time to write a letter to his family in late June:

25 June, 1944
Dear Folks,
The big guns are roaring and our planes are in command of the skies and Jerry with his crack troops are trying to throw us back into the sea but he has American Paratroops to contend with and we have our own ideas about being thrown anywhere . . . as a result, he is backing up to get a running jump at us and each time he backs up we keep him company. As you have read in the papers, we have had hand to hand and bayonet to bayonet combat and have dug him out of his holes with just plain American intestinal fortitude and good fighting equipment. It might be interesting to note we have been awarded a Presidential Citation . . . nice eh? Write when you can. . . .
Love Cec

By June 27, 1944, the 101st Airborne Division was relieved of their frontline positions beyond Carentan by elements of the 83rd and 90th infantry divisions. The various subunits of the 101st boarded trucks that took them north, past recently liberated battle areas at Carentan and St. Come du Mont, then veered northwest via St. Sauveur le Vicomte (recently liberated by the 82nd Airborne Division), then on northward to various positions in and around Cherbourg to mop up and provide security as the damaged port was being cleared and made operational again.

Before leaving the Cherbourg area to return to England for the next mission, Len Langford of HQ 2/502, LMG Platoon, wrote to his future wife, LaVerne, about his current situation:

4 July, 1944
My Dearest . . . it is a bright, sunny day for a change. Some of the boys have gone to the beach for a swim. My turn probably comes tomorrow. Honestly, I haven't had a decent bath for a month! I probably don't look too bad, but the feeling is there, just the same. My jump suit is in terrible shape. I won't wash it cause they get light, and a bright uniform makes a beautiful target. I don't want any snipers taking pot shots at me, if I can help it. A couple have already, and it's not comfortable feeling . . . I've been studying how to get this souvenir into this letter. It's a piece . . . from the parachutes we used to jump here. It isn't from my chute—I left mine too fast, not worrying about taking it! Everyone wears a camouflaged silk scarf. I doubt very much if they are wearing part of the same parachute they actually jumped into France with.

CHAPTER 5

ENGLAND, SUMMER 1944

Len Langford of 2/502 wrote to LaVerne again after returning to England in July 1944. Some excerpts from his letter reflect bitter personal views of the war in regard to the affluent class of French refugees:

I spent much of a day in the port of Cherbourg . . . it wasn't a bad town. The people in the city were glad to see the Yanks or at least pretended to be happy about the whole thing. There was no end of flags waving and tricolor ribbons on their lapels. Their famous war cry was [translation] "Long live the Americans, any chewing gum, candy, cigarettes?" The cigarettes were hard for them to get, because they were crazy for them. One Frenchman told me they cost one hundred francs a pack or two dollars! And money was scarce there, except for the select few that you always find in every country.

I pity the "poor" French peasants, but as for the rest—all of them in fact—I wouldn't give a damn for the whole bunch! I just can't stomach them! Even over here [England], there are Frogs galore—wealthy people that got out or were chased out during the German occupation and are just sitting around waiting for France to be liberated so they can go back to their "beloved" country—parasites, waiting for someone else to do the dirty work. They didn't have guts enough to stay there, so they left and let the poorer class bear the suffering. I recall one incident in London, in an exclusive hotel.

General Eisenhower talking with Corporal Leroy Gravelle of I/502 PIR. Gravelle and Chester Elliot were with Cornelius Owens hundreds of yards south of Bridge No. 4 at Carentan when Owens was fatally wounded by a German bullet. This happened on Sunday, June 11, 1944, hours before Cole's bayonet charge. *Signal Corps*

We were having tea, and across from us were two Frogs (female) and a 4-F Frenchman—dressed in the best of clothes. They were jabbering away, entirely unconscious of a war going on. I had just returned from France and comparing those poor ragged French people with these wealthy [censored] made me see red! This is a helluva way to fight a war—feeling the way I do about things. A man doesn't go through war just hating the enemy alone. Gosh, I'm getting excited—guess I should cool off a little before finishing this . . . Keep writing and keep loving me.

Yours Forever,

Len

In England during summer 1944, one of the most unusual events was a fistfight between two 501st officers. Lieutenant Ben Stevens of Great Falls, Montana, became

The Taylor brothers. In a scenario similar to that in *Saving Private Ryan,* a 101st Airborne trooper lost two of his three brothers, both killed in action. Stokes Taylor (far left) was a member of the 80th Airborne AA/AT Battalion in the 82nd Airborne. Stokes was killed in the Battle of the Bulge in heroic action against 1st SS Panzer troops at Trois Ponts, Belgium. He was awarded the Distinguished Service Cross posthumously. Jim Taylor, USN, was killed aboard the original cruiser *Quincy,* when it sank near Guadalcanal. Ironically, the *Quincy*'s namesake *USS Quincy II* fired support for 101st Airborne troops in Normandy. David Taylor was first sergeant of regimental HQ/502 PIR. He survived the war as did Ben Taylor, far right, who joined the U.S. Army Rangers. *Tom Taylor*

unhappy with Capt. James T. Brennan, a 1st Battalion medical officer. They fought between the tents at Hamstead Marshall for a full hour, until both were too bloodied and weary to continue.

Many combat jumps for the 101st Airborne Division were planned but eventually cancelled that summer. On a couple of occasions, the troops actually went to airfields, received invasion money, ammunition, rations, and briefings before the missions were canceled. A small task force of 377th Artillery personnel sailed to the continent to be on the drop zone when one of these jumps was to take place. When the mission was canceled, the members of the task force had to return to the United Kingdom to await the next real deployment.

Many of the men who had survived the Normandy Invasion were still licking their wounds, both physically and psychologically. The veterans reflected on why they had survived while many close buddies had perished. Always, there was the question of who else would "get it" before the war was finished. The never-ending mourning for lost friends had only started.

British Field Marshall Bernard Montgomery had devised a massive airborne operation. Had it succeeded, the war in Europe might have ended by Christmas 1944.

Ike and General McAuliffe inspecting some towering glider infantrymen in England. The helmet stencils of these soldiers identify them as members of 1/327 Glider Infantry Regiment (GIR). *Tom Mallison*

Members of HQ 3/501, summer 1944. They had recently moved to tents at Newbury from stables at Lambourne, England. New twin buckle combat boots had also been issued to replace the jump boots, a very unpopular policy that was eventually rescinded by army administrators. Stacey Thompson second from right, standing, and John A. Alexander, second from right, kneeling, were killed together in a barn north of Eerde, Holland, by a German night patrol. Norbert Kowalski, far right, kneeling, was a T-5 radioman who was cited for bravery in the Hill 30 attack south of Carentan. He would be killed by a German 88mm artillery shell near the town of Mont, Belgium, east of Bastogne. *Chuck Bahr via Mary Santiago-Bahr*

Division communicators in England, summer 1944. Among those pictured are Daniel Shearer, recently transferred from HQ 3/501 to Division Signal Company, Lt. Col. Sidney Davis, holding map board, 1st Lt. Bill Johnson, C.O. of Division HQ Company, and Lt. Oliver Handlesman, recently transferred from 401st Glider Infantry to Signal Company. *Signal Corps photo from Wierzbowski collection via Nadine Wierzbowski-Field. Identifications via George Koskimaki*

Paratroopers of the 82nd and 101st Airborne divisions, as well as their glider-borne units, would invade the German-occupied Netherlands by air. By landing along a pre-designated route, they could secure a number of bridges over numerous rivers and hold them open for British armor, driving north from the Belgian border. The final bridge, over the Neder Rhine River had to be captured, held, and crossed by this armored task force for the mission to succeed. The Brits could then skirt the industrial Ruhr to the north and make a stab for the German capitol at Berlin.

The British 1st Airborne Division would land at Arnhem, farthest north in this new Allied Airborne corridor to capture and hold the final bridge over the Rhine. While this plan sounded good in theory, it would prove too ambitious in scope to ultimately succeed. The project diverted many thousands of gallons of gas from U.S. armored forces, which were now stalled at the German border. Also, the objective lay between the German Fifteenth Army, still in place along the Atlantic coast and the German border. Operation Market-Garden underestimated the resources that the German military could throw into counterattacks to thwart Allied intentions. Also, the presence of the two SS Panzer Divisions of 2nd SS Panzerkorps at Arnhem was not known to Allied intelligence. A large, costly, bloody, and ultimately failed operation was in the offing.

During summer 1944, two separate combat missions were planned that took the troops as far as the airfields before being cancelled. General Taylor addressed the mass of troops shown assembled here and apologized that the latest mission had been scrubbed. When he promised the troops that he would get them another combat mission as soon as possible, someone booed. *Signal Corps via Nadine Wierzbowski-Field*

APO 472, U. S. Army
15 September 1944

<u>MESSAGE FROM THE DIVISION COMMANDER</u>

Men, at last we have the real thing. We're headed for the German lines of communication through HOLLAND, to seize the important bridges on the route of the 2nd British Army to GERMANY. Marshal Montgomery's troops at this very moment are surging forward and we must have the bridges if the British advance is to roll.

We must work fast. Every man must hit the ground running to his prearranged point of assembly. Every man must know the importance of the bridges at ZON, VECHEL and ST OEDENRODE. If you land near these bridges, stay there. Drive off any Germans who are about. Dig yourself in to cover the bridge with the fire of your weapon. Officers and demolitions experts, look for explosive charges and remove them. The bridges must be taken fast and taken intact.

I have talked to you before about supply discipline. Everyone in BELGIUM and HOLLAND is short of food and ammunition. We must not lose a bundle or leave behind a ration. Make every shot count, especially those of the mortar squads and of the artillery.

We go into this fight to help the British forward. We can give this help not only by seizing the bridges but by keeping the roads clear of prisoners, civilians and our own troops. We can help by covering the flanks of their columns and by preserving the wire lines and the boats and barges on the canals. The British will help us by bringing us supplies and evacuating our wounded. And they will lend us a strong force of tanks to give us the type of support we had from the American tanks at CARENTAN.

We are the first American troops into HOLLAND. To the Dutch and to our British Allies we are individual ambassadors of the United States. We must conduct ourselves as such at all times.

My last word is this. We have a clear cut airborne job. It might be our last one, so it must be done well. I promise this Division the same aggressive leadership which carried it to victory in NORMANDY. I expect a D day performance from every officer and man.

Maxwell D Taylor
MAXWELL D. TAYLOR,
Major General, USA,
Commanding

To be read by every jumpmaster and glider leader to his stick just prior to enplaning. Then <u>DESTROY</u>.

This letter is an extremely rare artifact. Note the last sentence indicating that these sheets were to be destroyed after each jumpmaster read the message to his troops. *George Lage Jr.*

Soldiers of the 101st Airborne participating in this mission would be a combination of surviving Normandy veterans and newly arrived replacements who were doing their best to be trained and assimilated into their new squads, platoons, companies, or batteries. The Normandy veterans now knew the reality of what a combat deployment meant and would approach the coming missions with a sober and realistic attitude. Still believing they were unbeatable on the battlefield, however, there was confidence in the ultimate victory. As to individual doubts, Glen Derber of the 501st wrote:

> I realized I wasn't the largest or toughest guy in the outfit, but I wasn't worried about the possibility of hand-to-hand combat. I knew that as long as I had a single bullet left in my rifle, I would never have to deal with that.

In mid-September 1944, the troops were alerted to prepare for another combat mission. This time it would actually come to pass. The biggest difference from Normandy was that the combat assaults, parachute jumps, and glider landings would take place in daylight. Also, much more of the 101st Airborne Division would be inserted into battle by gliders, with relatively few soldiers crossing the Channel by sea. The thousands of glider-borne infantrymen, artillerymen, engineers, medical, and HQ personnel would require several consecutive days of airlifts to deposit all of them in the Netherlands.

A group from the HQ 81mm Mortar Platoon, 1/506 PIR posed in England in early September 1944. Standing (left to right): Richard C. Newell, Charles J. Becht, four unknowns, Dudley, and Joseph Gates. Kneeling: Albert Merrill, Leo Bert, Lester "No-No" Nowlin, Osie Burton, Elmer Krall, Roscoe Brinson, and Bill Grovenburg. A close look at Osie Burton reveals that he attached two pockets that were removed from the chest of an M42 jacket to both shoulders of his newly issued M43 jacket. This is a rarely seen modification. *Bill Kennedy via A. Borrelli*

CHAPTER 6

HOLLAND, PART I: LIBERATION OF THE CORRIDOR

At about 1300 on Sunday, September 17, 1944, the first elements of the 101st Airborne from the 501st PIR began jumping in the sandy area between Veghel and Eerde, Holland. The remainder of the 501st would jump to the northwest at Drop Zone A-1 near Heeswijk. Having the element of surprise, the 501st drops went mostly unchallenged. Elements of 1st Battalion and RHQ moved from Drop Zone A-1 toward Veghel from the west. They left a rear guard near the Heeswijk castle, which was later mostly wiped out. The rest of the 501st moved from Drop Zone A to Veghel, securing road and railroad bridges over the canal and river in the area. Initial resistance was light.

Down on Drop Zone C, it was a different story. Although the weather was clear and perfect, considerable antiaircraft fire greeted the 506th and 502nd regiments as they left their C-47s at more than one thousand feet altitude. Some C-47s were hit and shot down. Sergeant Gordon Yates, the company radioman for H/506, wrote of the jump:

Captain Richard Meason was quite a guy—we were close. He was my company commander; I was his communications chief. He's dead now, partly because some shrapnel was never removed and he was in pain from then on. [While standing up for the red light] Captain Meason received some flak around the midsection. Not much bleeding, but several punctures, as though metal was inside. He said, "Hell, you can't evaluate me [here], we're behind the lines. Let's go!"

Three officers from regimental HQ/506 taking a break at the side of the Vlokhoven church in Eindhoven, Holland, September 18, 1944. Left to right: Lt. Schrable Williams, Lt. Bruno Schroeder, and Lt. Edward S. Haley. *John Reeder*

At left, on September 17, 1944, Col. Howard R. Johnson, commanding officer of the 501st PIR, chats with Gen. Lewis Brereton, commander of the 1st Allied Airborne Army, before boarding a C-47 for Holland. Colonel Johnson jumped from the first plane in the lead serial at Drop Zone A near Eerde, Holland. Below, on September 18, Brig. Gen. Anthony C. McAuliffe was photographed with an unidentified Air Corps colonel before boarding a glider with troops of the 327th GIR. *Signal Corps via Steve Mrozek*

I was wounded around the face by the same flak that got Meason. A piece [went] through my upper right lip [evidently spinning], knocked out 5 teeth and left out through my mouth. I was spitting blood and teeth. I received aid from Captain Feiler [regimental dentist] and moved out.

With wounds such as those just described, both Captain Meason and Yates certainly could have justified unhooking their static lines and returning to England on the plane to receive proper medical attention. Instead, they opted to make the parachute jump and to continue fighting despite their serious wounds. This was common behavior within the 101st Airborne Division.

The paratroopers coming to ground by the thousands on Drop Zone C assembled quickly on the signal of various-colored smoke grenades. Members of each battalion ran toward their predesignated color. A few troopers landed close enough to colored smoke from their sister regiment to run to the wrong signal. But this minor confusion was soon straightened out, and the battalions began rapidly moving on their missions.

Before the 1/506 could clear the drop zone, they saw two CG 4-A gliders circling overhead collide in midair and crash to the ground. There were some survivors, but the troopers could devote only a short time to trying to free them from the wreckage and had to move south through the forest to seize the bridge over the Wilhemina Canal in Son before the Germans could blow it up. Major General Maxwell D. Taylor had jumped with 1st Battalion of the 502nd PIR, but being on the same drop zone as the 506th after landing, he opted to follow 1/506 in their bid to seize the Son (Canal) Bridge.

Meanwhile, Lt. Col. Robert G. Cole's 3/502 headed west to attempt to capture the canal bridge at Best, Holland. The 1st Battalion of the 502nd headed north off the drop zone to take Sint Oedenrode and establish an outpost, and 2/502 went into a brief reserve status at Wolfswinkel.

While 1st Battalion of the 506th moved south through the woods, 2/506 moved due east off the drop zone, encountering a German flak unit twenty yards past the road that would become known as "Hell's Highway." Without breaking stride, members of Dog Company wiped out this small German detachment, then turned south directly down the highway, heading toward the Son Bridge from the north.

Members of F/506 who were with Dog Company would destroy a German 88mm flak gun near the west side of the road with bazooka fire. First to reach the Son Bridge from the north were Staff Sgt. Frank Anness and Ray Taylor of Dog Company. With them was a replacement who had recently joined their company. These troopers could not have known it at the time, but the Germans had positioned entrenched troops near the bridge and behind the North Brabant Sanatorium in the previous week, also wiring the bridge with demolition charges in anticipation of an Allied attack. Seeing that crossing the bridge without the rest of 2nd Battalion was suicidal, Anness and Taylor ran back north to collect the rest of their company. They alerted the stragglers to hurry forward, and then returned to the area just north of the bridge.

Their replacement buddy had decided to make a fast recon across the bridge to the far side. He was coming back across when the Germans blew it up. Anness and Taylor ducked into a small alley between Dutch homes on the east side of the road about fifty yards north of the bridge. Debris from the bridge explosion rained down for an extended period. A huge steel angle iron thudded onto the ground a few feet from where Anness and Taylor were standing. Members of Company A 506th watched the explosion from a different perspective, several hundred yards west of the bridge along the north bank of the canal.

Captain Moe Davis' company had taken severe casualties from two 88s that were fired directly at them from sandbagged emplacements facing north into the woods. The German guns were positioned on the north bank of the canal and used tree bursts, and later, direct fire to inflict many casualties on Company A. In a final desperate rush, the two guns were taken and soon thereafter the Germans detonated the bridge.

US Airborne Actions, D+1, Operation Market-Garden

Captain Eli H. Dixie Howell, the 506th 1st Battalion operations staff officer, was walking along the north bank waving an orange smoke grenade. He had activated it and it was spewing forth colored smoke. A German sniper fired from across the canal. The bullet hit Howell's face at an angle, removing one of his eyes. Recently commissioned, Lt. Francis Fleming was wounded in both knees, ending his combat career.

Lieutenant Colonel James LaPrade, the commanding officer of 1st Battalion, 506th, swam across the Wilhelmina Canal along with Pfc. George "Birdlegs" Dickson of C/326 AEB. They used planks from a rickety wooden fence, securing them with jump ropes to the remaining footings of the destroyed bridge to form a makeshift

When Leslie Harris of I/501 learned that a troop carrier pilot from his hometown was among those flying 3/501 to Holland, arrangements were made for Harris to jump from his plane. Pilot John Henry Peterson (left) was Harris' cousin by marriage. Leslie Harris (right) and his entire stick were flown to Holland on Peterson's plane. *Leslie Harris*

means for much of the 506th PIR to cross to the south bank.

Their mission was to head south into the city of Eindhoven to meet British armor coming north from the former front lines in northern Belgium. A few elements of the 506th would remain in Son to provide security for Gen. Maxwell Taylor, the 101st ABD commanding general. Taylor's command post was established in De Sonnerie, a religious institute several hundred yards north of the canal. Across the road was the North Brabant Sanatarium into which medics of the 326th Airborne Medical Company moved their operations to treat the wounded of both sides from the fighting in that area.

Members of the 326th Airborne Engineer Battalion began working to restore a decent bridge in the area where the original Son Bridge had been blown up. The 506th PIR would march part of the way to Eindhoven on September 17, sleeping in fields beside the highway at Bokt that night. The assault into the north end of Eindhoven would resume on the morning of September 18, led by elements of 3rd Battalion.

Late on September 17, the 1st Battalion of the 502nd PIR had entered Sint Oedenrode and engaged German troops in the large medieval cemetery behind the church. Other elements outposted the roads heading north from Sint Oedenrode to Veghel and to Schijndel. Other roads leading to the west were also secured.

Lieutenant Colonel Robert G. Cole's 3/502 was heading west toward the town of Best, Holland. Some elements probed south through the Zonsche forest in a bid to capture the canal bridge in front of Best. A small mixed group of H/502 PIR and C/326 AEB troopers were isolated and trapped along the north bank of the canal, just east of the bridge. They were unable to secure the bridge and would watch helplessly as the Germans also destroyed that particular crossing with explosives.

Two troopers from D/501 wearing Griswold rifle cases, newly modified with extensions to allow the M1 Garand rifle to be jumped fully assembled. *Ken Moore*

Captain Robert Jones had two-thirds of Company H at the opposite (north) edge of the forest when one of his men shot a German motorcyclist who was leading a sizable column of trucks containing German infantry troops. An unwanted battle then erupted, with one company trooper being killed immediately. Jack Dunwoodie, another Company H man, cradled him in his arms as he died. Fighting in this area would rage all night, with German artillery and mortar concentrations exploding into the treetops above American troops sheltering in the forest. In the next two days, the battle at Best would continually escalate as hundreds of German troops poured in to the area via train, arriving from Dutch cities north and west of the U.S. Airborne corridor.

Members of Service Company, 506th PIR, on the runway before Holland. Note the silhouettes of C-47s parked in the distance. *Mrs. Gerald Loraine*

By evening of September 17, 501st troopers had secured the Veghel-Eerde area and prepared to repulse German counterattacks while awaiting arrival of the British armored columns of 30th Corps. The area between Sint Oedenrode and Veghel was only outposted lightly and that segment of Hell's Highway was mostly vulnerable to being cut by German forces. The first night of U.S. Airborne presence in this corridor, a recon and intelligence patrol from the 502nd PIR went up the highway from Sint Oedenrode, clear to Veghel, and established contact between the Deuce and Col. Howard R. Johnson's 501st PIR.

A long stretch of highway extending beyond Uden to Grave was also mostly without U.S. presence, creating a gap in the bridgehead between forces of the 82nd and 101st Airborne divisions. In the coming two weeks, as British armor inched up Hell's Highway toward Arnhem, these gaps would have to be filled. Sections of the road which were cut by enemy attacks had to be continually reopened to British traffic by various elements of the 101st Airborne Division.

The 1/502 held Sint Oedenrode, and the 3/502 had the woods along the south edge of Drop Zone C, although the Best Bridge was no longer a viable objective. Crucial Dutch towns along the meandering road known as Hell's Highway served as bases of operation from which American troops fought to keep the highway open. This became, in essence, the mission of the 101st in the first phase of Operation Market-Garden.

THE 506TH ATTACKS INTO EINDHOVEN

On the morning of September 18, 1944, Company H of the 506th led off the assault from Bokt into Eindhoven. After wiping out German infantry pockets in the fields on the outskirts, the 3/506 troopers entered the north edge of town along Vlokhoven Street and began clearing German troops one house at a time.

Members of the regimental S-2 platoon of the 501st PIR donning parachutes and equipment for Operation Market-Garden on September 17, 1944. The parachutes used for this mission were T-5s modified with the addition of a quick harness-release device, making these forerunners of the later mass-produced T-7 design. Staff Sgt. John F. Tiller, of Boaz, Alabama, stands at far left. *Signal Corps via P. Adamec*

Vincent "Sharky" Tarquini was one of the boldest members of How Company, and after clearing a house by jumping in through a large glass window while firing his rifle, he demonstrated how to clear an entire city block using a single hand grenade. Tarquini would approach a German-occupied house and toss a grenade in the window on the near side of the building. He would then run to the opposite side of the building and shoot the fleeing Germans down, one-by-one, as they came pouring out. Tarquini then went inside, retrieved his grenade (he never pulled the pin), and repeated this scenario on each successive house.

Sharky Tarquini was a short trooper who resembled "Yogi Berra on a bad hair day." Miraculously, he emerged from World War II combat without a scratch.

Reaching a significant curve in the road, Captain John Kiley, the operations staff officer of 3/506, was shot dead by a sniper who fired from the steeple of the Vlokhoven church. Also on Vlokhoven Street, Don Zahn and Godfrey "Jon" (pronounced YON) Hansen sought cover in a Dutch home on the right side of the street. Hansen was a former college student and mountain climber from California.

As Zahn moved deeper into the house, Hansen stood in front of the large living room window. The sniper in the church tower could not target Hansen's head due to the angle from which he was looking down from the steeple. Instead, he fired through the window at Hansen's midsection and inflicted an agonizing and mortal wound. Zahn carried the dying trooper out into the garden at the rear of the house. These two troopers, having much in common in education and intelligence, had been very close friends. Shortly before Hansen breathed his last, Zahn walked out of the garden as he could not bear to watch him die. Hansen's last words were, "Tell Collette I love her," referring to a Red Cross girl the troopers had known in England. This episode left Don Zahn badly shaken for a long time afterward.

Bill Galbraith of Item Company fired a clip of .30-06 M1 rounds up into the sniper's window and then sprinted to the church entrance. The sniper evidently fled,

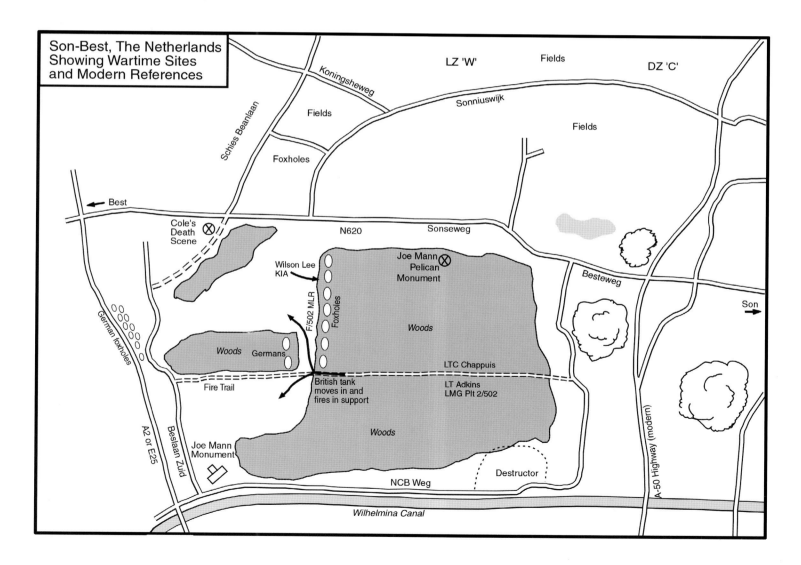

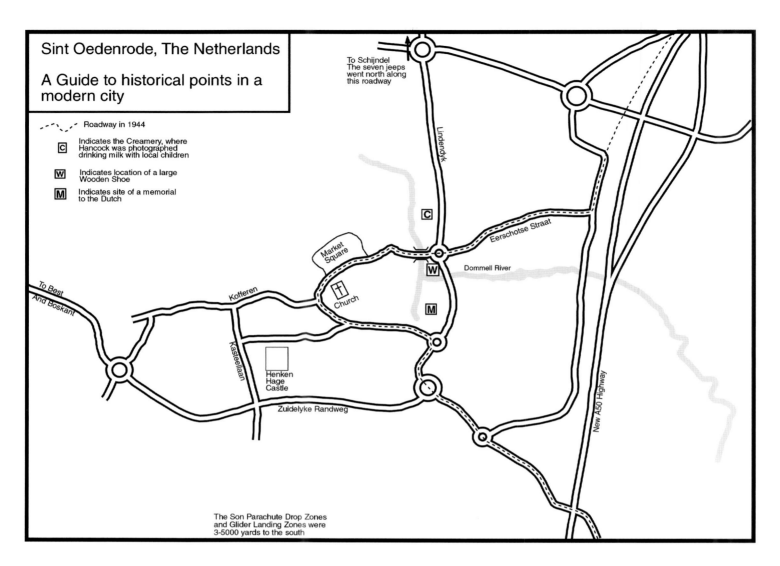

Sint Oedenrode, The Netherlands

A Guide to historical points in a modern city

- - - - Roadway in 1944

C Indicates the Creamery, where Hancock was photographed drinking milk with local children

W Indicates location of a large Wooden Shoe

M Indicates site of a memorial to the Dutch

To Schijndel
The seven jeeps went north along this roadway

Lindendyk

Eerschotse Straat

Dommell River

Market Square

Church

To Best
And Boskant

Kofferen

Kasteellaan

Henken Hage Castle

Zuidelyke Randweg

New A50 Highway

The Son Parachute Drop Zones and Glider Landing Zones were 3-5000 yards to the south

running down the long, winding spiral staircase of the bell tower. As of 2006, Bill Galbraith's bullet holes could still be seen in the rear wall of the bell tower behind the sniper's window.

Continuing deeper into Eindhoven, two dual-purpose German 88mm flak guns again held up the progress of the 3/506 on Vlokhoven Street. Exploding against nearby Dutch buildings, 88mm flak rounds killed some troopers and badly wounded Bill Galbraith, ending his World War II combat days. Those German 88mm flak guns were flanked by members of Company F, who used a mortar, rifle grenades, and M1s to destroy the German crews and capture both guns. Hank van Zeldern, a Dutch teenager in 1944, recalled that a third German 88mm was situated in the living room of a Dutch farmhouse, on Barrier Weg, but it never came into play as the route of the 506th bypassed it at some distance.

Colonel Robert Sink soon established his regimental command post in a school beside the Vlokhoven church. Here, a British Recon car entered Eindhoven after circling the perimeter and made first contact between XXXth Corps and 506th troopers. However, as the fighting progressed deeper into the city of Eindhoven, it became necessary to move

HQ/506 into the Catholic Center building closer to the middle of the city. The 506th would liberate two additional Dutch churches in Eindhoven; first St. Catharina's beyond the Dommel River Bridge, then the Paterskerk near a canal. The large Phillips Electric Company high-rise office buildings were cleared by members of A/506.

In various neighborhood streets, vengeful Dutch people now carried out reprisals on accused collaborators, shearing off the hair of the females and shooting many of the male turncoats. Thousands of Dutch civilians poured into the streets offering apples, ice cream sandwiches, beer, and other treats to the paratroopers. Kissing, dancing, singing, and celebrating liberation day with orange bunting displayed everywhere, the populace was in a joyful frenzy. Sergeant Gordon Yates of H/506 recalled, "Most of all, [it was] the sincerity and happiness of the Dutch people at being liberated. They were laughing and crying at the same time, saying, 'We are so happy you have come!'"

The various reprisals and celebrations would seriously delay the flow of northbound British traffic. Even without the crowds, the proposed route up Hell's Highway involved many twists and turns just to get through Eindhoven. Hank van Zeldern recalled the route: "Up AA Listereweg to Strumsedyk, to Eind, to Rechterstraat, to Demer, across the railroad to Fellenoord, to Bschdyk, to Frankreichstraat, to Woenselstraat, then to

The sky above Eerde, Holland, was filled with parachutes, as members of the 501st PIR, minus 1st Battalion, jumped at 1300 on September 17, 1944. *Albert A. Krochka*

Members of the 327th GIR march to waiting gliders on September 18, 1944. This regiment would secure the area southwest of Son, while other elements helped the 502nd PIR in clearing the Zonsche forest north of the Wilhelmina Canal. *Signal Corps via Nadine Wierzbowski-Field*

Vlokhoven, finally north out of the city to Son and points north."

Able Company troopers boarded British tanks of the 15/19 Armored Regiment and patrolled to the northwest of Eindhoven, while elements of 2nd Battalion probed toward a German Panzer staging area at Helmond via Nuenen. Company G was sent to secure the airfield west of town.

The city was struck by a German air raid on the night of September 18–19, resulting in the deaths of a number of local Dutch residents. Some Company G men would be detailed to retrieve unexploded German bombs later that day. It required three troopers to lift each bomb, and they laboriously carried the deadly duds over to the nearest canal and tossed them in. Jim "Pee-Wee" Martin still gets angry when he thinks how ridiculously hazardous that assignment was.

Because some of the 506th troopers had pulled out of Eindhoven before the air raid to perform recon duties on the outskirts of the city, many Dutch residents falsely assumed that the Americans had prior warning of the raid yet didn't inform them of the danger. This caused a brief period of resentment until the Americans explained that the raid had been as much a surprise to them as to the Dutch victims. Positive relations were resumed, and the people of Eindhoven would continue to share a bond of friendship with their liberators extending well into the next millennium.

JOE MANN AND THE BATTLE FOR BEST, HOLLAND

The first afternoon, Sunday, September 17, 1944, elements of 3/502 headed southwest from the drop zone, and one platoon cut through the Zonsche forest to the Wilhelmina Canal in an effort to capture the bridge east of the town of Best. Joining with the Company H men were some engineers from Company C of the 326th AEB. This force came under heavy fire, and many of the troops ran into the woods and headed back in search of larger groups of friendly forces.

Stranded near the bridge were Lt. Edmund Wierzbowski of H/502 and a small group of his men along with some Charlie Company engineers. The U.S. group was unable to capture the bridge and watched helplessly as it was eventually exploded by German demolitions. The Germans came under repeated attack by Wierzbowski's force, who fired a bazooka at the Germans and caused damage to their positions, including the destruction of an ammunition dump.

Private First Class Joe Mann of Reardan, Washington, was the aggressive individual bringing the fight from his small, outnumbered group to the local Germans.

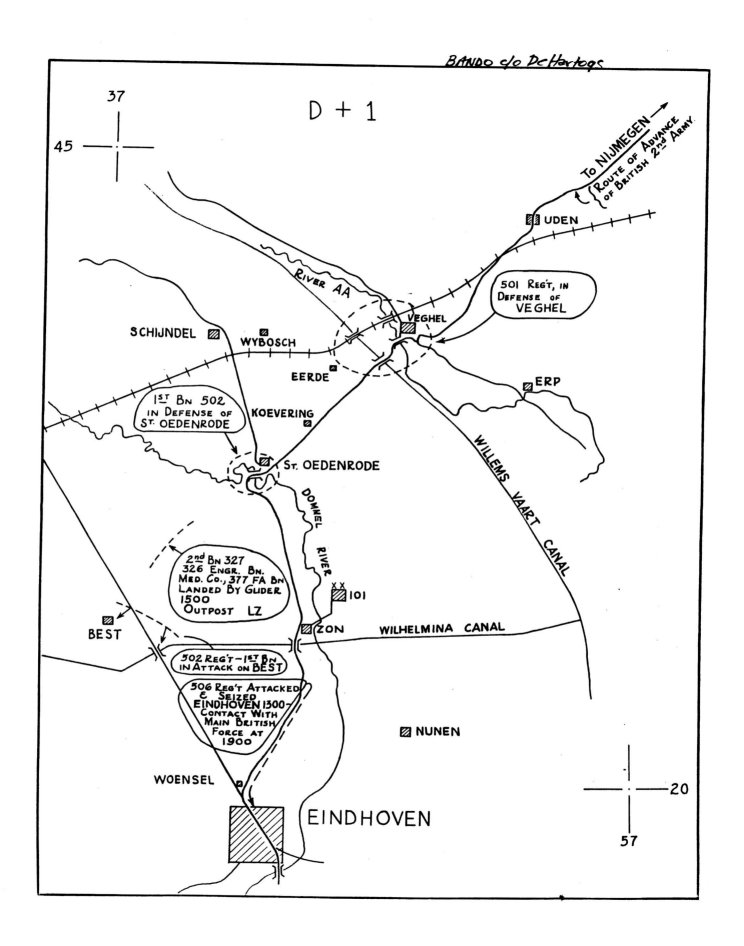

D + 1

To NIJMEGEN →
Route of Advance
of British 2nd Army

UDEN

RIVER AA

501 Reg't, in
Defense of
VEGHEL

VEGHEL

SCHIJNDEL
WYBOSCH

ERP

EERDE

1st Bn 502
in Defense of
St. OEDENRODE

KOEVERING

WILLEMS VAART CANAL

St. OEDENRODE

DOMMEL RIVER

2nd Bn 327
326 Engr. Bn.
Med. Co., 377 FA Bn
Landed By Glider
1500
Outpost LZ

XX
101

BEST

ZON

WILHELMINA CANAL

502 Reg't — 1st Bn
in Attack on BEST

506 Reg't Attacked
& Seized
EINDHOVEN 1300 —
Contact With
Main British
Force at
1900

NUNEN

WOENSEL

EINDHOVEN

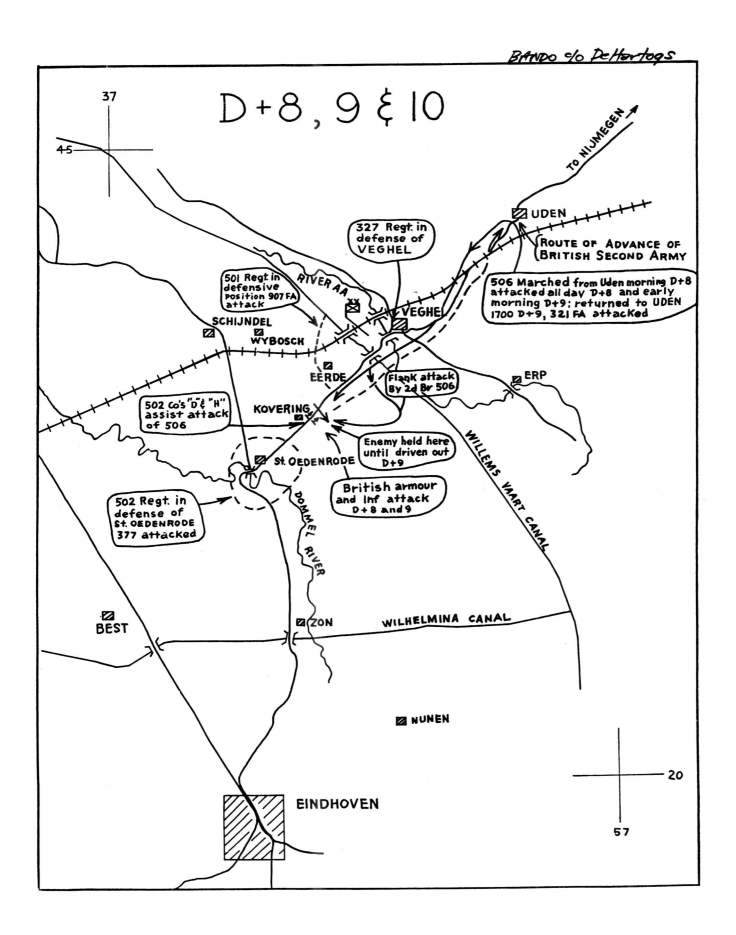

BANDO c/o DeHartogs

D+8, 9 & 10

37

45

TO NIJMEGEN

UDEN

327 Regt. in defense of VEGHEL

ROUTE OF ADVANCE OF BRITISH SECOND ARMY

RIVER AA

501 Regt in defensive position 907 FA attack

506 Marched from Uden morning D+8 attacked all day D+8 and early morning D+9; returned to UDEN 1700 D+9, 321 FA attacked

SCHIJNDEL

VEGHEL

WYBOSCH

EERDE

Flank attack By 2d Bn 506

ERP

502 Co's "D" & "H" assist attack of 506

KOVERING

Enemy held here until driven out D+9

St. OEDENRODE

British armour and Inf attack D+8 and 9

502 Regt. in defense of St. OEDENRODE 377 attacked

WILLEMS VAART CANAL

DOMMEL RIVER

BEST

ZON

WILHELMINA CANAL

NUNEN

20

EINDHOVEN

57

At left and below, after spending a night near Bokt, Holland, the 506th PIR attacked the city of Eindhoven with a plan to meet northbound British armor there. This was no cakewalk, as depicted in *Band of Brothers*. Led by 3rd Battalion, they suffered numerous men killed and wounded as they fought their way into town. A sniper in the steeple of the Vlokhoven church killed Capt. John Kiley and Pfc. Godfrey Jon Hansen. Two 88mm dual-purpose artillery pieces on Woenselstraat inflicted more casualties. These guns were flanked by members of F/506, who eradicated their crews with rifle grenades and small arms fire. *John Reeder*

Members of E/506 in Eindhoven. Left to right: unknown, Amos Taylor, Sgt. Carwood Lipton, McLaurin, Bill Kiehn (later KIA), and Campbell T. Smith.
Pratt Museum, Ft. Campbell, KY

Wounded several times, Mann's arms were both rendered useless and bandaged as he remained in a firing position with others who could still fire weapons.

On the morning of September 18, German attacks on Lieutenant Wierzbowski's position eventually captured it. A hail of hand grenades and small arms fire preceded a rush by the German infantry. Machine gunner Vincent Laino, C/326, was among those furiously shooting the attackers until he was blinded by a grenade blast. When another German grenade landed in the trench behind Mann, he realized he could not toss it out because of his wounded arms. Mann yelled, "I'm taking this one!" and lay back on the grenade, absorbing its blast and thus saving the lives of his companions. Without a whimper, Mann said, "My back is gone," then died.

Soon thereafter, his surviving companions, including Lt. Edmund Wierzbowski, were taken prisoner and marched to a nearby German aid station. They were able to grab weapons while the Germans were not paying attention, capture the aid station, and return to the American positions with a batch of prisoners.

Less than two miles northeast of Mann's heroic action, the remainder of Lieutenant Colonel Cole's 3rd Battalion was engaged in fierce combat with ever-increasing numbers of German troops from many assorted units. In reaction to the Market-Garden landings, trainloads of German troops were being diverted to the Best area from Amsterdam and other Dutch towns outside the battle zone. So many Germans would

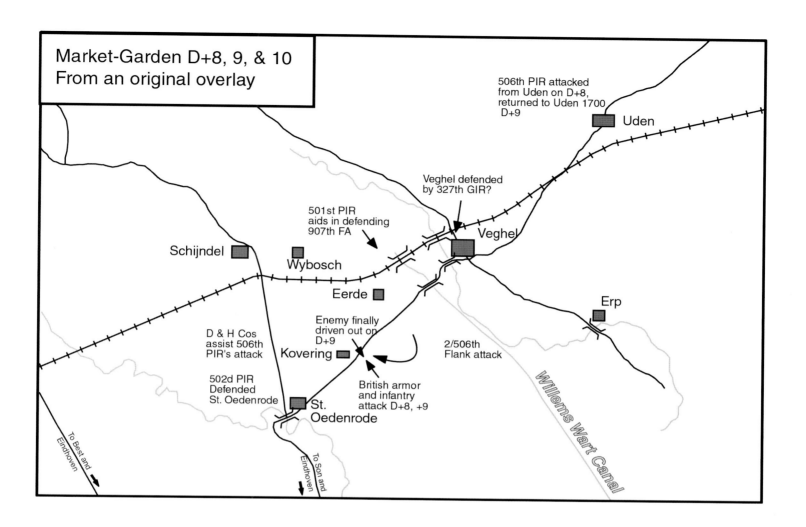

Market-Garden D+8, 9, & 10
From an original overlay

506th PIR attacked
from Uden on D+8,
returned to Uden 1700
D+9

Uden

Veghel defended
by 327th GIR?

501st PIR
aids in defending
907th FA

Veghel

Schijndel

Wybosch

Erp

Eerde

Enemy finally
driven out on
D+9

D & H Cos
assist 506th
PIR's attack

Kovering

2/506th
Flank attack

Willems Wart Canal

502d PIR
Defended
St. Oedenrode

British armor
and infantry
attack D+8, +9

St.
Oedenrode

To Best and
Eindhoven

To Son and
Eindhoven

While the 506th was securing Eindhoven, and 3/502 was moving toward Best, 1/502 took Sint Oedenrode and sent patrols probing west toward Donderdonk and Olland. Early in the fighting there, Lt. Mort J. Smit was seriously wounded when he knocked down an incoming German stick grenade and it exploded, setting off a fragmentation grenade that was hung on his hip. Captain Hancock used Smit's camera to snap this photo of Smit being evacuated while feeling the effects of a morphine injection. *Mort J. Smit*

arrive in the coming days that the town of Best never was captured by 101st or British Guards armored forces, despite their eventual local victory above the Wilhemina Canal and west of the Drop Zone C area. Lieutenant Colonel Chappuis' 2nd Battalion of the 502nd had been alerted to move west and reinforce Cole's troops. They departed Wolfswinkel and joined the fighting near Best late on the 18th.

THE BATTLE AT BEST

Lieutenant Colonel Cole had requested air support, but the rocket-firing Allied planes overhead were strafing too close to Cole's front line. He went out into an open field in front of the trees where his men were dug in to personally adjust the recognition panels on the ground. As he stood shielding his eyes from the sunlight, a sniper's bullet struck him in the temple and fatally wounded him. Cole's men dragged his body back into the woods, placing him in a shallow foxhole that was too short for his long body.

There he would remain until the following day. Cole had been recommended for the Congressional Medal of Honor (CMH), a result of his leadership in the Carentan bayonet charge, and he was still awaiting this award at the time of his death.

After securing Eindhoven and probing to the east and west of that city, the 506th PIR was back on Hell's Highway retracing their steps north to Son and beyond. This photo shows members of regimental HQ/506 PIR taking cover in a field near Hell's Highway on the journey north toward Veghel. *John Reeder*

A house in the open field north of 3/502's main line of resistance (MLR) was believed to be the source of the bullet that killed Cole. A trooper from Item Company named Robert Boyce observed a German attempting to escape from the house and shot him down. The men of 3rd Battalion assured themselves that Cole's slayer had been killed and his death avenged.

Joe Mann would also receive a posthumous CMH for his self-sacrificing heroism near the Best Bridge. It is interesting to note that the only two CMH recipients in World War II's 101st Airborne Division were both members of the 3rd Battalion of the 502nd PIR, both of them killed within twenty-four hours and two miles of each other as the crow flies when they died.

Medics of the 377th PFAB and DIVARTY on Hell's Highway. All Market-Garden forces were pushing toward Arnhem and the German border. *Wierzbowski collection via Nadine Wierzbowski-Field*

One of the German weapons that fired persistently into 3/502 positions on the 18th was a 20mm gun situated quite a distance to the north. Chester Elliott of I/502 left his machine gun long enough to borrow a trooper's .03 rifle from the adjacent foxhole. Running the sights up to seven hundred yards, Elliot was able to drop one of the 20mm gunners, whose body draped over the top of the weapon. After hitting a second crewman, the gun stopped firing for the rest of that day.

The 2nd Battalion troops launched a counterattack into deadly fire on September 19, working west across the highway that connected Best to Eindhoven. The attack headed slightly northwest, guiding on the Best church steeple. Captain LeGrand "Legs" Johnson, located west of the highway, was wounded in the shoulder. The Germans had an MLR at that part of the highway, with two parallel lines of foxholes and riflemen facing east.

Legs Johnson was shot in the head while being evacuated to a field hospital by jeep. His runner, T-4 Charles Dohun, found his body in a "dead pile" at Son later that afternoon and forced a surgeon (at gunpoint) to operate, saving the captain's life.

South of the spot where Johnson was initially hit in the shoulder stood several two-story buildings where many German troops spent the night of September 18–19; most of them were killed when they came out of those buildings on September 19 to man their firing positions.

Johnson's Fox Company withdrew from Best to their original line of foxholes, which ran north from the area where Joe Mann had been killed. While there, Sgt. Wilson Lee was KIA by a 20mm hit to the midsection, John Hovey was grazed across the side of his face by a close bullet, and many other troopers were wounded.

Meanwhile, elements of the 327th GIR were clearing the Zonsche forest south of the drop zone and working westward, with a squadron of twelve British tanks diverted from Hell's Highway. One of the British tanks (which was diverted from Hell's Highway at the direction of Maj. Allen W. Ginder), arrived via a logging trail and fired support for F/502 with its main battery, sending rounds to the northwest and southwest.

The 502nd was in a precarious situation, facing a large force of German troops, when the British tanks arrived to assist them. This turned the tide, and more than 1,100 German troops were taken prisoner, thus ending the crisis on the west flank. The impressive bag of prisoners was quickly organized by Lt. Joseph Pangerl, the IPW officer of the 502nd, and herded east to the vicinity of Son. A strafing Allied plane killed a few of the POWs and threatened to stampede the entire group, but order was maintained and the survivors reached Hell's Highway for further evacuation to the rear.

Also on the 19th, along the canal east of Son, the Germans launched an attack with six Panther tanks and accompanying infantry in an attempt to capture or destroy the new bridge being built to replace the one blown on the 17th. Members of HQ 1st Battalion and C/506 fired across the canal at the German attackers from a berm on the north bank, while members of A/506 and some individuals from division HQ engaged the attackers directly—on the south side of the canal. Colonel Ned Moore of division HQ manned a bazooka that struck one of the Mk V tanks.

Eventually, all the attacking vehicles were knocked out, and the German infantrymen who were not killed faded back. Newly commissioned 2nd Lt. James Diel, former

Reg Davies

Anatomy of a Silver Star Action

On September 19, 1944, 2/502 was attacking through the Zonsche forest on the flank of 3/502, trying to turn the tide in a desperate situation. Advancing west across a field, Company F was pinned down by effective fire from a quad-20mm antiaircraft gun that fatally wounded Sgt. Wilson Lee and wounded several others. The German AA gun was horse-drawn and was delivering fire from a stopped position on a road.

Lieutenant Colonel Steve Chappuis got around the left flank of the gun crew and realized he needed an effective weapon to knock out the 20mm guns and their crew. Spotting Reginald Davies, a member of the 2nd Battalion light machine-gun platoon, Lieutenant Colonel Chappuis personally asked Reg if he could work his way close to the 20mm crew and take them out with his LMG.

Reggie began dragging his A6 LMG along the road in a crawl, approaching the gun crew from their right flank. His assistant gunner crawled along parallel to him in the roadside ditch holding aloft the belt of .30-06 armor-piercing ammunition. When Reg got about one hundred yards from the gun crew, they noticed him approaching.

While the 20mm's kept firing toward F Company, two German riflemen opened fire on Reg and his assistant with Mauser rifles. With the element of surprise gone, Reg opened fire on the gun crew, watching his tracers find the target. He killed the security men, the gun crew, and the horses and kept firing until the ammunition supply exploded. This was accomplished with the total expenditure of less than sixty rounds of ammunition. Chappuis personally wrote Reg up for a Silver Star that he received soon thereafter.

Two members of regimental HQ/502 in a foxhole on the edge of Drop Zone C. Both have personal weapons close at hand as one writes and another reads a letter from home. The following day, shortly after the duo vacated this hole near a large haystack, a C-47 resupply plane was shot down and crashed at this exact spot. *Len Swartz*

Members of C/502 with prisoners taken outside Sint Oedenrode, Holland, circa September 18, 1944. *Mort J. Smit*

The Landing Zone W area seen from above, with gliders still in place at their final rest positions. Capt. Evans C. Thornton, former aide to Gen. William Lee, was a 502nd PIR staff officer assigned as liaison to the 1st Allied Airborne Army for Operation Market-Garden. After spending several days in the landing area above Son, Thornton was withdrawn from the invasion area via ground transport and then flown back to 1st AAA HQ in England. He used this photo to brief General Brereton and the other Allied Airborne staff officers. *Thornton via Jake Crellin*

SCALE.

Members of the 506th inspect a captured self-propelled gun mounted on a Czech armored chassis. This vehicle belonged to the Panzerjager Kp613 of Panzerjager Battalion 657 and was captured on Hell's Highway between Son and Sint Oedenrode. *John Reeder*

first sergeant of E/506, was now assigned to A/506. He was killed in this battle, when he single-handedly charged one of the enemy tanks with explosives. Also lost in the battle was a trooper who jumped into the canal and drowned while attempting to swim to the north bank.

The troopers who were dug in on the north bank discovered how devastating the fire from a high-velocity 75mm gun could be. A bazooka was fired from the left flank, serving only to draw the nearest tank's attention to American presence on the north bank. A German 75mm tank round hit a tree on that flank spraying fragments into Lt. Frank Stone and collapsing a sizable tree, which fell across his body. Shrapnel from the same shell sprayed Lt. Harold Cramer, stripping much of the flesh from his legs; he would die from his wounds several hours later. Over on the right flank, Lt. Wayne Winans was killed when a German machine-gun burst struck him in the head as he looked over the top of the embankment. These officers were all members of Charlie Company of the 506th.

Other incidents that developed in the fighting to keep the corridor open for the British Guards Armored Division resulted in the 501st PIR defending Veghel against numerous attacks. The first one came along the canal from Hertogensbosch during the first night, in which a probing German battalion hit E/501 in the early hours of September 18. After a fierce battle, the German battalion was repulsed, and its survivors retreated back the way they had arrived.

Next, the 1st Battalion of the 501st made a sweeping maneuver against German forces that were getting ready to attack Veghel from the northwest, in the

A closer view of Allied officers examining the captured self-propelled gun. Colonel Sink stands at center, with back to camera, Maj. Clarence Hester at right. Note the British tanker wearing a black beret, standing at left. *John Reeder*

Heeswijk–Dinther sector. Lieutenant Colonel Harry Kinnard's troops maneuvered skillfully and captured hundreds of Germans, who were then paraded through Veghel to POW cages. Colonel Johnson then sent his 1st and 3rd Battalions on a night attack to the west to disrupt German forces staging for an attack in the Schijndel area. Although the incursion was successful, the U.S. forces were withdrawn the next day because the Germans had cut Hell's Highway near Koevering and 2/501 had all it could do to hold Veghel. The 3rd Battalion returned to Eerde, soon to be joined there by 1st Battalion.

Fighting to secure Eerde would require taking and holding the sand dunes at the northwest edge of town. A dramatic charge was led by Lt. Harry A. "Monk" Mier's 3rd Platoon of Able Company, while Able's other platoons provided covering fire. Lieutenant Colonel Kinnard came right up to the front lines and gave advice as to where to position the machine guns. Ed Posnek, firing his LMG in a supporting role, would shoot many Germans that day. During the melee that followed, Lt. Harry Mosier would be seriously wounded, and Lt. Cecil Fuquay would die immediately from the concussion of a nearby exploding shell—without a visible mark on him.

As Lieutenant Mier prepared to give the order to charge, he was crouching beside Pfc. Eddie Gulick, whom he describes as, "a little, gutsy SOB." When Mier gave the order to "fix bayonets!" though, Gulick told him, "Lieutenant, you've lost your *mind*!" Mier told his attackers to prepare hand grenades. On a given signal, they threw them all at once, which Mier says, "shook hell out of the Germans."

Mier's men then jumped up and rushed into the midst of the enemy to do close-combat with them. As Lieutenant Mier charged into the sand dunes, his heart was pounding and he was so pumped with adrenaline that he could not hear firing, only the roaring of blood in his ears. As if acting in a silent movie, he ran—firing from the hip—and watched Germans falling as his men added their firepower to the assault.

One Able Company trooper locked into a hand-to-hand struggle with a much larger German. The pair fell to the ground, with the German rolling over atop the Geronimo trooper. Lieutenant Mier drew his M-3 trench knife, rushed up to the struggling pair, and stabbed downward into the German's back, withdrawing it, and plunging it in again and again. On the third stab, he left the knife planted and pushed the dying German off to the side. Then he continued advancing, while again firing his weapon. An officer who witnessed this ferocious attack later wrote, "I doubt if any group of men could have held their ground against it."

Medic George Whitfield of the 326th AMC operated a medical evacuation jeep with Capt. Henry Barnes. Under direct fire from a German tank near Koevering, Holland, the duo evacuated many wounded soldiers, mainly English and German. For his death-defying bravery in accomplishing this, Whitfield was awarded the Distinguished Service Cross. *Whitfield via Terry Poyser*

Survivors who tried to flee from the assault of 3rd Platoon were mowed down by the machine guns and small arms of the other platoons. When this battle ended, the 1st Battalion of the 501st owned the Eerde sand dunes, and Monk Mier's intrepid paratroops had written another bloody victory into the annals of U.S. Airborne warfare.

Other German attacks on Eerde were repulsed by Company G on the north in epic struggles, as machine gunner Melton "Tex" McMorries proved instrumental in stopping the numerically superior enemy. On the east side of Eerde, only five hundred yards from the church in the center of town, members of H/501 (later supported by Dog Company troopers sent from 2nd Battalion) did furious defensive work to hold the Germans at bay. German paratroopers in the area were identified from several regiments, including the 6th Para, which had fought against the 101st in Normandy. Students sent from the Hermann Göring Panzer Division's training school, at Amersfoort, Holland, were also identified in the fighting.

After 3rd Platoon of Company H had lost both their platoon leaders—as well as platoon sergeant Norman N. Nelson—to enemy fire, a private named Fred Schleibaum assumed the leadership role in that unit. One afternoon, he told Carl Beck to reposition his LMG and cover a certain area near some trees in the distance. Having done his own reconnaissance of the enemy position, Schleibaum had been his own I&R/S-2, and he now made his own estimate of the situation and his own attack plan. Schleibaum explained how he would take a few men around the flank of the German position and open fire, which he anticipated would cause them to flush into Beck's field of fire. The plan was implemented, and this is exactly what happened. Schleibaum had been a grape farmer in California and Beck describes him as "a horse of a man." This example illustrates how outstanding men in the enlisted ranks of the 101st Airborne could take over and lead by the strength of their own talents and initiative, even after all their assigned troop leaders were dead or wounded.

The Germans launched numerous attacks against Veghel, mostly coming from the east. But on the September 23, 2/501 was sent southwest on an attack to reinforce 3rd Battalion at Eerde. The

While other units were engaged at Eindhoven, Son, Best, Sint Oedenrode, and Koevering, the 2/501 PIR defended Veghel against many German probes, while 3rd Battalion outposted Eerde and 1st Battalion swept the northwest approaches to Veghel, between Dinther and the Aa River. In the photo, John J. Sullivan of D/501 has just flushed two Germans from hiding at the edge of Veghel. *Signal Corps photo*

Larry Cormier (right) and an unknown wounded paratrooper from B/501, taking a break in Veghel. Cormier had already lost his best buddy, Jack McNally, killed in action in Normandy. Cormier would also be KIA soon after this photo was taken. *Dutch Photo via Bob Burgess*

Members of the 101st Airborne Division artillery staff pause to talk with Dutch civilians in the corridor. Traffic on the highway behind them was rather constant. *Wierzbowski collection via Nadine Wierzbowski-Field*

attack across open ground turned out to be for naught. Soon after arriving on the outskirts of Eerde, most of the battalion was recalled to Veghel to ward off the latest attempt to sever the British convoys on Hell's Highway.

The attack cost 2/501 some valuable men. Kenneth Reiller was shot and killed as he ran across the open ground toward Eerde. T-4 Joe Mero of HQ_2 had performed heroically in helping to decimate German attackers the day before. On the 23rd, however, Joe reached a tree-lined dirt road north of Eerde and was fatally wounded by shrapnel. He would survive to be evacuated and even managed to write a letter home before succumbing to his wounds, sixteen days later. Elements of the 506th moving up from Son would reinforce the 501st at Veghel and extend the 101st presence up to the town of Uden.

A German document captured by the 508th PIR was passed along to 101st Division G-2, which published it in a daily order on September 28, 1944. The memo gives information, advice, and instruction to defenders of German static positions, and—as evidenced by the following excerpts—contains some interesting lines:

A recon team from H&H 501st PIR S-2 paused for a photo in the corridor before embarking on a tour of Nijmegen in the 82nd Airborne sector. At the time this took place, the city was still in German hands. The Geronimo S-2 troopers hitched a ride to that sector with the British convoy. This unauthorized recon trip cost the life of King R. "Red" Palmer. Several men in this photo won worldwide fame six weeks later as members of the "Incredible Patrol" that was featured in *Life* magazine. Pictured from left to right are: Frank "Chief" Sayers, Bill Canfield, Richard "Smoky" Ladman, Frederick J. "Ted" Becker, and Roland J. Wilbur. *Canfield Photo via Roland J. Wilbur*

It is essential to beat the enemy ruthlessly, wherever we can catch him. Every soldier, every German man, has to defend himself to his last cartridge and fighting ability. Everybody has to realize that enemy paratroopers or terrorists cooperating with them are unable to take prisoners, since they cannot afford to spare guards for captured troops. Counter terror is the best defense against this.

The enemy uses picked men for paratroopers, men who are familiar with all kinds of gangster methods and who are even dangerous when wounded. Searching for weapons of wounded POWs is essential. A comrade is to cover the searching soldier with a loaded weapon. Beware of gangster weapons, which can be fired through the pockets by means of concealed wires, in the position even of hands up. There is also a possibility that the enemy wears a German uniform. Hence: don't be trusting . . . Conserve ammo—aimed firing only—for it might be necessary to hold the position for days, until relief might come up. Use rifle for individual enemy, not the machine gun.

Over at Eerde, southwest of Veghel, 3/501 fought an isolated war, later joined by British armor, 1/501, and Company D from 2nd Battalion. Most German attacks came from the northwest and east. Northwest of town was a sizeable section of sand dunes and A/501 made a bold sweep through those dunes to disrupt assembling German attackers. This photo shows prisoners taken in the aftermath of the sand dunes battle. *Signal Corps, Wierzbowski collection via Nadine Wierzbowski-Field*

A lend lease Sherman M4 tank manned by a British crew passing through Veghel. The sign on the tree indicates that the tank is passing the command post (CP) of the 2/501 PIR (Klondike White). *Bruce M. Beyer*

Guy Whidden's Miraculous Escape from Death

Guy Whidden was a gunner in the LMG Platoon of HQ 2/502. On September 18, 1944, while walking through the woods west of Son carrying his forty pound 1919A6 LMG, Whidden got lost and separated from friendly troops. He wandered alone for some time along a road where intermittent mortar shells were exploding.

Suddenly, from behind a clump of bushes, a large, stocky German solder leapt out and tackled Whidden to the ground. Guy Whidden was pinned, lying on his back, with the forty-pound machine gun across his chest and the large German lying atop the gun. Whidden could not reach his carbine or trench knife. The German worked his way up to a sitting position, then he drew his P-08 Luger pistol and placed the muzzle against Whidden's face.

The eyes of the two enemies met; Whidden guessed that the German was in his forties and old enough to be his father. Suddenly the German's eyes took on a look of compassion. Whidden could almost read his thoughts, and he got the impression that seeing him reminded the German of someone younger, someone he cared about—perhaps a son back in Germany? In a few seconds, the situation changed, from Whidden assuming he was about to be killed to the German handing over the Luger and surrendering to him. They walked together for many minutes in search of American lines, not as captor and prisoner, but more "like traveling companions." Guy Whidden brought the German in to the 2/502 area as his prisoner. Soon thereafter, Whidden was seriously wounded in the leg by an exploding shell. As a result of this wound, Whidden was sent back to the states, and after recuperation he served as an A-stage instructor at the Parachute School for the rest of World War II.

The 101st Division's G-2 report for the following day described a little known, but rather interesting, enemy unit that was identified as operating in the Hell's Highway corridor:

> PW Report: A new unit was identified when a PW was taken today from Luftwaffe Jager Battalion. According to PW, this is a specially trained GHQ recon battalion, whose personnel work in patrols of five unobtrusively dressed (PW wore a sniper's tunic, civilian trousers, and blue, high-necked sweater . . .) So, apart from the unobtrusiveness, might have been taken for a British officer. [He was] carrying no pay book or personal belongings.
>
> They are armed with machine pistols. Their task is to penetrate our lines and record our dispositions, tactical signs, etc. The battalion arrived three weeks ago, from Italy, where they had lately been employed in the north, stalking Italian partisans and Allied armies. They are under command of Oberst Ewald, who is stated to command all troops in Hertogensbosch. PW claimed to have been in Veghel yesterday and identified the Kangaroo Division.

By late September, the portion of Hell's Highway south of Uden was mostly secured from German efforts to sever it by means of local actions. In retrospect, the 101st Airborne survivors of the Market-Garden mission would ruefully remind all that they did accomplish their assigned mission and it was in no way their fault that

Above and left, hundreds of Germans captured by 1/501 PIR in Lieutenant Colonel Kinnard's "broom and dustpan" sweep near Dinther, on September 21, 1944, were paraded through jeering Dutch crowds in Veghel. Company C had provided the blocking force near Heeswijk as companies A and B swept a force of Germans into them. A total of forty Germans were killed, and 418 were taken prisoner (forty of whom were wounded). *Bruce M. Beyer*

the British armor could not reach its objectives. From the Everest of postwar hindsight, we now know that the expenditure of gasoline and lives would have been better spent elsewhere on the western front in late 1944. But with political pressure on General Eisenhower to hold the Anglo-American coalition together, he gave in to Montgomery's demands and Operation Market-Garden became a doomed reality.

The Corridor and Hell's Highway phase of Market-Garden was ending—the era of the muddy, bloody island was about to begin. The entire 101st Airborne Division was alerted to move north, to be used as supporting infantry in Montgomery's army for a prolonged time period, which would last most of the next two months. During this time, the 101st would subsist on British rations, along with whatever food they could scrounge from local Dutch houses, farms, and liberated jam factories. Moving unit by unit in truck convoys, the 101st Airborne Division would leapfrog past the 82nd Airborne, which had been fighting hard since September 17 in the area surrounding Nijmegen. They would cross the Nijmegen Bridge over the Waal River and stage at various places including Elst, Slijk, Ewijk, Andelst, and Zetten, eventually tying in with British forces and forming an L-shaped line from Dodewaard to Opheusden and to the area east of Driel, with main lines facing west and north.

An unknown glider trooper visiting the temporary grave of a fallen buddy at the cemetery north of Son, Holland. Note how one identity tag was tacked to the center of each wooden cross. The crosses were burned several years later, as bodies were either returned to stateside families or permanently interred in the U.S. military cemetery at Margraten, Holland, under marble markers. This dramatic and haunting image brings home the costly reality of human lives lost—even in a "good war." Frank Hoffman collection via R. Campoy

CHAPTER 7

HOLLAND, PART II: THE ISLAND

Arriving on "the island" on October 4, the 506th initially staged at Zetten before moving northwest to outpost a town called Opheusden. Artillery batteries set up firing positions east of Zetten at Hemmen from which they could fire westward to support the 506th and 1/327 GIR. The island was so called simply because it was a sector of land with rivers on all sides, making it impossible to arrive or depart the area without crossing a body of water—the Waal River on the south and the Neder Rhine on the north.

Opheusden was expected to be a quiet sector as American paratroopers first moved in to assume its defense from the British. This was not to be the case. October 5 and 6, 1944, proved to be horrendous days of fighting for the 506th PIR at Opheusden. Elements of a German Volksgrenadier division attacked repeatedly all day coming from west to east.

In town, near the large windmill that became a first aid station, elements of the 1st Battalion of the 506th fought the Germans to a bloody standstill. Captain "Red" Minton of B/506 established a defense perimeter just west of the aid station. The 506th troopers were supported by .50 caliber machine guns and British-made six-pounders from the 81st Airborne AA/AT Battalion, and later by British troops of 5th Battalion Duke of Cromwell Light Infantry. The three hundred Brits attacked to the westward in rows, and all but thirty were mowed down by the German Volksgrenadiers and their mortars and artillery.

The train station near the Linge Canal at the south edge of Opheusden. It changed hands numerous times in the heavy fighting that took place in the area during the first ten days of October 1944. *Signal Corps*

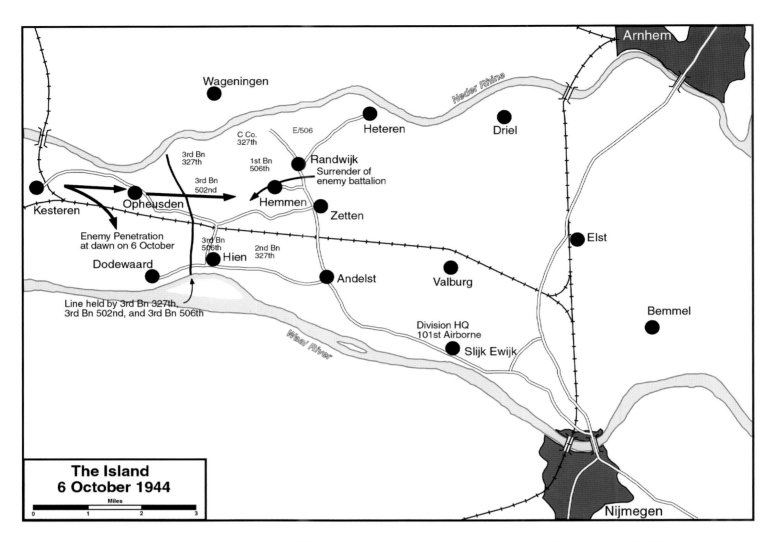

The Island
6 October 1944

The Germans counterattacked with supporting armor, and their tanks wended their way right into the town of Opheusden. During the seesaw fighting in town that day, 1st Sgt. Bill Knight of C/506 had two M1 rifles shot from his hands, both of them destroyed. The scabbard of his M1 bayonet was pierced in the metal part at the top by shrapnel, but Sergeant Knight emerged unscathed from the fighting.

Sergeant Edgar Dodd of B/506 was a husky trooper (two hundred pounds) who had been a member of the original parachute test platoon. Dodd lay wounded near the base of a wall, and German troops were resting right on the other side. Sergeant C. A. Mitchell and others drove near in a requisitioned medical jeep, and then they quietly loaded Dodd and another wounded trooper, who was placed in the front seat. The jeep took off briskly and delivered the wounded to the aid station in the large wind-mill near the north end of Opheusden. Soon after Sergeant Dodd was taken into the windmill, a direct hit by the main battery of a German tank destroyed the jeep that had conveyed him, killing the passenger in the right front seat. This was William J. Yorko, also of B/506.

The interior of the aid station looked like a slaughterhouse. Bob Flory was among the wounded, talking to Don Patton, who was skewered with two long pieces of

In early October 1944, the 101st Airborne leapfrogged past the 82nd Airborne, crossed the Nijmegen Bridge, and found themselves southwest of Arnhem in an area surrounded by rivers and nicknamed "the island." In contrast to the small German "tankettes" encountered in the Corridor, the 506th encountered Mark VI Tiger 1s, while the 502nd at Elst met Mk V Panthers. Normal airborne armament (i.e., bazookas, six-pound antitank guns, and 75mm pack howitzers) was effective only at point-blank range against these iron monsters. The Panther pictured was found abandoned near Elst by HQ/502 PIR troopers. *Joseph Pangerl*

shrapnel that were piercing completely through his leg. Catholic chaplain John Maloney was standing upright, holding a plasma bottle over a badly wounded trooper and refused to duck, even when close-exploding shells sent shrapnel whizzing through the inside of the aid station.

Sergeant Charles Weise, another casualty of B/506, was so badly wounded that he barely avoided being placed on the "dead pile." Weise joined hands with Don Patton as Patton began praying aloud. Weise later wrote:

It seemed like immediately the war stopped. We were not getting shelled. The medics stopped to listen. It was a very stirring moment in my life. As soon as he stopped praying, shrapnel came in again and struck one of the doctors in the abdomen. He fell backwards, grasping his innards, and the medics got busy trying to care for him. But the religious concept was so fantastic. . . .

A farm at Slijk Ewijk, Holland, on the Island, briefly occupied by the 502nd PIR. After a glance at the map, American troopers referred to this place as "Slicky-Wicky" (the Dutch pronounced it *Slike Ay-VIKE*). One afternoon, a huge 210mm German artillery shell exploded here, fired from the north side of the Neder Rhine River. Joe Pangerl, a newly promoted captain, recalls that as the shell came in, it caused everyone's knees to buckle from the sudden displacement of air before it impacted and exploded. Pangerl's former roommate, Richard Daly, of regimental demolitions, narrowly escaped death when the exploding shell blew mud all over him. This deliverance from death was only temporary—Lieutenant Daly would die in a different explosion a month later. *Joseph Pangerl*

LT BURNS, "I" CO WITH
PATROL IN NO-MANS LAND
ON THE "ISLAND"

An interesting double exposure with Lt. Richard Daly (close-up at top) superimposed on a group of I/502 troopers about to embark on a patrol near Wely, Holland, in October 1944. Standing near center, facing the camera is Lt. Bob Burns, an I Company platoon leader.
Joseph Pangerl

The surgeon who was blown back into the aid station in this incident was Lt. Cyrus Worrell, who had a small hole in his abdomen from which his intestines were oozing. Worrell, who was assistant battalion surgeon for the 1st Battalion of the 506th would lose several feet of intestines and suffered other internal injuries from this incident.

Lieutenant Bill Pyne, the commanding officer of Charlie Company was wounded in the chest and evacuated. Lieutenant Albert Hassenzahl of 3rd Platoon became the new acting CO. Hassenzahl was standing in the doorway of a Dutch building watching mortar and artillery shells exploding nearby when he looked across the street and saw two of his men, who were equipped with a bazooka, crouching in a ditch. A sudden ESP flash caused the lieutenant to call the men over to join him in the doorway. As soon as they arrived, a German shell exploded on the exact position they had just vacated. Hassenzahl said, "When this happened, it really spooked all three of us. [But] as I recall, both of those men were killed soon thereafter." The 1st Battalion would join the general withdrawal from Opheusden that evening.

3RD BATTALION OF THE 506TH
AT THE SOUTH END OF TOWN

Earlier that morning, Lt. Col. Oliver Horton, the 3rd Battalion commander, was fatally wounded while walking along the railroad tracks near the Linge Canal at the south end of town. Both sides expended a terrific amount of artillery and the batteries of the 377th PFAB and 321st GFAB were pouring hundreds of rounds of 75mm pack howitzer shells into the southwest perimeter of Opheusden from their gun pits near Hemmen. By sheer force of numbers, the Volksgrenadiers overran entire squads of 506th paratroopers, including Sgt. Charles Richards' squad from Company H. Miraculously, some of these overrun elements not only survived but escaped to fight again. These German elements were also supported by tanks.

Down near the railroad signal station, by the road that crosses the canal, Company H of the 506th reconsolidated their line and held out for hours. Sergeant Don Zahn and Sergeant Frank Padisak were actually running 1st Platoon of Company H, as their replacement platoon leader, Lieutenant Stroud, had deferred to their experience after Staff Sergeant Clawson went MIA. Zahn's troops held the railroad station, then, later that afternoon, withdrew to a woods several hundred yards south of there.

Before withdrawing to the east, Sgt. Ralph Bennett found himself in the railroad signal station after most of his buddies had withdrawn. He suddenly saw a squad-size

East of Opheusden, Holland, an abandoned quarter-ton truck (jeep) bearing markings of the 321st GFAB is examined by a lieutenant of regimental HQ/327 Glider Infantry Regiment. *Signal Corps*

element of German infantry walking broadside past his window at a range of about thirty feet. They were not aware of his presence in the building. Ralph swung his Tommy gun into action, spraying the group from side to side, as the rapidly hammering .45 slugs knocked all the Germans down. He watched as pieces of flesh and field gray uniform material flew away from the bodies of his unsuspecting victims. Ambushing these men from such close range was a horrible experience that Ralph could not erase from his memory. For years after World War II ended, "Those guys chased me, in my dreams," Ralph said.

He was soon joined by Lt. Alex Andros, who had faded back to this position from the original Company H line about one-third of a mile farther west. The lieutenant and sergeant now found themselves to be the rear guard for withdrawing troops. They grabbed a 60mm mortar tube and eight rounds of ammo for it. Using only the tube, Sergeant Bennett planted the end of the barrel on the ground, and using only estimation began firing rounds at the line of German infantry that was about to overrun their location. Aiming with the tube "almost straight up" due to the proximity of the attackers, Bennett fired all eight rounds before joining the withdrawal with his officer. Lieutenant Andros, who had fed those mortar rounds into the tube, later wrote Sergeant Bennett up for his heroic work, which took a toll and slowed the advance of the rampaging enemy that day. Sergeant Bennett was awarded the Silver Star for his actions.

A city block north of them was the company command post. Sergeant Gordon Yates, the company communications sergeant, found most of his communications lines had been severed by artillery fire and the radio went dead. He decided to take the initiative to organize the clerks, cooks, and runners into ammunition carrying parties, supporting the riflemen who were firing at (in Yates words) ". . . a solid mass of krauts [who] poured over the railroad tracks in our battalion sector. They were in plain sight but there were just too damned many of them. Our men were using up all their ammunition and it couldn't slow down the attack."

Holding out as long as possible, Yates also received the Silver Star for his valuable actions that day.

In one of the withdrawals, Sgt. Harry Clawson, who had been blinded by a close explosion, got left behind in a Dutch house. Clawson, a former Eagle Scout and a Normandy-era Silver Star recipient, was captured and taken to a German field hospital. Clawson was discovered to be in possession of many German military decorations that he had looted from dead and captured enemy soldiers earlier in the war. This is presumably why he was murdered and deliberately buried in an unmarked grave along with a trooper from HQ 3/506 named Morris Thomas. Their bodies were accidentally discovered by a Dutch farmer many years after World War II ended.

During the peak of the afternoon's fighting, a .50 caliber machine gun had assisted the incoming U.S. artillery in taking a considerable toll of the German infantry who were attacking eastward along the south side of town. Don Zahn recalled the gun being in a sandbagged position, several hundred yards west of the railroad stop and at the south edge of the rail embankment. However, Lt. William Joe, a Chinese American of Battery D of the 81st Airborne AA/AT Battalion, stated that another .50 caliber gun belonged to a section of D/81, led by Lieutenant Hare, and that the gun was manned

by a Corporal Lindsay. Lieutenant Joe thought that the .50 caliber machine gun was closer to the railroad station. Joe wrote in a March 1988 letter to George Koskimaki, the 101st Airborne chronicler from Signal Company:

> The men later reported that in the far distance, the enemy was crossing over the RR track to the south side of the tracks. I'm told that Lindsay's gun didn't stop them, but it certainly slowed them down. We had .50 caliber ammo, loaded for antiaircraft fire—two-ball, armor-piercing, explosive (blue tipped magnesium), and tracer. I can imagine when the rounds hit the rails, cross ties, and rock ballast, there was a helluva ear blasting sound, [with] red tracer skittering in every direction and the bright flash of exploding magnesium rounds. One of my men told me later, ". . . first you see the enemy soldier, [and] when a .50 caliber magnesium round hit, there is a big white flash, then you see this object [man] fly backwards." He sounded quite awed.

During the Holland campaign, each of the three firing batteries of the 377th PFAB was equipped with six 75mm pack howitzers instead of the previously allotted four. This was done as a precaution in case some of the guns were lost, as had happened in Normandy. The 321st had only two firing batteries, also equipped with six 75mm pack howitzers each.

On the evening of October 5, after the fighting died down, Sergeant Padisak took a walk from his isolated woods south of the canal to the far northwest corner of the field below the railroad line. Hundreds of German troops had tried to come around the left flank of the U.S. positions that day, and scores of them had been massacred by

Machine gunner's view, looking across the road atop the main dike at the Neder Rhine River, somewhere between Heteren and Driel, Holland, October 1944. Although the main dike was situated hundreds of yards inland from the river, German bridgeheads in the area were dug in on the opposite side of the dike road, with their backs to the river. (The main German forces were across the river on the north side of the Neder Rhine.) The tall chimneys visible near the river give some idea of how far away the water was from the main dike. (A shallower, minor dike was built close to the river.) Each chimney marks a brick kiln. Brick factories flourished where clay from the riverbanks was harvested and baked. *Eugene Brierre*

Captain Pangerl accompanied a patrol conducted by A/502 into enemy lines west of Dodewaard on the Island in October 1944. In this splendid study, Lt. Delmar D. Idol, an A Company platoon leader, is scanning suspected German positions using 6x30 binoculars. *Joseph Pangerl*

artillery fire missions of the 377th and 321st artillery battalions. In addition, the .50 caliber machine-gun crew, mentioned previously, had also interdicted those flanking troops and cut them to ribbons.

Sergeant Zahn learned that the killing field was a place of horror when the hardened and calloused Sergeant Padisak returned at dusk from touring the battleground. He related that physical evidence indicated the Germans had been sent into the attack carrying only weapons, ammunition, and wearing their steel helmets. Finding themselves in a rain of artillery shells and .50 caliber machine-gun fire, some of them had tried to dig holes with their steel helmets because they weren't even equipped with shovels. A huge number of them had been slaughtered while trying to scoop out a little cover with their helmets. The sheer quantity of mangled bodies and their gruesome appearance left Padisak greatly disturbed. The wreckage of a crashed C-47 with British markings was also in that area; it had been shot down early in the Market-Garden campaign after dropping supplies to the British paratroopers at Arnhem.

The 506th PIR withdrew to the west, crossing a footbridge over the Linge Canal and taking up positions near an orchard situated west of the village of Hemmen. The confused situation the following morning was described by Bill Grovenburg of HQ 1/506:

The 1st Battalion moved back one night and set up a defense in an apple orchard. A German unit evidently followed us. At daybreak, they sent somebody forward, carrying a white flag. Our platoon sergeant met with the Germans. The Germans had made contact with our heavy weapons company consisting of mortars, bazookas, and machine guns. They wanted us to surrender, and we thought they were surrendering. Someone threw a grenade, wounding our sergeant, and the battle started. Initially, the machine gun section was our main defense. Someone in the mortar platoon jumped up, grabbed an 81mm mortar, and others followed.

The mortars were set up behind a pile of apples, and a fire control unit started selecting targets. A rifle company then flanked the Germans and attacked with mortar and machine gun support from HQ Company. The German unit finally gave up and surrendered. The prisoners outnumbered the total survivors of 1st Battalion.

During this intense battle, more Germans who had been moving east along the railroad line to the south rushed north to join in the fray. Company B machine gunner Glen "Red" Reeder shot an estimated total of more than eighty Germans in this engagement with his LMG, a possible record within the 101st for a single engagement.

Several members of the 81mm mortar platoon were shot in the head in this battle, including Barney Becker, who survived partially paralyzed, and Charles Becht, who had a bullet pierce his skull at the corner of his eye socket, grazing his brain and exiting behind his ear. This removed his ear drum but only grazed both his eyeball and brain. Miraculously, he would return to full duty after hospital recuperation.

Norman Closson was not as fortunate, taking a direct hit to the head, which killed him instantly. Unknown to Closson at the time was the fact that his English girlfriend was expecting his child. Sadly, Closson died never knowing that she would later give birth to their daughter. Don Burgett of Company A was near Classen when he was killed, and he has described this shootout in his book *The Road to Arnhem*.

Company C had only twenty-six survivors at this time, led by Lt. Albert Hassenzahl and Lt. Guthrie Hatfield. Hassenzahl told one of his men, Mariano Sanchez, who "had eyes like an eagle," to direct mortar fire into the trees where the German battalion was located and to walk an 81mm barrage across that area. "You could hear the Krauts screaming as the shells exploded amongst them," Hassenzahl later recalled.

It was Company C that circled the German position and persuaded the German survivors to come out and surrender. In the process, though, their lead scout, Harold Forshee, was shot dead. When the first Germans came out to surrender, Lieutenant Hatfield drove them back into the trees by shooting at them with his .45. The surrender was eventually accomplished without further loss of life, and Sanchez was thrice written up for a Silver Star, but the award never came through. Sanchez would be killed in action on December 21, 1944, in the woods near Luzery, Belgium.

Maj. Louis Kent, regimental surgeon of the 506th PIR, with medic T/4 Paul Miller in October 1944. This photo was taken in Andelst, Holland, on "the island."
Kent Photo via Dudley Cone

Hettrick's War: Forward Observation Hunches Enabled Artillery to Turn the Tide

Lieutenant Hettrick, still acting as a forward observer for the 377th PFAB, lived in a Dutch house on the main street of Zetten. He would spend several days on the line, supporting various rifle companies, then rotate to his rear location for some time off the line. Hettrick wrote about some action during the fighting along the main dike facing Wageningen across the Neder Rhine River (vicinity of Opheusden):

From Zetten, our Battery CP, we went up a string of houses along the dike and picked the last one as our new outpost. We were assigned to the 327th Glider Infantry Company C, commanded by Capt. Walter Miller. Shortly after getting settled in our new setting, I looked over the area [beyond] the dike, taking note of any enemy positions or emplacements. These bits and pieces [of info] can come in handy when things get popping.

It did not take too long for things to start happening, as the German artillery started firing about 150 yards down our side of the dike—just as it happened in Normandy. We guessed the krauts were adjusting artillery for a forthcoming attack on our position. A fire mission requires two basics: range and deflection. The Germans had now gotten the range and needed only to swing the pieces 150 yards to the right, giving them very fast and accurate fire. Recipients of this fast accurate fire [do not] get any warning. It seems the enemy had learned their lessons well since the invasion of Poland.

Knowing what the enemy was up to, I immediately warned the captain of a probable attack. He alerted his company and I checked the German lines for any indication of an assault. I did see a long trench, just over the enemy side of the dike. My hunch was that this was probably [their] troop build-up area. I called in a fire mission and adjusted the fire onto this trench. After about thirty or forty rounds, I called, "Cease fire, mission accomplished. . . ." The captain came up to see what was happening (white rags were waving from the German trench). We thought at first that it was a surrender, but that was too simple a deal. It turned out to be two German nurses with some helpers to carry out the wounded from my artillery concentration.

After about an hour of this evacuation, the white flags disappeared and the war was now back with us. In looking over the area earlier, there was this trench and now [I saw] another, further back. I fired again at a bit longer range and got the survivors a second time, so it was a repeat performance. After the dust settled, I was about to nail them a third time when Captain

Miller came up and said, "Lieutenant, I think you've killed enough Germans for one day." He was a really nice guy, so I didn't hassle him too much. So he said, "Lieutenant, make that an order . . . ," How could you refuse an order so gently but firmly put?

The next day, the Germans launched a full-scale artillery bombardment on our company position. They threw everything at us but the kitchen sink, and the CO said it was the heaviest shelling [they had] received so far. Enemy shells severely damaged the upper front of my OP, but we kept our counter fire going until they brought up SP guns and proceeded to finish off [the house containing] our OP.

My radio operator and I had to seek refuge downstairs in the back of the house. Infantry Sergeant [Joseph R.] Fitzgerald was on the kitchen floor, on his hands and knees, under the kitchen table. I yelled at him to lay flat on the floor to avoid getting hit . . . steel fragments were bouncing off the door jambs and sending brick fragments all over the room. I finally had to take cover in the next room in a huge potato bin.

Finally, the shelling stopped and we knew that the enemy infantry was now attacking our immediate position. We raced up the stairs and, seeing the situation, immediately called for artillery support . . . the [SCR] 300 radio was full of shrapnel holes and the antenna was bent like a corkscrew, but I ordered my radio operator to send a fire mission. I had to really yell at him, and he finally complied, and the beat-up radio worked fine.

By this time, the krauts were right on top of our company position. I asked fire control to drop our range fifty yards. They at first refused, because you cannot break a one hundred yard increment. I told them that we would be overrun with tremendous casualties. We received what we needed and the last salvos broke the attack, thank God. But there was a price for my fifty yard, extra close artillery fire.

Some of our men were also wounded, and I made the rounds to apologize. But the GIs assured me that it was a small price compared to what the damage would have been if I had not pulled an artillery no-no. Even though our artillery had broken up the attack, there were still enemy milling about dazed, and I reached for my scoped M1 rifle and shot up a slew [more than twenty] of these survivors. For the actions of myself and my radio operator, Captain Miller put us in for the Bronze Star Medal and also a promotion to first lieutenant for me.

At a 101st Airborne reunion in NYC [1947] Captain Miller saw me as I passed his table of guests and called me over. He introduced me to his friends as the FO who saved his company from certain death. Very flattering indeed, after the [war] was long-since over. I never forgot him. How could you forget guys like him and his men?

Richard Brinkley visited Barney Becker in San Diego, California, after the war and discovered that Barney could still drive a car and shoot a rifle at the range, though his left arm was lame and he had to walk with a cane. Unable to accept living with a disability, Barney would take his own life about ten years later.

Around October 7, elements of the 327th GIR took over the 506th line east of Opheusden. The new line was considerably east of the 506th's former position, which caused initial objection from 506th commander Colonel Sink. When he was persuaded that containing the Germans to the west was the main consideration and that the precise location of the lines was immaterial, Sink relented in relinquishing real estate previously held by his regiment—at a high cost.

ACTIONS FARTHER EAST ON THE ISLAND

As 1st and 3rd battalions of the 506th battled in and near Opheusden, 2nd Battalion held positions along the Neder Rhine near the village of Randwijk. Here, a reduced battalion of Waffen SS troops was wiped out in a brilliant action staged by Company E of the 506th, under the command of Captain R. D. Winters. East of 2/506, 2/501 held the dike from just east of the ferry crossing road (northeast of Randwijk), to and including the village of Heteren. The 3rd Battalion of the 501st held the line east toward Driel, while 1/501 held the rest of the line to the railroad bridge at Coffin Corner. Coffin Corner was formed where the dike road met the railroad bridge, which crossed the Neder Rhine below Oosterbeek, Holland. (Oosterbeek is a suburb west of Arnhem.) The MLR in this sector was dug in along the shoulder of the dike road, on the landward side of the main dike, facing the Neder Rhine River. One evening, a German armored and infantry attack was halted by C/501 near Coffin Corner. On another day, when companies A and C traded positions, more friendly troops were lost, including William C. McClain, from Uniontown, Pennsylvania; shrapnel from a tree burst detonated a hand grenade on McClain's belt, inflicting ghastly damage, which proved fatal.

A German lieutenant named Kurt Martin from Jena commanded the last German bridgehead on the south bank of the Neder Rhine River from his command post at the brick kiln east of Veghel. In this area German troops were dug in right across the road from 501st troopers on the embankment of the main dike. The British who previously held this position had tolerated the presence and proximity of the German troops, but troopers of Company G of the 501st soon drove the enemy MLR back to the brick factory at the river's edge. The survivors evacuated the factory, fleeing to the north shore in shuttle boats, which crossed during darkness. G/501 machine gunner Melton "Tex" McMorries and another gunner, Bob Baldwin, were instrumental in driving the German forces from the main dike. During the second week of October 1944, elsewhere along the Neder Rhine MLR, Colonel Howard R. Johnson was fatally wounded by an 88mm artillery round that was fired from across the river.

Lieutenant Colonel Julian J. Ewell would assume command of the 501st as Johnson's successor. One of the very first crossings of the Neder Rhine to the enemy side was made by Lt. Ronald Speirs of 2/506, who made a solo night crossing on October 9 to recon the German positions near Renkum. Speirs' presence was discovered, and he was forced to swim back to the south shore, chased by German bullets, one of which wounded him in the posterior. For this intrepid act, Speirs received the Silver Star. More night patrols risked crossing to scout the German shore, including a 327th GIR patrol and several others mounted by 3/501. The Second SS Panzer Corps was thought to be on the Arnhem side of the river, but all U.S. patrols failed to bring back any prisoners as the month of October dragged on. On the night of October 22–23,

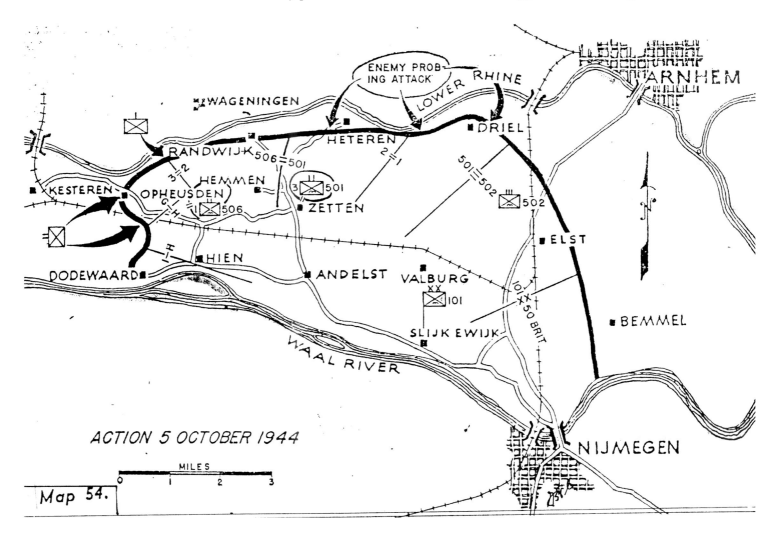

ACTION 5 OCTOBER 1944

MILES
0   1   2   3

Map 54.

German prisoners captured near Renkum, Holland, by the "incredible patrol," led by Lt. Hugo Sims. This seven-man group returned across the Neider Rhine with thirty-two prisoners, including SS Capt. Walter Gartner (seated at left with fur collar). Capt. Werner Meier, commander of IPW Team No. 9, 501st PIR, stands at right. *Joseph Pangerl*

1944, a rescue operation was mounted in darkness to bring back more than one hundred British Airborne survivors from Arnhem, who had been hiding in Dutch barns and cellars for weeks. This rescue was primarily a 2/506 operation, although it was supported by members of G/501.

A week later, near the end of October, the famous "incredible patrol" ventured across the Neder Rhine, spending several nights in a Dutch house on the Arnhem-Utrecht highway. On this patrol, six troopers, led by Lt. Hugo S. Sims Jr., captured thirty-two Germans, including SS artillery captain Walter Gartner, and miraculously shuttled them in raft relays, across to the American-held southern shore. This unusual and daring raid was reported in detail in an issue of *Life* magazine (January 15, 1945, edition).

NEARING THE END OF THE ORDEAL ON THE ISLAND

After Opheusden, various units of the division were juggled around, and the 3rd Battalion of the 506th ended up moving from the extreme west flank to the east end, near Coffin Corner. This area was originally liberated by Commonwealth forces and turned over to the 501st, who held it for six weeks. During this period, patrolling along with an exchange of mortar and artillery fire was the norm for both sides. Lieutenant Joe Doughty, now commanding Company G of the 506th, wrote to his wife:

> Back in a reserve area again, after a week of absolute hell. This whole operation has been hell. 54 days of it. One can't describe the things that happen over here—to have to just stay in a position and hold it, with the krauts looking right down your throat, and stay in a hole, sweating out barrage after barrage after barrage of mortars and 88s, with those screaming meemies thrown in every so often, just wondering when the law of averages is going to catch up to you, and put one right in your hole. . . . I've seen some good men go to pieces and have wondered about myself more than once. I have never in my life prayed in the true sense of the word until I came to Holland. A sense of humor has been the only thing that has kept our crowd sane at times, and this last week was one of

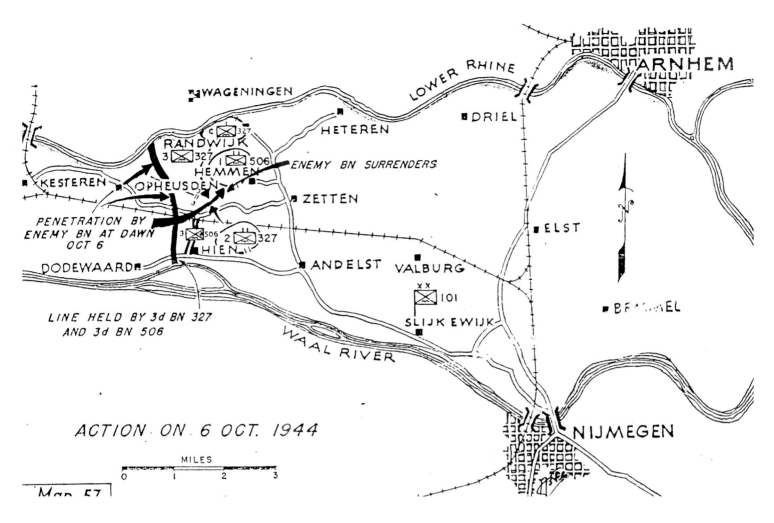

ACTION ON 6 OCT. 1944

MILES
0   1   2   3

Map 57

them. It got bitter cold and rained, and holes filled with water from the bottom, due to this part of the country being under sea level.

The mud was four inches deep and you couldn't even move except under cover of darkness, yet there wasn't a groan or a mumble from a man. What a bunch—the finest soldiers in the world! Yep, we are on the right side and know it.

We have taken a lot of prisoners and they all want to quit; it is only the true fanatics who prevent so many of them from coming over to us.

I have seen life in its simplest form, where it was as cheap as dirt, where you would see one of your best friends one minute and an hour later say, "Well, he was a swell guy."

Those are things that people at home will never see or understand. They will never know fear as we see it, to be so damned scared (that) you aren't ashamed of it, and when it's past, joke about it, to console yourself. I never knew what scabies were until I came here. When you are compelled to wear the same clothes, week in and week out, not being able to wash or take them off, you get these things. I read (your letter) in my little hovel. Boy, every time I think of that place, I shudder. The only things that lived around there, that

Hettrick's War: A Sixth Sense for Survival on the Island in Holland

DONALD J
HETTRICK
2ND L   FA

We moved down the dike to try to locate the position of the German [artillery] observers. They had the high ground and could place artillery fire on us any time they needed. We picked a row of houses and moved into the fifth one, as it had a piece of slate missing from the enemy side of the roof. Using a ladder, I was able to get a good view of the enemy areas. We set up the SCR 300 radio and reported in to battalion HQ. They had to know our exact location, so they could plot our position in relation to the artillery pieces and also to the targets.

I watched for many hours and saw nothing to indicate the enemy OP. Suddenly, my sixth sense kicked in and I knew it was time to evacuate this spot right now. I shouted to my driver, "Let's get the hell out of here!" He had been warned that when I said leave now, it was imperative to get moving. We raced out of the house, into the jeep, and up to a house at the dike. We had not been there for very many minutes, when a 200–300mm shell hit the just-vacated house. It was blown to smithereens [as were] almost all of the houses on either side. Just another close shave by my Guardian Angel. . . .

Our new OP was a large brick house with a big storage room in back, plus a very large hayloft over the living quarters. It took a very long ladder to reach the upper brick wall for a spot to view through two or three missing bricks. It did not take the enemy long to realize [they] had a nosey observer, and they had a sniper take pot shots at the hole in the brick wall. Unfortunately, I was there, watching them. On an impulse, I leaned back just as the first bullet hit next to my face, just as I backed away. Again, way too close for comfort, so I left as quickly as I could clamber down the long ladder. A few fragments nicked my face but the bullet ricocheted with a screech to my rear.

I was getting awfully tired of these close encounters. That night, some infantry GIs shot a German just as he sneaked up to the house. The next morning, I saw his body and found that he had a flamethrower [with the obvious intention of] wiping us out. Again, we were lucky that he had been spotted and shot. It occurred to me that the German Wehrmacht was trying to get rid of me and my driver. They were quite persistent.

The incident described above took place along the main dike, facing the south shore of the Neder Rhine River, at a point east of Opheusden.

---

hadn't been killed by artillery fire, were a few pigs and a cat. Even they used the ditches and sneaked around under cover of bushes and trees. That cat walked out on the road one day and they threw about 18 rounds of artillery at it. What a place! I'll tell you all about that spot some day.

At the end of November, the 101st Airborne Division began leaving "the island," one unit at a time. Most of the division was gone when the Germans placed a large aerial bomb in the dike on the south bank of the Neder Rhine River, just east of the Oosterbeek railroad overpass, and blasted a large gap in the embankment. Because the current of the river flows westward, and the bomb was strategically placed so that the current would flow southwestward right through the curve where the new hole was made. The water flowed under the viaduct and rapidly flooded the area between Coffin Corner and Randwijk. The last men to be evacuated from this area were issued metal cans for flotation devices, and British boats collected them a few at a time, from Dutch rooftops, where they were roosting to avoid drowning.

CHAPTER 8

BASTOGNE

Remembering they told me when I volunteered for the paratroops that my chances for coming out alive would be only one out of ten, I had the mindset that if I could kill one enemy before they got me, we'd be even. After Holland, I knew we'd win.

—Glen A. Derber, 2/501 PIR

At the beginning of December 1944, the weary survivors of the Holland campaign moved in to the stone French army barracks at Camp Mourmelon near Reims, France. They arrived by truck convoy, coming south from "the island" in a zigzag route, and passing through many towns on the way. The one-story barracks had more recently been occupied by German Panzer troops. About three thousand new replacements arrived in the following days and weeks and were distributed to the various companies. Some time was devoted to small unit tactics and calisthenics, and small groups began going on passes to Paris, where the attractions of *Place Pigalle* (aka "pig alley") were the most popular. For soldiers who misbehaved significantly, American MPs had opened a jail known as the "Paris detention barracks". Soldiers incarcerated there for less than capital offenses were often sprung after one of their company officers arrived to vouch for them and ensure their return to duty. The 82nd Airborne was also stationed outside Reims, so some brawls resulted when troopers of the two divisions met in town. A schedule was made, allowing troops of each division to visit Reims on alternating nights. All the independent parachute and glider-borne RCTs and battalions of the ETO were assembled in the Reims area as the ETO's tactical reserve force. Troopers of the 101st Airborne expected to get a respite from the fighting until the

An unidentified Screaming Eagle posed beside the wall of the Bastogne cemetery that was situated right across the road from the complex of Belgian army barracks. The 101st Airborne Division headquarters was later located at that same complex. *F. Hoffman collection via R. Campoy*

return of warm weather. The front seemed to have stabilized at the German border, and it did not seem likely that the badly whipped Germans who had retreated across France in the fall could cause any significant trouble until the return of warm weather. Furthermore, many weapons and other equipment had been turned in for maintenance or repair, and the Screaming Eagles were not fully prepared for a return to the shooting war. It seemed that the imminent arrival of Christmas represented hope for the future and optimism for the present. However, Adolf Hitler's minions had been preparing for many weeks to launch a massive counterattack on the western front, with the Belgian port city of Antwerp as their goal.

A massive German offensive along fifty miles of front at the eastern border of Belgium caught the U.S. Army by surprise on the morning of December 16, 1944. Many weeks in preparation, this attack, which utilized the 5th and 6th Panzer armies, roared through the previously quiet sector with an agenda of vengeance and terror. Hitler's large gamble of troops and material would exhaust Germany's last reserves. Because of the large bulge it formed on situation maps of that sector, American troops labeled this Ardennes campaign the "Battle of the Bulge." Of the thousands of Panzergrenadiers, Volksgrenadiers (VG), Fallschirmjagers (FJ), and support troops, many individuals were aggrieved by the loss of family members in Allied bombing raids. They now found their opportunity to turn death and terror back upon the Americans who had wrought destruction on their homeland. Their offensive did spread panic and death—for the brief time that it lasted.

The Bulge would become the largest pitched land battle fought by U.S. forces in Europe, and despite the fact that a fifty-mile front amounted to a small fraction of the length of the Russian front, many of the premier units of Germany's elite forces had

When the division moved out in truck convoys to Bastogne on December 18, 1944, the 502nd PIR was among the last to depart Camp Mourmelon. On that afternoon, while awaiting orders to board trucks, Capt. Joseph Pangerl snapped this photo of mainly 3rd Battalion officers. At far left is Lt. Corey Shepard (Company I) and Lt. Ralph Watson (Company G). Seated at bottom right is Lt. Graham "Armey" Armstrong, of regimental S-2. *Joseph Pangerl*

Bastogne bound. Of all Bastogne-related photos, this one has been the most misidentified. The trouble began in 1948 when the smiling trooper at center was misidentified in the divisional history *Rendezvous with Destiny* as being Francis Mellet of E/506. That trooper is actually Francis L. Gillis of F/501. Since *Rendezvous with Destiny* first appeared, this photo has been wrongly identified as E/506 in several books on that company. The actual identities of the troopers standing, left to right are: unknown, Emerson Rhodes, John Megaw, Frank Nardo, Daniel Newton, Blanchard Carney, Fletcher "Doc" Gainey, Hayden Faulk, Francis Leo Gillis, William H. Wilson, unknown, James Culbreth, and 1st Sgt. Herschel Parks. Of the aforementioned, Gainey lost a leg on January 10, 1945 in the Bois Jacques, and James Culbreth and 1st Sgt. Parks were both KIA. The helmet of the second unknown trooper clearly shows markings for 2/501 PIR, of which F/501 was a part. Dick Winters, the most famous commander of E/506, knew Francis Mellet well. In 1989, he told the author of this book that the smiling trooper pictured at the center of the photo was *not* Mellett. Winters went on to say he didn't recognize any of the men in this photo. The author asked Winters to ensure that the mistake was not repeated in Ambrose's book *Band of Brothers*, which was being written at that time. The photo was, however, misidentified in Ambrose's history of E/506 and has been misidentified in at least two subsequent books. *Albert A. Krochka*

been assembled for participation in this assault. The 1st, 2nd, 9th, and 12th SS Panzer divisions, as elements of the 6th Panzer army, broke the U.S. line in the north sector, accompanied by Fallschirmjagers and Volksgrenadiers, as well as Volksgrenadier foot soldiers and horse-drawn artillery. On the south sector, ranging westward from the area where Belgium meets Luxembourg, the 5th Panzer army deployed such venerable units as the 2nd Panzer and Panzer Lehr divisions and the Fuehrer Escort Brigade. The sweeping Bulge battleground can be divided into many individual sectors of local fighting as well as three main sectors. The main sectors were: 1) the area between the German border and Camp Elsenborn on the north; 2) the central sector ranging westward from St. Vith through Vielsalm, Manhay, Grandmenil, Sadzot, and Celles; and 3) the southern sector, with the road network hub of Bastogne, as the main geographic prize, lying about fifty miles west of the German start line near Diekirch, Luxembourg. For several days before the U.S. Army's strategic reserve divisions (82nd and 101st Airborne divisions) entered the Bulge, fighting in that sector was characterized by a war of retreat and delay. While some American units were quickly surrounded and convinced to surrender, others fought tenaciously against great odds, exacting a heavy toll and costly delays on the German attackers.

The Ardennes region of Belgium is characterized by winding roads and many mountains. The vast majority of the terrain is not suited for deploying armor, unless the vehicles remain road bound. This fact made things somewhat easier for the defenders, and American engineer units caused great consternation and delay by blowing bridges over the rivers in the area. This forced the German vehicle columns to make wide and time-consuming detours while the blown bridges were reconstructed. Time was of the essence for Hitler's minions, as bad weather for the first week of the offensive would aid them greatly, keeping Allied planes grounded. As it turned out, after December 23, clear skies would permit Allied air power to inflict

After debarking trucks near Mande St. Etienne, west of Bastogne, some troops arrived in time to get a few hours of sleep before moving east at dawn to meet the enemy. Parts of the division marched down the main street of Bastogne, going out to the east and north sectors. Other units bypassed Bastogne when taking up their fighting positions and never marched through the city itself. This view shows members of 2/506 PIR moving north on the Bastogne–Houffalize Road (N30), from a point just north of the seminary. *Signal Corps*

devastating losses on German vehicles, but cold temperatures and the worst winter western Europe had seen in fifty years would make the battleground and the weather significant enemies for all who had to endure those hostile weather conditions. From the particular perspective of the 101st Airborne Division, they had only a few weeks earlier been sent to the rest camp at Mourmelon le Grand, short of personnel.

The newly arrived replacements were being gradually integrated into their companies. The veterans of Holland had turned in many damaged and worn-out weapons for repair or replacement. When they were alerted to a rushed move back into the combat zone, much equipment and weaponry (as well as ammunition) was simply not available. The replacements had not yet been fully trained and absorbed into the division.

Scores of men were also enjoying passes to Paris when the alert came on December 18, 1944. The survivors of Normandy and Market-Garden were incredulous when they heard the news that they were being committed to battle again this soon. Trucks started departing for Ardennes from Mourmelon, the morning of December 18, one unit at a time. They were still departing that evening. The convoys rolled northeast, past World War I battlefields and massive cemeteries, where the dead of the previous world war lay buried. The

Members of 2/506 PIR, photographed almost a mile north of the seminary. The camera is facing southwest across the N30 highway and retreating armored vehicles can be seen in the field across the road. That area is now filled with houses built after World War II. Identified in the photo of marching paratroopers from D/506 are: Laymon Massey (far right), John Kliever, "Whitey" Merritt, Sergeant Cook, and Dick Gleason. This shot of paratroopers moving out to meet the enemy has been published many times and has been claimed by the 501st, but the tall houses in the left distance still stand today and have definitely established this as the N30 road to Foy, Noville, and Houffalize. *U.S. Army*

convoys continued on in full darkness, with headlights turned on, in violation of usual night blackout precautions. Time was also of the essence for the American reserves heading up to salvage victory. The 82nd Airborne departing from Camp Suippes, France, had preceded the 101st Airborne, passing west of the city of Bastogne and continuing north another forty miles to Werbomont, Belgium. Here, that division's regiments and attached units would disperse in many directions to block German units that had spread all over the map in the north and central sectors of the Bulge. General McAuliffe's advanced party, traveling north toward Werbomont by jeep, decided to make a detour from Sprimont, Belgium, into the town of Bastogne en route. The purpose was to confer with Gen. Troy Middleton, whose VIIIth Corps headquarters was situated in Bastogne. This meeting proved to be of fateful consequence when they decided to reroute the entire 101st Division to form a line in front of Bastogne, instead of following the 82nd the rest of the way to the Werbomont sector. Thus the stage was set for the most famous World War II triumph of the 101st Airborne Division. All the years of functioning as a team, the grueling training, the deadly proficiency, and battle wisdom gained the hard way in Normandy and Holland were about to reach their fulfillment and culmination in a deadly confrontation. This test of wills and battlefield superiority would spell the beginning of the end for Hitler's Wehrmacht. In the process, a lot of blood would be spilled in the frozen hell known as the Battle of Bastogne.

Motorized elements of the 101st Airborne began arriving near Mande St. Etienne, Belgium, in the west suburbs of Bastogne in the wee hours of the morning on December 19. After marching various short distances, the individual subunits were told to sleep on the open ground, with or without the luxury of foxholes, to get some rest before moving out at dawn. Elements of the 28th Infantry Division, which had retreated forty miles in the face of the German onslaught, were still moving westward, not convinced that anyone could stop the enemy at Bastogne. This was a dramatic and confused situation, wrought with panic and fear, until the Screaming Eagles arrived with no intention of yielding

Elements of the 501st made first contact with advancing Germans east of Bastogne on December 19. F Company fell back from the vicinity of Magaret and dug in with D and E companies on the approaches to Bizory. As evidenced by this photo of Walt Lengieza and Lt. Joseph Harman (3rd Platoon of F/501), the ground was still mostly devoid of snow on the 19th. Lieutenant Harman was killed in the first German attack against the east flank on December 20, 1944. The 1st Battalion of the 501st dug in south of 2nd Battalion at Neffe, while 3rd Battalion took up positions to their right at Mont. The second big German attack on the east perimeter hit the 3rd Battalion area on the night of December 20–21. German losses in these attempts were so significant that they did not try to force their way into Bastogne from the east again. *Daniel Newton*

Among the other units supporting the 101st at Bastogne were tanks of CCR, 9th Armored Division, which fell back on Bizory from roadblocks in the Mageret–Longvilly sector. This M5 light tank of the 9th Armored was photographed at Bizory by Dan Newton of F/501. *Daniel Newton*

in the face of the German army. With elements of the 82nd Airborne also digging in to the north, stability had been restored to the Ardennes, and the first nails had been applied to the coffin of German failure in the Bulge. American paratroopers, the bad boys of the U.S. Army, had arrived and would stand, fight, win, or die while presenting the advancing Germans with a type of foe they had not encountered since launching their offensive on December 16. Could the battle weary, underequipped Airborne soldiers prevail in this encounter? The Allied cause was staking everything in their belief that they would.

The strong presence of German troops and armor east of Bastogne was obvious and well known. Less recognized was the fact that moving west alongside the masses of retreating American infantry were small groups of advancing German infantry, who bypassed Bastogne as early as the morning darkness on December 19. Members of C Battery of the 377th PFAB describe skirmishing with small German elements encountered on the way to their gun positions on the hill at Savy that morning.

As early as the evening of December 19, Clyde Yaist of C/377 picked off eight Germans who were trying to stealthily approach the C Battery gun pits. Yaist was a crack shot with an M1 rifle and had been positioned in a concealed spot in front of and below the firing batteries to provide security for them. This "artillery sniper" using a Garand rifle without benefit of a scope was placed in a battery security assignment by his first sergeant, Fred Fitzgerald. As Germans tried to sneak up a draw toward the U.S. artillery positions in the fading light of December 19, they were picked off one at a time by rounds fired by Yaist, from a position they couldn't see and were not aware of until it was too late.

General McAuliffe knew that the main German elements were following close behind the retreating American infantry troops, and he initially planned to hold a regular line, running from north to south in front of Bastogne. This line would form a wall to block progress farther west by the advancing German divisions. But circumstances would turn the left flank of that planned wall, with rapidly advancing German forces wrapping around the north and west sides of Bastogne, eventually forcing the defenders into a circular, 360-degree defense perimeter. Many of the German forces that had bypassed Bastogne continued westward toward their goal of the Meuse River and Antwerp, leaving other forces behind to deal with Bastogne.

The 501st PIR was initially sent east of Bastogne to make contact with the enemy as well as to consolidate with miscellaneous engineer and armored forces, who already manned roadblocks in the vicinity of Magaret and Longvilly. Combat Command B (CCB) of the 10th Armored Division had already arrived at Bastogne after detaching from the rest of their division in the vicinity of Luxembourg. Their three available combat teams, each one named for its commander, were spaced from north to south along the east approaches to Bastogne. Team Desobry was farthest north, soon to be joined by the 1st Battalion of the 506th at Noville. Team Cherry supported the 1st Battalion of the 501st due east of Bastogne, while Team O'Hara between Wardin and Marvie, southeast of the town, was initially to support 3/501, but their main role would be in support of the 327th GIR's 2nd Battalion. A small force from CCR, 9th Armored Division, fell back on Bizory and would remain there in support of Lt. Col. Sammie N. Homan's 2/501 PIR.

The 705th Tank Destroyer (TD) Battalion had driven many miles south from the vicinity of Liege to support the forces at Bastogne. Equipped with the new M18 tank destroyers (TDs), the 705th arrived at Bastogne just in time, before the town was surrounded by German forces. Tank destroyers of this battalion were dispersed to various parts of the perimeter in four-vehicle teams to support various parachute and glider infantry battalions.

In one of the earliest actions, Company I of the 501st was sent to outpost a little village near the road to Wiltz, at the south edge of the U.S. line forming east of Bastogne. This intrepid group had the misfortune to encounter numerous tanks and a battalion of armored infantry from the Panzer Lehr Division. In a lopsided forty-five-minute battle, Item Company withdrew from Wardin with heavy losses and retreated to the high ground west of the town, in piece-meal fashion. Stragglers trickled back to Bastogne with word that the company had been wiped out. Indeed, collecting all the survivors would take time, but a total of about 85 troopers eventually re-assembled from the company of 140 that had entered Wardin that day. Losses at Wardin had been high indeed, but perhaps not as bad as initially thought. So the company's actual losses could be termed something less than "wiped out," as had been originally reported. Survivors of the Wardin battle still complain that while they were being decimated by elements of Panzer Lehr, they could see tanks of Team O'Hara sitting on high ground to the southwest. Those friendly tanks never moved to assist them and, in fact, never even fired a round in their support.

The 1st Battalion of the 506th PIR, under Lieutenant Colonel LaPrade, was sent north into Noville to join with Team Desobry from the 10th Armored Division in holding that place as long as possible. This put 1/506 way out in front of the rest of that regiment, which had dropped off at Foy to dig in and establish a main line of resistance south of that hamlet. Lieutenant Colonel LaPrade assumed command of troops from both the 1/506 and 10th AD. He was killed on December 19, when a tank retriever parked in front of the two-story building used as his command post was hit by German artillery thrown at the tank retriever. The artillery also wounded

Two paratroopers with and without a white sheet for snow camouflage, stand in front of a 9th Armored Division tank at Bizory to demonstrate the contrast in visibility. Hayden Faulk (left) and Walt Lengieza (right). *Daniel Newton*

Desobry. Major Robert Harwick was then placed in command of the 1/506. The soldiers in Noville were facing massive numbers of German vehicles and troops, but the heavy fog that enshrouded the area served to protect them from annihilation by the enemy who permeated their positions. After holding the town for almost twenty-four hours, the battalion received orders to withdraw to the Foy area, taking as many vehicles and friendly wounded as possible.

As will be described, the division hospital and most of its staff and medical supplies were captured at Crossroads X at Sprimont. The identity of the German unit that captured the hospital has not been positively established and G-2 situation maps for December 19–20 indicate that although German forces were known to be on the southwest perimeter, their unit identities were unknown. The 502nd's IPW report for December 20 identified elements of the 304th Panzergrenadier Regiment operating in the north sector, near Foy, and a G-2 report on December 22 states that the 6th Company of the 78th Volksgrenadier Regiment was split into ten-man squads armed with machine guns and MP40s, and dispersed into Recogne and other points on the north and west perimeter. It is possible that these were among the small, roaming elements that

Also in Bastogne were new M18 tank destroyers from the 705th TD Battalion, which drove south many miles from the vicinity of Liege under orders to reinforce Bastogne. They arrived just in time to join the perimeter forces that were being rapidly surrounded. Four TDs of the 705th joined 2/501 at Bizory, including the one shown. *Anacleto Leone*

were ambushed and killed in local firefights in and near the stream running between Foy and Savy, which was actually in the woods inside the main U.S. perimeter. Roving German patrols could appear almost anywhere on the west perimeter. It is also possible that elements of the 115th Panzergrenadier Regiment reached the southwest perimeter as early as the evening of December 20 and could have been the unit that captured the 101st Division hospital. Previous accounts have attributed that action to the 2nd Panzer Division, but that division's later presence far to the northwest, where they were eventually halted at Celles, indicates that they didn't remain in the Bastogne sector for long. Those elements of 2nd Panzer that were delayed in the area lingered on the north perimeter near Noville rather than moving to the southwest.

After December 20, the entire area was covered in a shallow layer of snow that would gradually accumulate until it reached knee depth in January. This classic shot shows typical perimeter positions adjacent to the Bois Jacques forest northeast of Bastogne in the sector held by companies A and D of the 501st PIR. In early January 1945, the fighting would move north into the woods, where the entire 501st and most of the 506th battled Germans on both sides of the railroad line. *Joe "Gopher" Sloan (501st photographer)*

CAPTURE OF THE DIVISION HOSPITAL AT CROSSROADS X

The division's medical company, the 326th AMC, established a surgical hospital in large tents at Crossroads X, a significant road junction about six miles west of Bastogne. Being on the opposite side of town from the German onslaught, which was headed from east to west, the location was wrongly assumed to be safe from the possibility of capture. The 101st's Division hospital, complete with medical supplies, doctors, medics, and wounded patients, however, would fall into enemy hands within a day of arriving at Bastogne. German motorized elements had already bypassed Bastogne, encountering the division hospital set up at Crossroads X.

Henry Hauser, a recent replacement who had just joined the 326th AMC after recuperating from wounds suffered as a combat medic in Normandy with the 83rd Infantry Division, was sent back to Camp Mourmelon in a truck with two other medics to haul more medical supplies up to Bastogne. When he tried to return, he learned that Bastogne was completely surrounded by German forces. Finally getting back to Crossroads X, after Patton's Third Army broke the encirclement on December 26, 1944, Henry said, "What happened to my company? They're all gone!"

On December 19–20, 1944, members of the 1st Battalion of the 506th took significant casualties at Noville, Belgium, north of Bastogne, and among those wounded was the tall, lanky Lt. Herb Viertel, a platoon leader in B/506. Viertel was a deadly combat soldier, who had taken a toll of the enemy in both Normandy and Holland. Wounded by mortar fire in front of the battalion command post in Noville, Viertel was loaded into an ambulance with other wounded and was lying inside that vehicle, awaiting treatment at Crossroads X, when the Germans launched their attack on the nearby surgical tents. Lieutenant Viertel ended up being captured while lying helplessly wounded in that ambulance and would be a

After the failed attempt of December 20, 1944, to break into Bastogne from the northeast, members of 2/501 PIR rounded up survivors from General Kokott's 26th Volksgrenadier Division near Bizory. *Dick Rowles via F. Gregg*

guest of the German government for the duration of World War II. Staff Sergeant Edward A. Miller, a member of the 326th AMC who had been with the outfit since prior to Normandy, wrote a detailed account of what led to the capture of the division hospital and his initial experiences in German captivity. Some excerpts follow:

> We were nearing our rendezvous, Bastogne, and being parked bumper to bumper on the road did not give me any feeling of security. There was snow of some depth along the roadside, although the road itself was clear. Early morning fog was slowly lifting as we saw the first signs of the havoc that Jerry was causing.
>
> Trucks were scurrying to the rear and armored stuff was likewise heading in the [same] direction. . . .
>
> What goes on, I thought. While the two rows of vehicles were halted, I yelled at some 28th Division boys in a kitchen truck. "Where are ya going? The fight is this way!"
>
> Someone yelled back, "Go ahead, boys, you'll catch all the hell you want, just a few miles ahead." Bastogne, it seems, was under fire, so we stopped at a crossroad a few miles west of the town. The crossroad spot looked important—and unprotected—and I for one did not like it. Refugees from the north and east were running and walking as quickly as they were able, in their efforts to get away before Jerry and the Yanks came together. The looks on their faces will be ever in my memory. . . .
>
> Woody and I tried to talk Captain Cohen out of setting up our station in the open. No dice! So up went three tents, a temporary station, until we could get into Bastogne. By 2 p.m., we were accepting a few casualties with the promise of many more to come. Corky, Kalla, Meador, Moose, and I had tried to dig shelters close to the treatment tents and close to each other. . . .

After 1/506 withdrew from Noville on December 20, 1944, they went into reserve behind the main 506th line below Foy. But 1st Battalion would soon be called up again to clear a German battalion from the woods northeast of Luzery. Foy (pictured) would become the center of contention, with several companies of the 506th attacking into the town on various days to disrupt German forces massing there for a possible concerted attack. Each time Foy was taken, 506th troopers would soon abandon the place, because Foy was surrounded on three sides by high ground and holding it was not a tactically sound idea. The last U.S. assault into Foy was made on January 13, 1945, by E/506. In this photo an abandoned German Mark IV tank sits on a road in Foy. *Albert A. Krochka*

At about 5 p.m., I was able to get a cup of coffee, but from then on, we were busy. [Dental] Captain Zumsteg came around with a rumor that we were surrounded, which didn't help our morale any, but I wasn't inclined to lend full credence to it, until Corky and I went looking for plasma at about 9 p.m. Corky had come into the tent I was working in around 8:30, although he was not on duty until 10 p.m. The amount of work on hand must have convinced him that his services were necessary, which indeed they were. We had about 50 casualties, some of them very seriously wounded, and were doing our best to handle them [many 1/506 troopers had already arrived from the fighting in Noville] when the sound of heavy equipment moving from north to south directly alongside our field made us take notice. I'm sure we all felt it was our own, until a volley of .50 caliber stuff sent us to the ground. Bullets whistled through the canvas as more guns joined in the din. Occasionally, something louder would sound off, and we all knew that Jerry had somehow managed to get behind or around Bastogne and had found our location. The firing was spasmodic, and during the moments of quiet, our officers who could talk German shouted the words which indicated that we were a hospital setup and not armed! The kraut paid no attention! The firing would awaken to new fury and

The body of a fallen German grenadier blends into the frozen ground at Foy, becoming part of the landscape.
Everett "Red" Andrews

Elements of 101st Division headquarters were actually in the town of Bastogne during the perimeter defense fighting, but they were subjected to continual artillery barrages and periodic aerial bombing by the Luftwaffe. Pictured here during the siege of Bastogne are message center personnel from Signal Company (this was at a forward command post near Foy, Belgium). Visible on the table are numerous M-209 code machines. Recognizable in the photo are (left to right): Earl Graessele, Eugene O. Bart (standing), C. K. O'Connell (holding phone), Ernest Koening, and John Medick. *Wierzbowski collection via Nadine Wierzbowski-Field*

we all lay as flat as the ground would allow. I was alongside of Captain McKee and can remember trying to keep a medical chest between me and the direction of the fire. My head was beside the pot-belly stove, but if it was hot, I didn't notice. During one of the lulls, Major Crandall asked me to assist in lowering a litter to the floor to get the patient out of the line of fire. I was amazed to see Query emerge from beneath the litter where he had ducked when the firing began! We lowered the patient and once more resumed our prone position as more bullets ripped the canvas and sped angrily out the other side. All about me I saw faces of men almost as scared as I was. My heart pounded like mad, and I almost hoped for the one with my number on it to come and claim its victim. I'm sure there was no "hero" in me as Jerry poured it on. By now, we could hear his infantrymen outside the tent and could plainly hear them calling to each other. We had blacked out all lights, but burning trucks just outside made this a useless precaution. One of the kraut halftracks was afire as well as three or four of our vehicles, and our tents were literally lit up like Christmas trees. The firing started and stopped several times between 9:50 and 11:30 [p.m.], at which time our division surgeon, Colonel Gold, was able to establish contact with a German officer, who accepted the surrender of the medical unit.

He issued orders that we were to board vehicles and be ready to move out in 30 minutes, after which time, the firing would be resumed. . . . I finally located Moose, who had been busy with the patients, and we managed to get on the same truck. Garnich was o.k., and I remember him saying as we pulled out, "If we turn left, we go to Germany. If we turn right, we're o.k." We turned left. The krauts drove very slowly, in a northerly direction, toward

Realizing that the American garrison in Bastogne was completely surrounded by German forces, General von Luttwitz, the 48th Corps commander, wasted no time in proposing that the Americans should surrender or face annihilation. There are no known photos of the surrender party visiting the Bastogne perimeter, but they entered the lines of 2/327 GIR at the southeast sector and were blindfolded and guarded while their proposal was being considered by the American commander. German-speaking trooper Ernest Premetz (top left) and Carl Dickinson (below left) were among those who escorted the Germans back toward their positions after they had received the famous refusal of "Nuts!" from General McAuliffe. Captain von Peters, a German medical officer, was among the ultimatum delegation. While returning in a blindfold to his lines, he said in perfect English, "I'd rather be walking in the park with my wife." Premetz and Dickinson

Houffalize, and all along the road, their infantrymen were concealed in the darkness. We stopped every few minutes, and at one of these stops, all of the officers were removed from the truck. I did not know it then, but a few of the enlisted men were also taken off to assist in caring for German wounded. The truck I was on continued in convoy all night, and riding was an uncomfortable nightmare. Near daylight . . . the boys who had been in different tents exchanged accounts of what had happened, and by piecing together we were almost assured that no one had definitely been killed, and as far as we knew, no one had been injured. That, of course, did not take into account the many on whom no information was available. Quite a few who had dug in near or into the woods might well have taken off and outrun their pursuers. The major himself had not been [captured], as he was on reconnaissance at the time we were attacked.

My musette bag was attached to the top of the trailer we were riding. The contents were beginning to fall out. . . . I opened a jar of chicken and passed it around in the truck. I had about a carton of cigarettes and some candy and was not sure I could retain them so I asked Andy Roach, a non-smoker, to hold onto a couple of packs of cigarettes for me. That turned out to be a wise move. The candy we ate, keeping only a K ration and a can of sardines. I was wearing arctics and a pair of German officer's gloves, which I held onto, rather foolishly I was told. Up to now, no search had been made, and several of the men had small arms which they disposed of, by tossing one part off the truck here and there, so the Germans could not make use of them. The sight of krauts riding our [captured] vehicles back and forth alongside the trucks almost brought tears to my eyes. I would gladly have watched them explode and blow their occupants to bits, but none did. The 20th of December was one of the longest days I've ever lived. The trucks moved slowly, if at all, and we were becoming more cramped by the minute. Several times, we had to go across country, to allow German armor the use of the roads, and many places we were reminded of the grim battles that had preceded the German advance. Our tanks were in the fields, mired deep in mud or lying on their sides. The tracks through the fields gave mute evidence

In the absence of any actual photos of the German surrender ultimatum delegation, this still from the MGM film *Battleground* provides some idea of how the German officers may have appeared. *UA/MGM films*

This photograph of 506th Pathfinders setting up radar devices atop a brick pile in the area between Luzery and Bastogne has become an iconic image of the 101st Airborne in World War II. Pictured atop the pile with a radar set is Pathfinder Jack Agnew. *U.S. Army*

of maneuvering to escape destruction, and the bodies of Yanks lay sprawled helplessly, along the roadside and even in the road, where vehicle after vehicle passed over them until they became a part of the muddy earth.

After detrucking in Luxembourg, this group of medical personnel was marched to a POW collecting center at Gerolstein, Germany. The author of this account and some of his friends were eventually incarcerated at Stalag II-A, where they remained until early 1945, when the advance of the Red Army caused their captors to move

December 23, 1944, brought a cause for celebration to the besieged defenders of Bastogne. The skies cleared, and formations of C-47s dropped desperately needed medical supplies, rations, and ammunition. Gliders would bring in surgeons and artillery ammunition. This was one of many examples wherein the troop carrier command's pilots proved their mettle and helped compensate for the many 101st troops who were misdropped back in Normandy. Clear skies also enabled Allied fighter-bombers to destroy columns of German trucks and armor that had collected around the Bastogne perimeter. *Donald Hettrick*

them west, on long, freezing road marches, fraught with starvation and physical ailments ranging from pneumonia, diarrhea, and diphtheria to tonsillitis and malnutrition. The survivors of this agonizing ordeal could never have imagined the suffering they would be subjected to as prisoners in the collapsing Third Reich.

THE GERMAN JUGGERNAUT HITS THE LINE EAST OF BASTOGNE

The strong German forces alluded to earlier were the 26th Volksgrenadier Division, under Gen. Heinz Kokott, and the Panzer Lehr Division, both of which would make significant thrusts against the east approaches to Bastogne on December 21 and 21. The morning attack on Bizory was launched early on December 20 by a battalion of 77th Grenadiers, supported by tanks. This first large attack against Bastogne was repulsed with heavy losses by 2/501 PIR, supported by four tank divisions of the 705th Battalion and assorted armor from CCR 9th AD. All 101st Division artillery of the 321st GFAB, the 463rd PFAB, the 907th GFAB, and the 377th PFAB was massed on the fields east of Bizory to rain destruction on those attackers. This gave the German commanders a false sense that the Bastogne defenders had a generous stockpile of available artillery ammunition. Although such ammo was actually critically short, this German perception made them reluctant to launch massive attacks against the Bastogne garrison in the following days. It is also of interest that the few tanks

This oft-published and famous photo shows troopers on the ground near Bastogne on December 23, 1944, dragging in newly arrived equipment bundles. Again, there are many versions of the identities of the two troopers depicted. Best evidence, as of this writing, suggests that Leroy Schulenberg is the smiling man in the foreground, while Archie Weindruch is the man in the rear. Schulenberg was a 506th Pathfinder and among those who had just parachuted in to mark a drop zone for the resupply planes. This might explain why his uniform and appearance are cleaner in comparison to Weindruch, who had been in Bastogne for five days. Both men were members of B/506 PIR. *Albert A. Krochka*

In the aftermath of the aerial resupply, these members of D Battery of 377th PFAB were in a happy mood. Pictured are a lieutenant, a jeep driver, and the battery first sergeant. This was taken in the fields between Luzery and Savy, Belgium. *Donald Hettrick*

supporting the attack on Bizory held back after one of them received a disabling artillery hit. None of the German tanks advanced close enough to 2/501's MLR, becoming a significant factor in that attack.

That night at nearby Mont, a battalion of Panzergrenadiers from Panzer Lehr made an attack against the east perimeter in darkness and were slaughtered in the rolling fields. The Germans encountered wire-fenced cattle pens in the darkness, which caused a fatal slowdown in their advance. Illuminated by flares, these hapless infantrymen were decimated by 3/501 small arms fire with support from 705th TDs. This was to be the last mass attack against the east perimeter of Bastogne.

Too little has been written about the epic stand of the 1st Battalion of the 506th at Noville and also the fight to clear the woods northeast of Luzery by that same battalion on December 21, 1944. A German Volksgrenadier battalion, reduced in strength by now, had infiltrated along the railroad tracks and taken up positions in a woods between the Bastogne–Houffalize highway and the railroad line that ran northeast out of Bastogne. Don Burgett gave a detailed account of the woods-clearing action in his book *Seven Roads to Hell*. Lieutenant Colonel Robert Harwick, who assumed command of 1/506 when Lieutenant Colonel LaPrade was killed, wrote his impression of the merciless attack to clear the isolated German battalion from those woods:

I took Meason's company (A) and Mehoskey's company (C), and carefully started through the woods to try and chase the krauts into the waiting company (B).

The woods here have been planted. The trees are all pine and fir, in neat rows, and with no underbrush. It was like a tremendous hall with a green roof, supported by many, many brown columns.

We moved . . . very slowly, feeling out each section of forest . . . there was some German artillery falling, the shells hitting in back and to our left, but nothing disturbed the quiet in the woods. The men moved softly; orders were whispers or motions. Then the rifle crack in front, just over there! There is no one standing, but helmets peer around trees, trying to spot the source. Just where did that come from? Then another, and now a burst of machine gun fire, the tracers bouncing from tree to tree, like a pellet in a pinball machine. But A Company has them spotted. A few low mounds of freshly turned earth

Meanwhile, back in town. The square toward the west end of the main street (now known as McAuliffe Square) was beginning to show signs of battle damage from bombing and shelling. The cameraman stood near what is now the visitor center, facing southeast across the square. *AP, Rosenfield collection via Joe Beyrle II*

An MP directing traffic across the street from McAuliffe Square, near the southeast corner of the main intersection; camera facing east along the main drag.
Joseph Pangerl

mark the outer foxhole line. The fire is returned and now a few greenish figures bound up and move forward, running crazily, then they are down again and have disappeared. C Company on the right has stopped at the shots on the left, but they now move forward again. A [Company] continues to work forward, and now the first call for "Medic!" C [Company] hasn't found anyone yet. I work past Zahn and his reserve platoon to be sure that A and C don't get separated. But there it is, C has made contact. A long burst of machine gun fire . . . again it rattles and bounces through the trees, and the men on the right go forward in dashes. Rifle fire is now heavy and crackles continuously. I pass the boy who caught that first shot, face down, still holding his rifle, his helmet a little off to one side. The prisoners come back. They are terribly scared and keep ducking their heads as the bullets buzz and whine. Finally, a close burst, and they dive for a foxhole. The guard takes no chances and throws a grenade in after them. We walks up to the hole and fires four shots from his carbine and returns to the fighting in front. Cruel? No. Calloused? Maybe. But the penalty for a mistake here is death. If you are a prisoner, you don't run; if a guard, you don't take chances. The fight was not long, but it was hard—it was bitter, as all close fighting is. A wounded man lay near to where I had moved. I crawled over. He needed help badly; beside him was an aid man, still holding a bandage in his hand, but with a bullet through his head. Prisoners were coming in. One, terrified, kept falling on his knees gibbering in German, his eyes continually looking here and there. Finally in English, he kept repeating, "Don't shoot me!" He finally fell sobbing on the ground and screamed as we lifted him. The rest had an attitude between this man and the coldly aloof lieutenant, who was so aloof, that somehow, somewhere, he got a good stiff punch in the nose. His dignity suffered, as he nursed the injured member. We made these prisoners carry the wounded back. In all, there were fifty-seven. C Company was still working on a group. When they finally quit, there were about thirty more prisoners. There were fifty-five German dead scattered through the trees, most shot as they climbed out of their holes and ran to others, further in the woods. The fifty-fifth German was made sure about this time, when one of the "dead" Germans was found to be trying to operate a radio on which he was lying. Not all were accounted for, so we reformed and began sweeping the woods toward the waiting company. We soon found them. Having reached the edge of the woods, they were afraid to take to the fields. Hastily they tried to dig in. They fired on our scouts. One squad worked around their flank. The fight was sharp and quick. Four Germans dead, three wounded, one prisoner. Thirteen broke from the woods and were taken prisoner by the company waiting.

Two members of Signal Company take their turns at providing security for division HQ on the east perimeter. Next to Milton Reese (below left, armed with an M1) is Frank Sheehan (below right). *Francis Sheehan*

Clement Hassenfuss and Frank Sheehan pose near a dramatic World War I statue that was situated at the crossroads in front of the seminary at the east end of the main street of Bastogne. After being struck by an incoming artillery shell, the damaged statue is now located on the sidewalk in front of the Bastogne church. *Francis Sheehan*

Back at our barns, we found that the wounded could not be evacuated. Bastogne was completely encircled. To make matters worse, our medical company had been captured and there was no surgeons and very few supplies for the doctors. . . the steady shelling of Bastogne from the circle of German positions began.

On the morning of the 22nd, General McAuliffe arrived and personally congratulated each platoon for the work they had done. The men were quite proud, in having been noticed and thanked by the general. But the general had a rough day ahead.

THE GERMANS PROPOSE A SURRENDER

During a lull in the action on December 23, a small group of Germans carrying a white flag entered the lines of 2/327 GIR southwest of Marvie, and the two officers in the group presented a written message that suggested that the surrounded and outnumbered American forces in Bastogne should surrender immediately or face annihilation by several German artillery corps. The officers were blindfolded and led to a forward command post of the 327th, while their message was carried to the 101st's divisional command post for a formal reply from the Bastogne garrison's commander. When General McAuliffe was handed the German ultimatum, he read it, became increasingly angry, dropped it to the floor, and replied "Aw, Nuts!" McAuliffe was known to his staff as an officer who never swore, but the word *nuts* was one of his strongest and most frequently used expletives. Minutes later, when his staff members informed him that the Germans expected a formal written reply, McAuliffe was at a loss for what to say. Lieutenant Colonel Harry Kinnard, the divisional G-2 said, "General, your first remark would be hard to beat."

"What was that?" McAuliffe asked.

You said, "Nuts," Kinnard reminded him.

All officers present seemed to approve of the idea, so McAuliffe wrote on a piece of paper: "To the German commander: NUTS!"

The American commander, Col. Joseph Harper, the CO of the 327th GIR was in the command post and was chosen to deliver the reply to the German officers who had brought the ultimatum to the perimeter. Harper took great delight in doing so, although none of the officers present when the reply was authored (including General McAuliffe) had any idea that this rather frivolous reply would become an immortal statement in the annals of military history. The simple, one-word response of "NUTS" was quite characteristic of (and widely endorsed by) the unconventional and cocky minions of McAuliffe's 101st Airborne Division. It defined their identity and attitude in a single, short word. Despite the gravity of the current situation, the soldiers on the U.S. perimeter knew that they were beating back every German attempt to take Bastogne, and in light of that fact, they thought a German surrender to *them* would be more appropriate.

After the German surrender delegation returned to their lines, the U.S. troops on the perimeter braced themselves for the threatened deluge of artillery. All that actually happened, however, was a small local attack, easily beaten back in the 327th sector,

and some relatively minor artillery barrages of short duration. The German bluff had been called by McAuliffe, and despite much hard fighting yet to come, the Screaming Eagles weren't going anywhere.

A G-2 report on December 22 indicates that Belgian civilians had seen more than forty German tanks and a like number of assorted trucks, half-tracks, and other vehicles at Givry, west of Bastogne, before December 22. It is significant to note that the Germans never launched an attack on any part of the Bastogne sector that utilized anywhere near that many armored vehicles at once. The biggest deployment of German tanks and self-propelled guns would come on Christmas morning against the west perimeter, and even that attack employed a total of less than twenty tanks and/or self-propelled guns. Certainly Panzer Lehr, sitting east of Bastogne, counted an even greater number of available armored vehicles in their lineup than those observed at Givry. The critical U.S. artillery ammo shortage was so acute before the aerial resupply of December 23 that elements of Panzer Lehr openly assembled east of Neffe milling around in plain view of 501st forces a few hundred yards away. When Lt. William Russo of C/501 requested artillery on this tempting target, he was asked via radio how many Germans he could see.

"It looks like a regimental review out there," Russo replied.

The requested barrage was denied. General McAuliffe decreed: "If you see 400 Germans in a 100 yard area, and they have their heads up, you can fire artillery at them . . . but not more than two rounds."

It was later learned that the German commanders had no idea of this critical American ammunition shortage and the early repulse at Bizory; utilizing all available artillery and a generous expenditure of ammunition had convinced them otherwise.

On Christmas Day 1944, the Germans launched several ambitious attacks on previously untested approaches in more failed attempts to break in to Bastogne. Well before dawn, Panzergrenadiers struck the town of Champs, held by A/502 on the northwest sector and were rooted out of Belgian houses by Captain Swanson's paratroopers. German infantry, supported by tanks, made a failed attack into Marvie on the southeast perimeter, while the biggest thrust broke the line west of Hemroulle on the west perimeter. About fifteen German tanks, supported by a battalion of Panzergrenadiers, penetrated the lines of 1/327 GIR, running a gauntlet of fire from 1/502, 463rd PFAB, 377th PFAB, and 321st GFAB. The last tanks and assault guns were halted at the tree line near the Rolle castle and in Champs. In this photo, an unidentified 101st trooper stands with his foot on the head of a dead German, with a KO'd Mark IV Panzer in the rear. *Albert A. Krochka*

Schuyler Jackson of HQ/502 was decorated with the Silver Star for disabling this Mark IV tank with a bazooka round. In this photo, paratroopers are examining the tank at a time when it was still basically intact. Allied planes would attack it repeatedly in the coming weeks, not realizing it was abandoned. By mid-January, it was blown wide open, with its turret sitting perpendicular to the chassis. *Joseph Pangerl*

Expecting the same powerful reaction to future attempts was one reason why they hesitated to send masses of men and armor against other Bastogne sectors. Also, consider the fact that the Germans were not willing to commit most of their available armor to attacks aimed at taking the town. This suggests that actually capturing Bastogne was initially a secondary priority on their agenda. However, by December 23, when the now-cleared skies allowed Allied fighter bombers to decimate much of the German armor surrounding Bastogne, the German forces in the area had missed their opportunity to go all-out in attacking with the armor they had initially brought there.

On the west perimeter, a small German recon column had been halted by elements of the 401st Glider Infantry Battalion, under Capt. Robert J. MacDonald. Again, when their vehicles were hit by antitank fire, the Germans backed off timidly instead of driving forward boldly. This repulse caused them to abandon further attempts to drive south, while circling the west perimeter from the north. The aggressive troopers of C/401 also succeeded in driving

A Mark III self-propelled gun knocked out in front of the Rolle tree line, also on Christmas Day. After being hit, the vehicle turned almost 180 degrees from its original direction facing the tree line. *Joseph Pangerl*

Captured grenadiers from the 115th Panzergrenadier Regiment, 15th Panzer Division, being lined up and inventoried by a member of regimental HQ/502 PIR after their abortive Christmas attack. *Hugh "Duke" Roberts*

Another Mark IV tank captured on Christmas Day in the 502nd sector. On the side of its gun mantle, this tank was named "Lustmolch" (the happy salamander), relating to a folk legend that salamanders thrown into a fire will not burn. Because the tank was still in running condition, it was driven to various parts of the perimeter for inspection by other 101st troopers. In this photo, troopers from 1st and 2nd battalions of the 506th (identifiable by their helmet stencils) are examining the tank. *Donald Hettrick*

enemy troops from a roadblock that other Germans had formed at Crossroads X after the capture of the division hospital. This roadblock force had shot up some retreating 28th Division soldiers, which brought the German presence there to the attention of the Glider infantrymen. Enemy troops manning that roadblock were no match for Lt. Col. Ray Allen's men, who counterattacked and drove them out with heavy losses.

Christmas Day was to be another day of significant German probes and attacks on the Bastogne perimeter. On Christmas Eve, members of G/506, still in their positions in the woods south of Recogne, built a huge bonfire but strangely did not receive a shelling in reaction. Homan's troops of 2/501 watched as German bombers worked over the city of Bastogne behind their positions. S-2 troopers in the Goose chateau in Bizory were serenaded by German Volksgrenadiers, singing Christmas carols, which was followed by a firebombing and infantry attack that set the chateau ablaze. Troops on line east of Bizory heard "White Christmas" broadcast on German loudspeakers as surrender leaflets floated down on their positions, while captured white

More Screaming Eagles examining the Mark IV German tank Lustmolch after its capture on Christmas Day 1944. *Donald Hettrick*

phosphorus shells came in occasionally, splashing the painful, burning chemicals over American foxholes. At about 0300, German grenadiers began rampaging out of the west into the town of Champs at the northwest corner of the perimeter. This village was held mainly by members of Captain Swanson's A/502 PIR, some of whom interdicted the Germans at the outskirts of town. Willis Fowler, firing his light machine gun from a wooden farm shed, took a heavy toll of the attackers as they ran broadside toward town on a parallel trail. A number of German troops did get into Champs, where vicious, close-in, house-to-house fighting ensued. It was a cruel way to ring in the day of Christ's birth. An unknown German officer scribbled some thoughtful words on the chalkboard of a schoolroom in Champs that morning. He wrote:

> May the world never see such a Christmas night again. To die far from one's children, one's wife and mother, under the fire of guns, there is no greater cruelty. To take away from a mother her son, a husband from his wife, a father from his children, is it worthy of a human being? Life can only be for love and respect. At the sight of ruins, of blood and death, universal fraternity shall arise.—A German Officer

With mopping up of Germans in Champs continuing into daylight on Christmas morning, the German force was neutralized with all the intruders either killed or captured. It is not known if the author of the schoolhouse message survived the fighting.

Lieutenant Jim Robinson, a forward observer for the 377th artillery attached to Swanson's company, called fire missions on the woods covering a hill west of Champs. More German troops were staging there to launch follow-up assaults into the town, but Robinson's fire killed and wounded so many that their plans were disrupted and those soldiers were unable to mount their intended attack. The main effort of Christmas morning originated on the west perimeter, south of Hemoulle, where about fifteen German SP guns and Mk IV tanks, accompanied by a battalion of grenadiers, broke through the lines of 1/327 GIR. The intruders were also met by infantrymen of C/502 and artillerymen of the 463rd PFAB. Some of the artillerymen fought as infantry when their positions were overrun. Among the 463rd artillerymen killed in an infantry mode that morning were Howard Hickenlooper and John T. Hall, both of Battery C. Hickenlooper was struck in the neck by a burst of 9mm rounds from an MP40, while Hall caught a burst of MG42 fire through the chest.

By the time the German armor neared the highway connecting Hemroulle to Champs, many different units were firing at the German force. Artillery from the

Hettrick's War: Christmas Morning on the West Perimeter

DONALD J HETTRICK 2ND L FA

Lieutenant Hettrick called fire missions on various German probes, which he witnessed on the west perimeter of Bastogne. This event probably happened on Christmas Morning 1944, when more than fifteen German tanks and a battalion of infantry crashed through the 101st perimeter near the boundary of the 327th/502nd Infantry regiments. Artillery from the 377th PFAB, 463rd PFAB, and 321st GFAB were all firing at once, as were the infantrymen. The 463rd was right in the path of the rampaging German armor and many of its artillerymen fought as infantry that day in front of Hemroulle.

Lieutenant Hettrick wrote:

As the enemy soldiers struggled through the snow, they made very good targets and I called in [requested] a fire mission on them. However, the FDC refused me, as my left flank needed it more. It was frustrating to see all these krauts and not even have my scoped M1 rifle with me. They advanced through a shallow valley at about two hundred yards and presented quite a target.

Suddenly, I noticed a group of German soldiers to my left and realized they were pulling a 57mm antitank gun and were setting it up to fire. Then they wheeled the gun around and aimed at my foxhole. Apparently, they guessed that I was an FO and a menace to them. They fired a round at me, which landed just short.

When I saw the gun, I had already started to call a fire mission, and at the first shot, I told the FDC that I had to get artillery fire at a checkpoint right next to the gun. A previous concentration had been fired on that spot, and the data had been recorded.

Now the antitank gun fired another round, which landed just beyond my hole. Now [they] had an artilleryman's bracket, and if you split the difference, you'll have a direct hit. I told fire direction if I did not get [the fire mission] right now I was dead. Just as I figured the Germans had reset their sights and were ready to load and fire, my rounds screeched over my head. [They] burst—just as I expected—an antitank round to hit my foxhole.

As our shells exploded, I looked up and saw the German gun and crew were gone via a direct artillery hit. I have seen many times that a refired concentration missed a target by a hundred or more yards. Temperature, gun shift at recoil, sight settings, all can cause misses. I was very lucky to have had one of the accurate firings—not only this gun crew wiped out, but the entire attack disappeared into thin air. I heard a story that Lieutenant Wheeler was on my right as a forward observer and lost his eyeglasses. [He] was crawling in the snow, searching for them, and the German soldiers bypassed him. He seemed to be no threat to them. Lucky again, Lieutenant Wheeler.

Interior photo taken near the loader's position inside Lustmolch. The shiny, angled opening of the main battery's breech can be seen at upper right. The wraparound bar is for recoil protection, while the black canvas bag hanging below it could hold ten spent 75mm shell casings. Identification of interior parts courtesy Wolfgang Kloth, 2nd Panzer Division. *Donald Hettrick*

75mm pack howitzers of the 463rd and 377th PFA battalions and the 321st GFAB all scored multiple hits on the German armor, making it impossible later to determine which units should be credited for destroying each vehicle. A group of cooks from C/377 left their positions on the hill near Savy and captured a Mk IV tank in running condition after tossing a grenade inside.

The surviving vehicles and their accompanying grenadiers, some of whom were riding atop the tanks, turned north and came up the highway toward the approach road to Rolle castle. An Mk III Sturmgeschutz was knocked out in the field below the tree line after hitting an M10 tank destroyer with its 75mm gun. Two Mk IV tanks made it to the tree line, with the first rushing past intact.

That tank and crew would hide in a patch of woods inside the U.S. perimeter for hours, until making a break for German lines through Champs that afternoon. This "maverick tank" would be destroyed by bazookaman John Ballard of A/502. Sergeant Sky Jackson of HQ/502 was officially credited with stopping the last Mk IV, which drove past the Rolle tree line a few minutes after the maverick tank had passed that point.

A batch of 502nd Service Company and RHQ paratroopers had rushed out of their billets near the Rolle castle and deployed in defense of regimental HQ. They

Here is an exterior view of the upper left front of Lustmolch's chassis, where an American antitank shell hit broadside, next to the driver's compartment. *Donald Hettrick*

decimated a bunch of German grenadiers with small arms fire in the field southeast of Sky Jackson's bazooka position. Elsewhere on the Bastogne perimeter on Christmas Day elements of the Panzer Lehr Division attempted to crash through the hamlet of Marvie on the southeast perimeter. Their tanks were stopped and their infantry decimated by members of the 2/327 GIR, supported by Airborne engineers of the 326th AEB. Although German bombers would return to rain destruction on the town of Bastogne after dark, the failed Christmas attacks meant that the surrounded garrison had survived the siege and had not been forced to surrender.

The vanguard of Gen. George S. Patton's Third Army relief force was driving a wedge through Germans besieging the south perimeter. First contact between the 4th Armored Division and elements of the 326th Engineers took place on December 26. The siege of Bastogne had ended, and unlike the defenders of St. Vith, the 101st had not been forced to withdraw or surrender the town to the enemy. It should be remembered that the 101st Airborne did not accomplish this feat alone. Surrounded in Bastogne were assorted troops from other U.S. divisions, which calculated in total numbers, nearly equaled the number of 101st troops defending Bastogne. Also surrounded during the siege of Bastogne were CCR 9th AD, CCB 10th AD, the 705th TD Battalion, the 35th Combat Engineer Battalion, the 158th Combat Engineer Battalion, the 58th Armored Field Artillery Battalion, the 420th Armored Field

More incoming German prisoners, guarded outside the wall of the town cemetery across the road from 101st divisional headquarters. *Wierzbowski collection via Nadine Wierzbowski-Field*

Artillery Battalion, the 755th and 969th Field Artillery battalions of 8th Corps (both equipped with 155mm howitzers), and armored infantry elements of the 10th Armored, supporting Team O'Hara. Adding the unknown number of stragglers thrown together to form Team SNAFU, from the scattered 106th and 28th Infantry Divisions and miscellaneous other units, the total figure of non-101st defenders of Bastogne is estimated to exceed 11,000 troops.

Elements of Patton's 4th, 6th, and 11th armored divisions, as well as the 35th, 87th, and 90th infantry divisions, would reach Bastogne, then swing eastward, pushing the Germans back toward the west border of their Reich. The most costly fighting for the 101st was yet to come, when counterattacks toward Houffalize and Bourcy, in early January 1945, faced elite German units that had been sent south to join the assaults on Bastogne. Among the forces identified in the following days were elements of Fritz Rehmer's Fuehrer Escort Brigade, the 1st and 12th SS Panzer divisions, and the 9th SS Panzer Division. Fighting on the 26th saw the Germans shift their probes to the area south of Bastogne from Senonchamps north toward Savy. This effort failed just as surely as the previous attempts. On New Year's Eve, part of the 6th Armored Division attacked east to liberate Neffe, Belgium. When that attack stalled in the face of German fire from the houses in Neffe, 1st Platoon of F/501 flanked the town and came in to clear it house by house.

At about this time, Sgt. Ed Pieniak of F/506 PIR saw his best buddy killed in action. It happened during a snowstorm in the Bois Jacques woods. Sergeant Pieniak later said:

> I was a jock, taller than most of the guys . . . as a survivor of Normandy and Bastogne, I was considered one of the "old men" of the company. As such, it was expected for me to be a role model for the new replacements, who observed and imitated me. So I kept a firm jaw and a stiff upper lip, even though inside, I was scared shitless. Well, one day during an artillery barrage, my best buddy since Camp Toccoa was KIA. I remember blubbering and sobbing, with tears flooding my eyes and snot flying out of my nose, as I stood over his body in the midst of a blizzard. I'm afraid I lost it at that time and I didn't care who saw me. All I could think of was all the days, weeks, and months of terror and suffering we had been through since Normandy. I was thinking: if he had to die in this war anyhow, why couldn't he have died at the beginning, instead of after enduring so many months of hell? Why did he have to get it here, in this miserable winter campaign?

On New Year's Eve on the north perimeter of Bastogne, forward artillery observers Paul Tertychny and Tom Splan had taken up a good observation position south of Monaville, Belgium. Their position was well concealed and a perfect spot from which to observe the German armor that seemed to be moving in to that area in increasing numbers. When a 502nd LMG crew set up about sixty yards to the left of them, the observers asked them to go away. "We're here to protect you guys, offer some security!" "We don't need you or want you. Get out of here and let us do our

Frozen foxhole living is illustrated in this shot of two Screaming Eagles suffering through the siege. Their subunit affiliation is unknown. *George Koskimaki*

Armored troops of General Patton's Third Army searching German prisoners taken in the drive to enter Bastogne from the south. *AP, George Koskimaki*

This Third Army relief force tank, commanded by Lt. Charles Boggess of the Fourth Armored Division, was the first vehicle to break through to the 101st near Assenois on the south side of Bastogne. The C-team, composed of tanks from the 37th Tank Battalion and soldiers of the 53rd Armored Infantry, shot their way through and met elements of the 326th AEB, ending the encirclement of Bastogne on December 26, 1944. *Guy Franz Arend*

jobs!" The paratrooper infantry gunners refused to leave, which proved to be a death sentence for Tertychny. A short time later, a German tank appeared several hundred yards in the distance. As the FOs began radioing a fire mission, the LMG crew opened fire on the German tank, which until then had not been aware of their presence. When the main battery of the tank fired, the round went nowhere near the machine gunners, instead scoring almost a direct hit on the artillery FOs' position. Tertychny was killed outright by the explosion and Splan was evacuated with one arm mutilated and multiple shrapnel wounds. The lesson again was clear: it was suicidal to open fire on a tank with bazooka or machine-gun fire when the vehicle was too far away to inflict significant damage. Attracting their attention nearly always carried severe consequences.

At the beginning of 1945, Hitler had still not given up hope in his Ardennes offensive. He diverted several SS Panzer divisions to the Bastogne sector, with the 1st SS going to the southeast of Bastogne, the 12th SS to the north and northeast, and the 9th SS to the northwest. Ever-increasing numbers of infantry and armored units of

Patton's Third Army were arriving up the lifeline from the south. The 35th, 87th, and 90th divisions began pushing eastward, while the 11th Armored prepared to drive north toward Houffalize. Before that could happen, the newly arrived German units struck in force at Bastogne on January 3, 1945.

The northwest sector between Monaville and Longchamps, Belgium, was held by elements of 2/502 and HQ 3/502. These parachute infantrymen, supported by artillery from the 377th and 81st Airborne artillery, found themselves fighting off a battalion of SS Panzergrenadiers and nearly twenty tanks and self-propelled guns, which proved to be a formidable force. An unidentified machine gunner in Easy Company of the 502nd remained behind in his position at Monaville and killed a truckload of SS troopers when his company fell back in the onslaught. This

Gen. George S. Patton wasted little time in decorating Brig. Gen. Anthony C. McAuliffe for his leadership in commanding the surrounded Bastogne garrison. In this December 26, 1944, photo, Patton is pinning the Distinguished Service Cross on McAuliffe. *U.S. Army*

trooper paid with his life, allowing his fellow soldiers a chance to escape being overrun, killed, or captured.

To the left of Monaville, D/502 put up a strong fight, while elements of Fox Company to their left, north of Longchamps, were partially overrun by sheer force of numbers. Ray "Calfboy" Blasingame of F/502 earned a Silver Star that day, hitting six German SP guns with bazooka rounds and knocking out several of them. While doing this, he was protected by Bert Ellard, armed with a carbine. His loader was Ray Gary, who initially wanted to retreat after being blown out of his foxhole by a close-exploding tank shell. Gary shouted, "They're going to kill us!" but he was convinced to stay low in the hole until the German armor was too close to effectively deploy their 75mm guns.

The Sturmgeschutze (self-propelled guns) were mounted on turretless Mk III and Mk IV tank chassis with nontraversible guns. This fact helped the paratroopers who faced them to survive. The German main guns could not be swiveled and could only be aimed effectively by turning the entire chassis of the vehicle in the desired direction. Blasingame waited for some of the vehicles to roll past his hole, before blasting them in the rear with his bazooka. Gary served as his loader, although in the excitement, he forgot to pull the pins on several bazooka rockets. Ellard was picking off the German infantry, which accompanied the vehicles.

The German armor sought out individual American foxholes on the open snowy ground; some would even park over the holes, flooding them with carbon monoxide. Others pivoted on their tracks over individual holes, crushing their occupants into the frozen ground. Seeing the inevitable consequences of this lopsided battle, some Fox troopers fled to the woods and escaped. Others on the left flank were able to mow down hordes of black-jacketed SS Panzer troops who had been deployed as infantry due to a

A lone Mark V Panther tank that penetrated the northwest perimeter before being disabled and abandoned. Captain Pangerl is of the belief that this tank was photographed south of Longchamps and east of Rolle before the 9th SS Panzer launched its attack on January 3, 1945. *Albert A. Krochka*

On December 27, 1944, another mass aerial resupply mission took place in the skies over Bastogne. A number of C-47s towed gliders filled with equipment to the landing zone north of Bastogne. The plane *Stardust*, pictured, belonged to the 92nd TCS and was shot down while towing a glider. The glider pilot, flight officer J. D. Hancock, cut loose and landed safely near the tow plane. *Stardust* successfully crashlanded after hitting the top of a hill, then bouncing and coming down in a field between Luzery and Savy. Lt. Donald Hettrick, a forward observer with the 377th PFAB, took this shot of the plane, piloted by 1st Lt. Martin Skolnick, who was the only member of the crew to be wounded in the landing. Walking past in the left foreground is a member of the 321st GFAB, identified by the cannonball stencil and tic at three o'clock on his helmet. *Donald Hettrick*

Hettrick's War: A Battle of Wits

Back at my OP again, early in the morning and very quiet. I was sitting in the snow next to the first of five haystacks, when a 502nd lieutenant around the other side yelled that German tanks were coming over the hill in front of us. Then, all hell broke loose and Lieutenant Carter was hit by the rain of tank shells and machine-gun fire. He screamed for help, but I could not move, as my foxhole was only about fifteen inches deep and absolutely no protection, but [I had] no place to go. You could not find foxholes with the deep snow covering the ground.

Fourteen panzer tanks moved to our right and stopped alongside the infantry foxholes, but one tank swung to our left, along the side of the haystack and only seventy-five feet away. . . . I jumped out and ran over to the next hole, which was a large mortar pit. As I jumped into the pit, I saw a figure slumped over in the corner and thought he was dead, but he opened his eyes and said that a tank was about to fire on us. . . . Sure enough, a round hit a bit short of me and I knew I was in for a very serious game of cat and mouse. I knew that I now had no place to run and had to somehow outwit the young, inexperienced German tank commander. When the next shell landed just over, I was obliged to get out and go for the house just above me.

Suddenly, I sensed what [I had] to do to escape this death trap. So I started to run up the snow-covered hill, knowing another round was about to be fired. I stopped and ran back about ten feet of the twenty I had gone. Sure enough, the gunner fired well ahead of me. I kept running like this but never making the same move twice in a row. After about six or seven rounds chasing me, I eventually reached the hilltop and climbed over to safety.

Lt. Donald Hettrick, England, 1945

As I leaned against the house stonework, I breathed a great, big sigh of relief; I had actually outwitted that German sonofabitch. My sixth sense had told me what to do and how to do it. The tanker fired a few more shells into the upper story to vent his exasperation.

As [dusk] fell, the tanker had to leave or get clobbered by whatever we could find. Before the tank departed I had to hit the john and removed all my harnesses to do what I had to do. That was when he fired another round. When I returned to the spot where I had been sitting and picked up my harness, it was shredded by fragments from the last round. [I] sure was glad I had to go to a slit trench, or I would have taken all those fragments along with my harness.

Someone upstairs was sure taking good care of me, and I also thanked God that the young, overzealous tankers did not have the accuracy the older men used to have. I have seen German [tank] gunners hit a man standing on a bridge, and another time, hit a man standing in an open window [where] I happened to be observing with binoculars. The krauts had fought all through Europe and knew the terrain intimately after four years of occupation.

Incidentally, I did have a small piece of something in my right knee after being chased up the hill by the German tank. It was somewhat touchy and a medic stopped the bleeding with some gauze and adhesive tape. Also, the shell that slashed my harness did not hit the two grenades or the .45 auto [pistol] that I carried.

The incident described probably took place on January 3, 1945, in the northwest perimeter (Longchamps sector).

---

shortage of armored vehicles. Their bodies dotted the landscape in the valley northwest of Longchamps, visible in sharp contrast to the snowy terrain where they fell.

Eventually, two-thirds of Fox Company was captured—the largest number of 101st Airborne paratroopers captured from a main line of resistance in any battle of World War II. Even Lt. Earl Hendricks, the company commander of Fox Company was taken prisoner. As the Fox prisoners were being rounded up, a barrage of friendly

artillery from farther back in the U.S. lines landed amongst the group, killing several men and wounding Frank C. Tiedeman, Lt. Earl Hendricks, Joe Kettering, and many others. The surviving POWs were marched east to Gerolstein, Germany, then moved on to Stalag XII-A at Limburg, Germany, from which they would be dispersed to numerous POW camps across Germany. Captain Raymond Smith, returning from wounds received in Normandy, would assume command of Fox for the duration of World War II.

After the battle, Company B of the 506th was sent to Monaville to relieve E/502. The body of the dead machine gunner who had stayed behind to cover the E/502 withdrawal was still lying behind a house where he had fallen. As the Easy Company Deuce men pulled out, trucks arrived to haul out the many bodies of Germans who fell in the attack.

"Take good care of our buddy's body," the Company E men told Bob Stinson of B/506. "That guy saved our bacon—we'll be back soon to have his body removed."

Stinson discovered a .50 caliber machine gun set up in the woods near Monaville, covering the left flank, but he could not be sure if the E/502 trooper who had taken such a toll of the German attackers had used that weapon or a .30 caliber light machine gun on January 3. Thus died another unsung hero of the 101st Airborne whose identity remains unknown and whose deeds went officially unrecognized.

Over on the northeast section of the perimeter, the Germans saturated the Bois Jacques forest with a seemingly endless barrage of mortar and artillery rounds. Tree bursts rained deadly steel fragments down at 501st troopers, along with showers of snow, pine needles, and branches. The 1st Battalion of the 501st would stay in reserve that day, while elements of 2nd and 3rd battalions crossed the railroad line and attacked the high ground north of the tracks.

Since December 19, G/506 had occupied a section of woods due south of Recogne, with no buildings nearby to warm up in. Sgt. James West made numerous forays into Recogne to shave and warm up. This photo shows a machine gunner with a modified A6 light machine gun. He has loaded the weapon with a partial belt and discarded the shoulder stock. The bipod is in use, which enabled the weapon to be quickly moved to other positions. Identity of the trooper shown is unknown, but he is a member of 3/506 PIR. _Joe Doughty via Kurt Barickman_

Another view of Stardust, taken from a rear perspective with the landing gear not in its usual supporting place. The C-47's fuselage clearly cants upward toward the tail end. *Donald Hettrick*

At the point where companies G and H crossed over on a wooden bridge, the forested ground on either side stood above the sunken railroad line, with the bridge going across some distance above the sunken rail line. The 3rd Battalion group fought their way uphill several hundred yards to find a strong concentration of enemy troops before being recalled to the start line.

A half mile to the northeast, a steel railroad bridge was crossed by D and F companies of the 501st. They pursued an enemy that kept fading back through the snowy pines and offering relatively little resistance. Company F lost more men killed in the rear, south of the tracks, where their company HQ personnel had stayed behind during the attack. Murderous artillery fire claimed the lives of Orris Loudermilk and 1st Sgt. Herschel Parks, who was awarded a posthumous Silver Star for giving his foxhole to a radio operator in the midst of a bursting artillery barrage.

Here's a shot of assorted members of 3/506 in the woods below Recogne. Interesting to note, the trooper in the right foreground is equipped with a captured German MP44 assault rifle. *Joe Doughty via Kurt Barickman*

Meanwhile, a battalion of the 26th SS Panzergrenadier Regiment, 12th SS Panzer Division, had circled with infantry and half-tracks around the rear of the 501st's 2nd Battalion position trying to bypass that regiment and head into Bastogne. The two reserve companies, HQ 2/501 and E/501, engaged the SS Grenadiers and half-tracks with small arms fire, causing them to be distracted from their goal of Bastogne. The vehicles drove close to the tree line, and American troops in their foxholes were pinned down by machine-gun and 20mm cannon fire. Some of the troopers were wounded or killed by this fire, and Bill Burge of HQ 2/LMG later observed: "While the Germans had us pinned down in our foxholes, they missed their chance to win

During a lull in the action at Neffe, members of HQ 1/501 PIR group together for warmth and companionship. *Dick Frame via Paul Bebout*

A 60mm mortar crew at Neffe at the end of December 1944. The embankment of the short commuter railroad track can be seen behind them. Since World War II, the steel tracks have been removed. John Versolenko of 1st Platoon of F/501 holds the shell, as John Henry Poe receives coordinates via a sound-powered phone. *John Versolenko*

Two paratroopers believed to be members of D or E Company 502nd PIR were photographed in their position near Monaville, where heavy fighting took place on January 3, 1945. *U.S. Army via Pierre Godeau*

this battle. Had the situation been reversed, and we had the Germans pinned down in their holes, we would've charged into the woods and finished them off."

The Germans didn't do that, and Lt. Joe McGregor and Staff Sgt. Frank McClure of E/501 were bold enough to move along the tree line, firing a bazooka at the German half-tracks. McGregor is credited with knocking out several of them, while McClure leaped aboard one of the vehicles, whose crew had been killed by McGregor, to turn the German machine gun back against the German infantry. Sadly, McGregor, who was KIA a week later, received his Silver Star for this action posthumously.

McClure, who was blown out of the abandoned half-track by an exploding 20mm round, was evacuated with serious wounds, and he received a Silver Star in the mail after returning to the states. Two outposts southeast of McGregor's action were situated on open ground, and F. Leo Gillis of Company E was instrumental in decimating enemy forces as well as evacuating the seriously wounded Pelham P. Noyes. Charles E. S. Eckman and Henry Schwabe also displayed uncommon courage by racing hundreds of yards, without cover, to a decimated U.S. outpost where they located and rescued Harry Coffey. Harry Artinger of the 2/501 LMG Platoon was

A splendid shot of a 2/502 light machine-gun position near Monaville. One trooper has covered the receiver of his M1 rifle with a torn-open K ration carton to keep the freezing rain off the mechanism. A bazooka at left is partially covered with a garment, and cardboard tubes containing rockets for the weapon can be seen at far left. More equipment can be seen, including a smaller cardboard tube containing a fragmentation grenade, a canteen cup, a .30 caliber ammo can, and more K ration boxes. The .30 caliber light machine gun can barely be seen at the far right of the photo. *U.S. Army via Pierre Godeau*

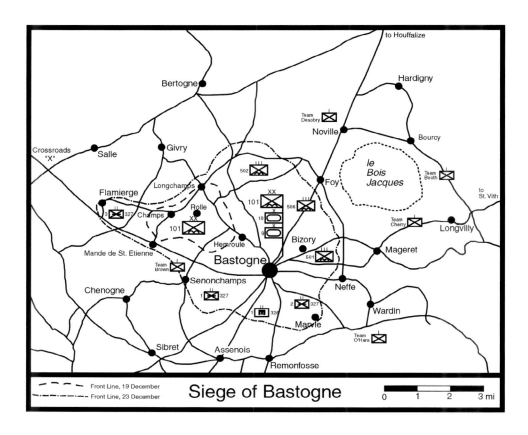

Siege of Bastogne

Front Line, 19 December
Front Line, 23 December

0   1   2   3 mi

among those killed. Back in the 1st Battalion reserve area, dozens of 501st troopers were wounded and killed that day, without even leaving their positions. The murderous mortar and artillery barrages rained devastation on them most of the day, with some individuals being hit more than once before being evacuated.

January 9, 1945, was a cursed day for Fox Company of the 501st PIR. For some reason, they were selected to attack and liberate the village of Recogne, Belgium, which throughout the siege of Bastogne had been in the 506th sector, facing the foxhole line of Company G. The 1st Platoon led off coming down hill from the woods and crossing open farm fields; the 2nd Platoon brought up their right flank along the main road into town from the south. When they got close to the village, German small arms fire erupted, hitting a number of troopers and pinning down the rest. The 3rd Platoon was added to the assault, coming in along the road as well. A number of troopers were killed and wounded, including Lt. Edward A. Matthews of 2nd Platoon and Pfc. Charles J. Merritts of 3rd Platoon. Survivors of the company finally rampaged into the town, killing and capturing a number of Germans, while others fled out the back way, heading north out of town. A mortar and artillery barrage soon followed, and Company E was sent in to help F in mopping up. During this phase, a sniper shot Lt. Joseph C. McGregor in the head, killing him. Mac had been shot in the head at Veghel, Holland, during the first night of Market-Garden. He had miraculously recovered from that near-fatal wound, only to be shot in the head again. The second head shot proved fatal. A half dozen 2/501st members were KIA at Recogne, and nearly thirty were wounded that day. Later that afternoon, Lt. Col. Julian Ewell, the regimental commander of the 501st PIR, was seriously wounded at Recogne, and Company F was withdrawn. They returned to their old foxholes in the Bois Jacques north of Bizory and were used in another attack through the woods on January 10. On that day, F/501 routed a German company, which was emplaced in dugouts between the trees; they lost Sgt. Paul Leeking KIA, several others wounded, and Sgt. Doc Gainey lost his leg.

Later in January 1945, the 101st Airborne Division was consolidating for a two-pronged counterattack, with the 506th PIR pushing north from Foy through Noville and Rachamps toward Houffalize. The 11th Armored Division and 17th Airborne Division were on their left flank. Meanwhile, the 327th and 502nd had swung around to the northeast to join with the 501st in pushing northeast toward Bourcy, following the railroad line that passed in and out of the Bois Jacques forest. Elements of the 6th Armored Division were pushing east, along their right flank through Oubourcy and Michamps. The 502nd took the lead in following the rail line toward Bourcy. They had close air support from P-47 fighter-bombers, but the 3rd Battalion advanced too quickly to the east and ended up in an area where they weren't supposed to be. This resulted in a 500-pound bomb being dropped on Lieutenant Colonel Stopka's battalion, killing him and wounding many others. Among the dead were Ernesto Burciago of HQ 3 and Troy W. Norris (Company I).

Rifleman of unidentified subunit manning a snowy position north of Bastogne with his Browning automatic rifle (BAR). By this time of the war, BARs were still not included on the official Table of Organizations and Equipment (TO&E) of a PIR rifle company, but most rifle companies in the 101st Airborne had managed to acquire some. They were integrated into each platoon and used to good effect. Despite their length of four feet and weight of twenty pounds, these weapons were considerably lighter than the M1919 light machine gun and could be employed with similar effect in a much more flexible deployment. *U.S. Army, Rosenfield collection via J. Beyrle II*

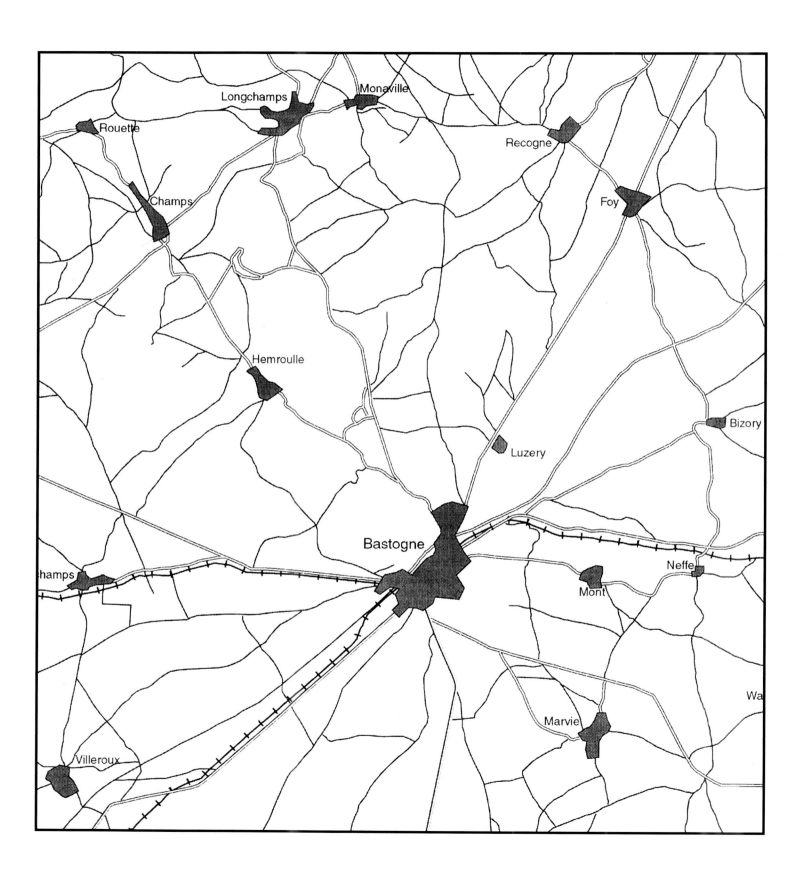

Troops of the 2/502 PIR, shifting positions in the northwest perimeter Monaville–Longchamps area, early January 1945. *Joseph Pangerl*

Looking north past the tree line west of the Rolle Castle. This shot was taken in early January 1945, after Allied planes again attacked the Mark IV tank destroyed by bazooka fire on Christmas Day. *Mike Musura, author's collection*

After being strafed and blown up two additional times by Allied fighter-bombers, the Mark IV tank destroyed by bazooka fire on Christmas Day west of Rolle was torn wide open, with the turret raised to perpendicular angles from the chassis. This photo of that tank, taken in early January 1945, is interesting because it shows the revolving turret mechanism of the tank. *Mike Musura*

Back in the states two years earlier, Burciago had miraculously cheated death when his parachute streamered on a practice jump. He had not deployed his reserve chute, but his main canopy caught at the top of a tall tree, which bent downward like a bow until his feet barely touched the ground, then raised him back up as it straightened out again. Stopka had succeeded the late Medal of Honor winner Lt. Col. R. G. Cole as commanding officer of 3/502. Now Stopka would be replaced by Lt. Col. Cecil L. Simmons, who became the third and final commander of that battalion, and the only CO of 3/502 to survive World War II.

Also KIA along the rail line while placing aerial recognition panels was Leo Pichler, a longtime member of the Deuce boxing team who was also killed by friendly fire from a P-47. The Germans faded back into Bourcy and continued east without pause. When the town was liberated two days later, it was abandoned, uncontested by the Wehrmacht.

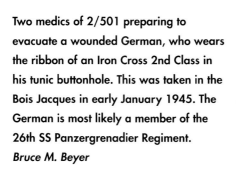

Two medics of 2/501 preparing to evacuate a wounded German, who wears the ribbon of an Iron Cross 2nd Class in his tunic buttonhole. This was taken in the Bois Jacques in early January 1945. The German is most likely a member of the 26th SS Panzergrenadier Regiment. *Bruce M. Beyer*

On January 5, 1945, thirteen members of the 501st PIR from Regimental Demolitions and Service Company were killed in the courtyard of the Bastogne Seminary, across from the church at the east end of town. The truck was loaded with land mines and men who were detailed to transport them to the front lines for burial. In addition to the load of mines on the truck, there were many additional stacks of land mines lying on the ground nearby. For no evident reason, the entire collection of mines exploded, killing all aboard and around the truck. A marker listing the victims is now posted on the seminary wall, thanks to the efforts of Julius Schrader, Leonard Cinquanta, and Richard O'Brien. *Jimmy Duggins, author's collection*

More German prisoners lined up on the main street in Bastogne. By mid-January, more than thirteen hundred POWs had been evacuated from the Bastogne area by various subunits of the 101st Airborne Division. The German cemetery north of Bastogne holds more than six thousand Germans killed between December 1944 to January 1945. Some of the solders buried there, however, were killed in other sectors of the Bulge. *U.S. Army*

An unidentified 101st Airborne chaplain gives last rites to two fallen SS Panzergrenadiers in a section of hardwood trees north of Bastogne in January 1945. *David White*

Some of the leaders who made the defense of Bastogne a success. Left to right: Col. Robert S. Sink, 506th PIR; Col. Curtis Renfro, division staff; Lt. Col. Paul Danahy, G-2; and Lt. Col. Pat Cassidy, 502nd PIR. *deTrez collection*

Three members of the 101st Airborne Division Signal Company pose with the town sign beside the wall of the town cemetery. This is across the road from the Belgian army compound that housed General McAuliffe's HQ. Pictured are Frank Sheehan, Milton Reese, and Benji Silverstein. *F. Sheehan*

A German-made dugout near the railroad embankment provided shelter for Capt. Pangerl of IPW Team 1, 502nd PIR, on the way to Bourcy, Belgium, in mid-January 1945. *Joseph Pangerl*

Two slightly different historic views were taken of the bullet-riddled sign held by members of the elite regimental S-2 section of the 501st PIR. The soldiers are, standing, left to right: Waldo Brown, James Ganter, Belgian civilian, Roland J. Wilbur, David Smith, Frank "Chief" Sayers, and Budz. Kneeling, left to right: Dunn, Frederick J. "Ted" Becker, Sgt. Bill Canfield, and Duane Henson. In the lower photo, Sgt. Eugene Amburgey at lower left, and the new 501st regimental photographer, Joe "Gopher" Sloan (second from right, standing), have joined the group. *Sloan Photo, Roland J. Wilbur*

The long, agonizing test of endurance ended for the frozen 101st survivors of Bastogne when they boarded trucks to head for the Seventh Army front in Alsace Lorraine, in eastern France. This began about January 19, 1945.

Sergeant Truax of Company D of the 506th PIR wrote: "I think we walked to Neufchateau. They put us in a building and a barn. After sleeping in a hole that long, I think we were suffering from hypothermia. We slept in a barn with warm manure. They loaded us on trucks and I started getting sick. We stopped at night, in Nancy,

Mid-January 1945, American tank tracks in the snow led to the town of Bourcy. The German defenders faded away, giving up the town without a battle. Another view showing some of the buildings in the town. *David White*

The fighting had moved away from town as two members of the 101st Airborne Division Signal Company helped Belgian civilians move their clothing and possessions back into Bastogne. Pictured are Benji Silverstein and Milton S. Reese. *Frank Sheehan*

Joe Halderman of B/326 AEB poses wearing a Mackinaw on a city street in Bastogne. The German prisoners visible behind him were put to work at clearing the road of rubble from the Luftwaffe bombing raids. *John Tocco*

A dead SS trooper was dumped in a grave at Noville, Belgium, by retreating Germans who didn't have time to cover his remains with dirt. After January 13, 1945, elements of the 506th attacked north, retaking Noville and Rachamps and advancing toward Houffalize, Belgium, with Patton's 11th Armored Division on their left flank. The 11th Armored had just arrived in the ETO, and the relief of Bastogne was their first combat. *Signal Corps, George Koskimaki collection*

In the absence of General Taylor, who was in Washington, D.C., to attend a war planning conference, Brig. Gen. Anthony C. McAuliffe had acted as divisional commander for the first week of the Bastogne fighting. This gave McAuliffe the opportunity to take his place in history when he replied "NUTS!" to a German surrender ultimatum on December 22, 1944. General Taylor later rejoined the 101st Airborne Division. Media hype had been swirling around McAuliffe after his "NUTS!" reply, stealing Taylor's thunder. There has been speculation that jealousy caused Taylor to promote McAuliffe, thus removing him, but he had already put McAuliffe's name forth for promotion to major general and division command. In reality, Mac's promotion after Bastogne was mostly due to the efforts of Gen. Troy Middleton, VIIIth Corps commander. General McAuliffe departed early in 1945, taking command of the 103rd Infantry Division. One of McAuliffe's aides, Lt. Ted Starrett, left with him to the 103rd ID, while his other aide, Vince Vicari, remained with the 101st. *U.S. Army*

Capt. Joseph Pangerl took this splendid photo of the snowy woods near the railroad line along the route to Bourcy. The officer at right, standing on the logging trail and holding rolled-up maps, is Capt. Robert Clements, former G Company commander, reassigned as regimental S-2 officer of the 502nd PIR. *Joseph Pangerl*

France. I was so sick I fell off the truck and defecated in the street. Some of us (also) had trench foot, bad."

The 101st Airborne was being sent to Alsace to bolster the lines that had been battered by Hitler's Operation North Wind, also known as "The Bitch Bulge," because it was another bulge-like Nazi counteroffensive staged near Bitche, Germany. The 42nd Infantry "Rainbow" Division had been mauled in that offensive, and the 101st would replace them somewhere along the Moder River near Haguenau.

Lieutenant Bill Sefton, now a platoon leader in D/501, says: "By now, we felt the war was a lousy business and that we had been ill-used. After a long, freezing truck ride, which was the most miserable aspect of the Battle of the Bulge to me, we were hardly cheering about having to go pull somebody else's chestnuts out of the fire."

CHAPTER 9

ALSACE-LORRAINE

Heading south to Nancy, France, then eastward to the French–German border, the 101st Airborne Division arrived in Alsace-Lorraine after January 20, 1945. This area had changed hands from Germany to France and back again over the decades, and much of the civilian populace spoke German. Their political loyalties remained uncertain. In recent years, the area had been ruled by Germany.

Locating Alsace on a map, it lies due west of the black forest, which is west of Stuttgart, Germany. South of Alsace are the Vosges Mountains. The 101st occupied an area that juts eastward into Germany, north of Strasbourg, due east of Luneville, and southeast of Metz.

Initially, the 101st Division relieved elements of the 36th Infantry Division in a mountainous region, but a few days later was shifted to the west bank of the Moder River to replace the 42nd "Rainbow" Infantry Division. On New Year's Day 1945, Hitler had launched a counteroffensive here, which was a smaller version of the Ardennes offensive. Locally, the Germans had managed to cross the Moder River and inflict significant losses on the Rainbow Division, which was newly arrived in the European Theater of Operations (ETO) at the time. It was feared that there would be more aggressive German action in this sector, but that proved to be unfounded.

The Germans in this sector were war weary, and aside from some patrolling, were content to maintain an unspoken truce. Some 101st troopers found themselves in towns that straddled the banks of the Moder and thus were able to move indoors for

Members of the 101st Airborne's divisional military police (MP) platoon in Alsace in early 1945. The divisional MPs began wearing a full-size painting of a Screaming Eagle shoulder patch on the front of their helmets in late 1944. *Signal Corps, Wierzbowski collection via Nadine Wierzbowski-Field*

Alsace lies in extreme northeastern France along the German border. The sector occupied by the 101st Airborne in January 1945 lies near Haguenau, which is north of Strasbourg, southwest of Karlsruhe and due west of Stuttgart. The town of Saverne was occupied by elements of 101st Division headquarters. *Signal Corps, Wierzbowski collection via Nadine Wierzbowski-Field*

the first time in more than a month. Others dug in at more rural sectors, but even those could periodically rotate back to barns, while doing their turn in reserve.

The Moder River was quite narrow and shallow enough at places to wade across. This knowledge could have saved some lives, as some troopers whose rafts capsized during night patrol panicked and drowned in neck-deep water.

Not surprisingly, the Germans had planted minefields of antipersonnel mines in some sectors of their east bank as security against these American incursions. Also, U.S. patrollers soon learned not to cross twice in the same place on subsequent patrols, a lapse that invited ambushes.

For the infantry squads, it was static holding and patrolling with the enemy in easily accessible range across a small water barrier, unlike the Neder Rhine had been on the island. For troopers who lived like the hunter, stalking their prey on solitary night forays, this period offered the opportunity to continue adding to their list of victims.

Melton "Tex" McMorries of G/501 had compiled a fearsome record of personal kills in Holland and Bastogne and would reach the enemy in Alsace by the only means available—night patrolling. But the ranks had been so decimated by Bastogne's casualties that Tex's platoon leader was loathe to allow the last three surviving old timers to venture into German lines together at the same time. Of this time period, Tex wrote:

Men of the 101st gathered in little groups, throughout the area, in dugouts, barns, houses, and in the open. Then, as the men gathered . . . the full recognition of the losses suffered by the units was realized . . . four and five men, where there should have been forty, 2 or 3 old faces, together with a few new ones . . . new yet old, in the way of battle, as only 30 days can make in a place such as Bastogne. . . . Something of these thoughts must have passed through the mind of my platoon leader, Lt. F. E. Sheridan.

He was never known to show a soft spot for any man nor any enemy.

As another patrol was called, three of the men who had been there while the 768th name was added to the wartime roster of G Company 501 PIR stepped forward . . . three men that had without a doubt made as many rough patrols as anyone could make and still be alive.

Lt. Sheridan said, "One of you three—and one only. The familiar faces are getting few, and if this patrol doesn't come back, there won't be any experienced men left to teach the others. . . ."

The three men objected and argued, one of the few objections ever raised to Sheridan's decisions. It was no challenge to Sheridan's authority and he knew this. It was not pity, nor feeling that led him to object, it was the cool

Members of the elite regimental S-2 platoon of the 501st PIR posed for regimental photographer Joe "Gopher" Sloan in Alsace. Standing, left to right: Frank "Chief" Sayers, William "Smokey" Ladman, Scover Bailey, Waldo Brown, Bill Canfield, unknown, and Roland J. Wilbur. Kneeling: Cobert Collins and Frederick J. "Ted" Becker. *A. Haines collection via Terry Webb*

During an inspection in Alsace, Gen. Maxwell D. Taylor talks with a first sergeant from 3/502 PIR as Lt. Col. Cecil L. Simmons, Capt. Richard Campbell, and Col. Steve Chappuis (regimental commander of the 502nd PIR) look on. *SLA Marshall collection, Carlisle War College via Jim Bigley*

realization of what the gamble implied. The patrol was to cross again, over the river and through the minefield into the German lines and capture a prisoner. No different from the many, many patrols these three had made before, that were common for all line soldiers.

Yet, somehow it was different. Edward Case looked ten years older; he had just recovered his eyesight from a potato masher explosion at Bastogne. Frank Serawatka looked no different, just a little leaner and meaner. I don't know how the other one looked, 'cause that was me.

These three men had been buddies too long; confidence in their abilities was mutual. The reaction of seven new men on a patrol was still uncertain. I know that Sheridan had a really tough decision. He thought: "These are the last of my really dependable men. Some other men (perhaps the best) will come back from the hospital, but which ones . . . when?" You must know it costs too much to find out. One mistake can cost a patrol, as well as a bad break.

Yet we knew that our chances, or the chance of one of us to make a successful patrol, would be increased if the three made the patrol.

This was argued and without offense to anyone, it was agreed.

A glider artillery trooper of the 907th GFAB aiming an M1 carbine somewhere in Alsace in February 1945. *Joe Mountain*

Henry Schwabe of the HQ 2/501 LMG Platoon was a German-born paratrooper from Pottstown, Pennsylvania. Because of his ancestry, Schwabe was treated with suspicion and not allowed to make the jump into Normandy. He did, however, parachute into Holland and distinguished himself in the Market-Garden campaign as well as at Bastogne. Tragically, while returning from a night patrol on the Alsace front, Schwabe gave the password with a German accent and was killed by a trigger-happy replacement.

Of his death, Glen Derber wrote: "The biggest emotional letdown I ever had was when Henry Schwabe got killed in eastern France. He was one of the men, who like me, lived a clean life. My belief that this would get us through safely was shattered."

Members of F/501 PIR standing in their field expedient chow line in Alsace in February, 1945. *Rudolph Korvas*

Members of Item Company, 501st PIR (I/501), who survived the battle of Wardin, Belgium (southeast of Bastongne), gather to talk in Alsace, February 1945. Left to right: Johnson, Ogle, Welch, Turner, and John J. "Moe" Higgins. Moe Higgins was from New Rochelle, New York, and his pose in this photo has become an iconic symbol of the 101st Airborne attitude. *Ogle Photo via P. Tessoff*

On February 13, 1945, 101st Pathfinders on detached service made a combat jump into the zone of the U.S. 4th Infantry Division to signal a resupply drop near Briealf, Germany. The jumpers originated from the 506th PIR. This photo depicts the Pathfinders examining K rations and smoke grenades after landing. *Signal Corps, Rosenfield collection via J. Beyrle II*

On March 15, 1945, the entire 101st Airborne Division passed in review for generals Eisenhower, Ridgeway, Brereton, and Taylor, as well as a host of other VIPs. The occasion was the award of the Presidential Unit Citation to the entire division for the defense of Bastogne, Belgium, in the recent Battle of the Bulge. This view of the reviewing stand shows an MP wearing the eagle patch painted on the front of his helmet. The marching troops wore four-pocket Class A uniforms with pistol belts, surmounted by steel helmets, and armed with shoulder weapons. *Donald Hettrick*

Derber did survive the war, and is still living as this is written in 2007. Don Castona of G/501 survived all the combat missions of the 501st PIR without getting a scratch. After VE Day, though, Castona was shot in the arm by a drunken French girl, who was waving a .25 caliber pistol around in a Paris saloon.

OPERATION OSCAR

Companies A and B from the 1st Battalion of the 501stPIR, as well as Company E of the 327th GIR, made a large raid across the Moder River on the night of January 31–February 1, 1945. This maneuver, called Operation Oscar, was a carefully planned incursion, utilizing artillery support and timed phase lines, all aimed at bringing back German prisoners. This was accomplished, and about a platoon of German infantry was ambushed and wiped out. U.S. dead included 1st Sgt. Joe A. Henderson of B/501 and Sgt. Ed Gulick of A/501. Phillip A. Nichols, a BAR man of E/327 GIR was awarded the Silver Star for his work in covering the withdrawal of his company across the Moder River. He and bazookaman Joe Seny (who also received the Silver Star) made numerous trips back to help evacuate the thirteen wounded members of their company.

As to prisoners, the 501st brought back one officer and twenty enlisted German POWs. E/327 captured one officer and fifteen enlisted men, killing an estimated fifty. Subsequent patrols across the Moder were made in February 1945 by elements of Able and Easy companies of the 506th. Those patrols have been detailed in books by Donald R. Burgett and David K. Webster. A total of seventy-seven German prisoners were taken by the 101st Airborne Division during their time in Alsace.

CHAPTER 10

BERCHTESGADEN AND THE END OF THE WAR

Striving to arrive first at Hitler's Alpine residential center, known as Obersaltzberg, the 101st Airborne Division found itself racing along the autobahn between Munich and Berchtesgaden with the French 2nd Armored Division. The autobahn was lined with hordes of surrendering German troops, many of them marching west still armed. In front of the racing Allied columns were still some die-hard enemy units, bolstered by SS troops and threats of the Feldjager Kommando, but imminent victory was in the air. German fighter aircraft, including FW-190s, ME-109s, and ME-262 jets lined the sides of the autobahn, grounded for both lack of fuel and trained pilots to fly them. The big prize was perceived to lie at the Berghof, Hitler's mountain home, where the monster himself might conceivably be captured and untold treasures liberated.

The thrill of the chase drove the DUKW convoy onward, until the advance was halted at Inzell by a blown bridge at a crucial crossing on the final approach to Berchtesgaden. The 2/506 detoured to a route that would pass through Bad Reichenhall but were halted again at the Saalach River by the obstinate commander of the U.S. 3rd Infantry Division, Maj. Gen. John O'Daniel. He effectively delayed further

SS Gen. Max Simon, a veteran of the SS Totenkopf Division and survivor of many campaigns on the eastern front, was the commanding officer of the 16th SS Panzergrenadier Division in 1945. Here he is discussing surrender arrangements for survivors of his division with Gen. Maxwell D. Taylor, as Lt. Col. Patrick Cassidy of the 502nd PIR looks on. *Signal Corps via Lawrence Schweiger*

Moving into the Ruhr area southwest of Duesseldorf on the west bank of the Rhine River in April 1945, the 101st took up positions east of Muenchen–Gladbach, Germany. The 377th PFAB, originally equipped with 75mm pack howitzers, had acquired a number of 105mm cannons while at Bastogne. This Ruhr pocket photo shows one of their 105mms under a camouflage net in a typical firing position in early 1945. *Donald Hettrick*

advance of the 101st Airborne. Thus elements of the 3rd Infantry Division entered Berchtesgaden on May 4, 1945, coming from the direction of Salzburg. The first elements of the 101st Airborne, as well as the French 2nd Armored Division, would arrive a day later. Hitler's house, the Berghof, had been recently bombed and the damaged building was further set afire by SS troops before the Allies arrived.

The first Screaming Eagles to enter Berchtesgaden (via several directions of approach) were elements of the 506th PIR, accompanied by the 321st GFAB and the 327th GIR. The 3rd Battalion of the 506th drew enemy 88mm artillery fire from the west flank, which hit several men, killing Pfc. Claude Rankin of H/506. Rankin became the last member of the 101st Airborne Division to be KIA before VE Day. The famed mountain conference center known as the Eagle's Nest was on the top of

A company-size night raid on Himmelgeist, Germany, by A/506 cost the lives of four troopers who were KIA by enemy fire on the east side of the Rhine, as well as several more, who drowned in the Rhine when their boats capsized under artillery fire on the return trip. Bob Morneweck was among the drowning victims. This photo was taken by Capt. William Kennedy, the CO of A/506 on return several days later to recover the bodies of Company A men who had been buried by the Germans near Himmelgeist. *Kennedy Photo via A. Borrelli*

Members of F/502 prepared for yet another night patrol across the Rhine River in April 1945. Pictured standing (left to right) are: John Hromchak, Lt. Edward L. Briant, and Dan McBride. Kneeling (left to righ)t: unknown, Russell Rogers, Franklin "Ray" Blasingame, and Roy Rapp. *Ray Blasingame*

Racing along the autobahn past Mannheim and Munich, the 101st encountered thousands of surrendering German troops, marching west and still carrying weapons. The main interest of those erstwhile enemies was now to escape the vengeance of the advancing Red Army. At the sides of the autobahn were many abandoned German planes—the Nazis lacked both the fuel and the trained pilots to put them in the air. They had been using the autobahn as a runway and concealing the planes under trees at the side of the highway to avoid destruction by the Allied fighter-bombers that ruled the skies in early 1945. The photo is that of a ME-262 two-engine jet fighter plane that was discovered by the 377th PFAB while en route to Berchtesgaden. *Donald Hettrick*

Kehlstein mountain—one mountain removed from Berchtesgaden. Vehicles could be driven most of the way up, but an elevator provided transport to the building at the summit. The SS had disabled the elevator before vacating the premises, so the final climb now had to be made on foot. The French got up to the Eagle's Nest almost an hour before the first 101st troopers climbed up there; they grabbed loot and scattered papers all over the mountainside. This was the beginning of a wave of wanton vandalism, looting, and even rapes perpetrated by the French as they ravaged the area in the name of vengeance. They also planted a French tricolor flag at the Eagle's Nest. Colonel Sink did not like what was happening, so he appointed the 2nd Platoon of C/506 to guard Hitler's house and allow nobody inside without a personal pass from General Taylor (high rank not being a qualifier in itself). Lieutenant Donald Zahn, who had been battlefield-commissioned after Holland, was commander of 2nd Platoon; his platoon sergeant, Leroy "Buddy" Gros, was a Cajun who could speak

More abandoned German fighter aircraft discovered while en route to Berchtesgaden. This photo shows members of the 326th Airborne Medical Company examining the vertical stabilizer of a FW 190. *Henry Hausser*

French. Sink eventually had Gros inform the French commander that his troops and their vehicles would have to vacate the Obersalzburg within twenty-four hours. This ultimatum would be backed up by use of military force if the French did not comply. The ultimatum was complied with and the French withdrew. Over at Bad Reichenhall, where the 907th GFAB had established a POW compound, some French troops paused to determine if any turncoats from the German foreign volunteer unit known as Charlemagne (utilizing renegade Frenchmen as soldiers) were among the men incarcerated there. Locating a dozen of the traitors in the Bad Reichenhall POW cages, the French troops reportedly shot them on the spot. Although some select troops, including Zahn's platoon, would remain behind to secure the Berghof and to reside in the nearby Berchtesgadener Hof hotel; although high-level Allied conferences and tours were held there, most of the division moved south after less than a week to outpost various Austrian towns more than fifty miles south of Hitler's Bavarian complex. The 326th AEB outposted the town of Lofer, while the 377th PFAB occupied Unken, Austria. The 502nd would be sent southwest to Mittersill, while the 506th outposted towns from Saalbach in the west to Taxenbach to the east, with Zell am Zee and Bruck

This former German army compound became a POW camp for surrendering Germans in April 1945. The 907th GFAB administered the camp. Among the prisoners held here were a dozen French traitors who had fought as members of the German foreign volunteer legion Charlemagne. *Donald Hettrick*

in the center. The farthest-flung 506th outpost eventually became the Company C group at Rauris and Worth, only a few miles from the northern border of Italy.

The 2/506 garrisoned the town of Kaprun, which had a sizable airfield on its west boundary, now occupied by POWs. Hordes of Wehrmacht personnel, fleeing the Red Army, passed into U.S. captivity in this area, with another large POW camp being established near Saalfelden, where Luftwaffe Field Marshall Albert Kesselring finally made known his intentions to surrender. "Smiling Albert" Kesselring was sent to Berchtesgaden, where he met with generals Taylor and Higgins. Hermann Göring had surrendered to elements of the 36th Infantry Division, but his wife was still living in the Fischorn Castle at Bruck, now the headquarters of Col. Charles Chase, the XO of the 506th PIR. Her Polish lady in waiting was also living in the castle and was found to be in possession of a rare Dutch painting, "Christ and the Adultress," by Vermeer, which was rolled up in a tube in her quarters. The painting was confiscated from her

continued on page 229

As American troops raced toward the prize of Hitler's home in Berchtesgaden, increasing numbers of German troops negotiated organized surrender. This scene shows surrendering German army officers conferring with officers of the 506th PIR near Bad Reichenhall, Germany, in late April 1945. *Don Brinninstool*

An officer of the 13th SS Panzerkorps, wearing an assault gunner's field gray wraparound jacket, confers with Maj. Hank Plitt of divisional G-2 and Capt. Joseph Pangerl (back to camera), between Munich and Bad Reichenhall in late April 1945. *David White*

Members of 3/506th PIR entered Berchtesgaden from a different direction than 2nd Battalion. Company H met resistance from an 88mm gun crew, which killed Pfc. Claude Rankin, making him the last member of the 101st Airborne to be KIA before VE Day. The buildings visible in this photo are still standing in the town of Berchtesgaden as of 2006. This photo was taken May 5, 1945. *Signal Corps, Wierzbowski collection via Nadine Wierzbowski-Field*

The complex of buildings that included Hitler's massive "Berghof" (mountain house) included several hotels as well as residences for top Nazi government officials. Because of the proximity of these places to Salzburg, Austria, this complex was known to the Nazis as the *Obersalzburg* (above Salzburg) area. Copies of this diagram were distributed to 101st Airborne troops occupying the area as a guide to who had occupied the various houses before their arrival. *Bill Sefton*

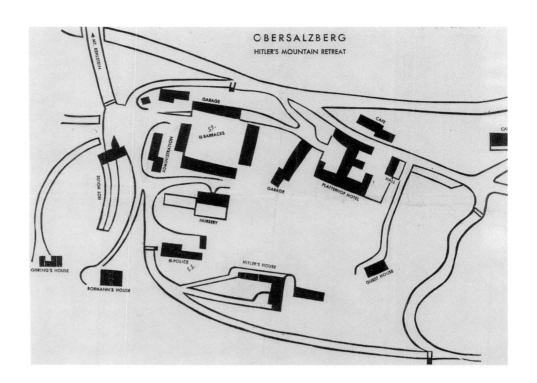

Capt. Harry V. Anderson, the fine arts and monuments officer for the 101st Airborne Division, displays a Dutch masterpiece by the famous artist Vermeer. This painting, entitled "Christ & the Adultress," had been removed from its original frame and given as a gift to the Polish lady in waiting of Frau Göring by Reichsmarshall Hermann Göring before the arrival of Allied forces in the Berchtesgaden area. This was among the many art treasures looted by Göring earlier in World War II. Frau Göring's lovely lady in waiting was living with her in the Fischorn castle at Bruck, Austria, when this painting was discovered rolled up in a tube and was confiscated by American officers of the 506th PIR. The painting was remounted on a temporary frame as shown and displayed with other treasures of the Göring art collection before being returned to a museum in Holland. Almost sixty years later, the version of "Christ and the Adultress" hanging in a Dutch art museum was pronounced a forgery by a team of Vermeer experts. Exactly when the substitution was made remains in question. It is even possible that the painting depicted was already a forgery. *Signal Corps, Wierzbowski collection via Nadine Wierzbowski-Field*

Sometime after the 101st Airborne occupied the Berchtesgaden area, Luftwaffe Field Marshall "Smiling Albert" Kesselring (center), sent word that he was in hiding at Saalfelden, Austria, north of Zell am Zee, where Colonel Sink had his regimental HQ for the 506th PIR. A contingent led by Lt. Ed Shames of E/506 came up from Kaprun, Austria, took the field marshall into custody, and conveyed him to the Obersalzburg area, where he posed for many photos with Gen. Gerald Higgins, assistant division commander (left) and Gen. Maxwell D. Taylor (right). Kesselring appeared to be perpetually smiling due to an apparent facial defect; because he was an enemy commander, many lower-ranking 101st troopers resented General Taylor's apparent fraternizing with him. *Signal Corps via Ed Ihlenfeld*

Hitler's famous mountaintop conference room "The Eagles Nest" (Adlerhorst), sits atop the Kehlstein mountain (next mountain adjacent to the mountain where Berchtesgaden is located). In this great photo by Capt. Joseph Pangerl of the 502nd PIR's IPW Team No. 1, the Eagle's Nest is visible at the top of the mountain, in the distance. It was possible to drive most of the way up to a parking lot, but the remaining distance to the top was meant to be ascended by elevator. SS troops had disabled the elevator before Allied troops arrived, making it necessary to hike the final hundreds of meters on foot. Elements of the French 2nd Armored Division arrived in the Eagle's Nest about an hour before the first members of C/506 got up there. *Joseph Pangerl*

A closer view of the Eagle's Nest, known with disdain to 101st troopers as the Crow's Nest and to modern tourists as the Kelhstein Tea House. This building was a marvel of engineering and was made at the direction of Martin Bormann, Hitler's secretary, as a present for the fuehrer's fiftieth birthday, in the late 1930s. It is said that Hitler disliked the place and actually visited it only a handful of times before World War II ended. *Signal Corps via Ed Ihlenfeld*

A view of the interior of the Eagle's Nest. Although these windows are twice the height of a man. *Signal Corps via Ed Ihlenfeld*

Sgt. George Allen, a 101st Airborne Division interpreter, reads important Nazi memos that SS troops had attempted to hastily destroy by burning as they fled the Berchtesgaden area. Some of the papers survived the flames and provided interesting intelligence on Nazi leaders and their activities. *Rosenfield collection via Joe Beyrle II*

Continued from page 224

and temporarily mounted on a skeletal frame. It was returned to a Dutch museum, but the specimen there was recently pronounced a forgery, making people speculate whether the painting liberated in 1945 was original, or perhaps a substitution that had already been made. Hermann Göring's train, loaded with art treasures (paintings and sculptures) that he had looted from numerous occupied countries during the Nazi rampage in western Europe, was discovered in the 101st's area. The train was put under constant guard, while many of its contents were displayed in a nearby building. Many Allied military visitors from various parts of occupied western Europe came to view Göring's art collection, courtesy of the 101st Airborne Division. Thus began a long, tedious, and complicated task of cataloging and returning the various treasures to their previous owners.

A Fourth of July party was planned for the 506th at Zell am Zee, where regimental headquarters was situated in the Grand Hotel. The nearby lake would be the target of a demonstration parachute jump by a team of troopers, who would parachute into the water. The original plan was for the descending troopers to fire flare pistols at one another in midair, but this was modified to igniting smoke grenades while falling.

The 501st PIR, soon to be deactivated, joined the division late at Berchtesgaden, coming from Mourmelon le Petit and having missed the drive through southern

After a brief stay in the Obersalzburg area, most of the subunits of the 101st Airborne Division were sent more than fifty miles to the south and southwest to occupy various towns in Austria. The 502nd PIR ended up in the Kossin–Mittersill, Austria, area, where patrols frequently ventured into the neighboring mountains to round up SS troopers who had not yet surrendered after VE Day. This photo was taken by Lt. David White and shows an officer candidate from the *Junkerschule* at Bad Tolz, Germany, surrendering in his black Panzer wraparound tunic. "JST" can be seen on his epaulettes. Note that the other SS trooper visible in the photo is still armed, indicating the odd circumstances in the days following the surrender of Germany. *David White*

A group of surviving medics from the 506th PIR's medical detachment posed in Austria for this photo in mid-1945. Standing (left to right): R. E. Wilson, H. Plaisted, unknown, W. Hodges, H. Haycroft, K. Ely, G. Myrick, Jacko, Drogesh, E. Woodside, C. Osteen. Kneeling (left to right): C. S. Henderson, R. Mueller, A. Valasek, P. Thompson, A. Sosnak, Capt. George M. Lancaster, Capt. W. Meyers, F. Fabian, R. Lutz, C. J. Kurtz, C. S. Burke, M. Barnhart, J. Halpin. *Fred Bahlau*

Before leaving Austria, the 101st Airborne Division participated in athletic competitions with numerous other infantry and armored divisions. These events were well attended by the brass and the 101st seldom lost track and field, boxing, or football games. Seated in the upper center are Gen. George C. Marshall, Gen. George S. Patton, and Gen. Maxwell D. Taylor. *John Gabor*

Members of HQ Battery 377th PFAB attending a mid-1945 assembly and displaying a variety of eagle shoulder insignia. *Bob Probst*

Germany from the Ruhr, due to their assignment as a SAARF reaction force. 501st troops were billeted in the SS barracks at Berchtesgaden for a brief time before being sent to Krimml, Austria. The 501st Regiment was inactivated at the end of July 1945, having never been an official TO&E member of the 101st Airborne Division. The 506th PIR was afforded that distinction in 1945, but the 501st would not be an official part of the division until its postwar reactivation in 1956.

When the 501st was disbanded, some troopers with high points were sent back to the states, while the rest were divided among other divisional subunits that still existed, such as the 327th GIR and 502nd and 506th PIRs. Later in the summer, the 101st

Where the Iron Curtain was raised, at the border separating the newly defined Soviet Union from the rest of Austria, Capt. James Nye, a survivor who had been with the 506th PIR since Camp Toccoa in 1942, shook hands with a Russian soldier in mid-1945. *James Nye*

The farthest flung town occupied by any 101st Airborne unit in Austria was the village of Worth, Austria, at the southeast corner of the division occupation area. This town was only a few miles from the northern border of Italy and featured a camp for displaced persons (DPs) from all over eastern Europe. The town was administered by Lt. Donald E. Zahn and his 2nd Platoon of C/506 PIR. *Donald E. Zahn*

While in Austria in 1945, all members of the division who had participated in the major campaigns of Normandy, Holland, and Bastogne were awarded Bronze Star Medals (in addition to any that individuals had been awarded for individual actions previously). Among the recipients who got the BSM at war's end to add to their total "points," and thus accelerate their eligibility for discharge, was Col. Robert S. Sink of the 506th PIR, shown wearing the medal. Sink was the only original regimental commander in the 101st to remain in command from beginning to end. *Donald E. Zahn*

Airborne Division moved to new billets in France, east of Paris, in the Auxerre-Joigny area. The division was transported to this region by 40 & 8 boxcars again, this time with shelves installed inside each boxcar to facilitate sleeping. Thus, the division was in France when the Japanese surrender was announced in August. This welcome news meant that the 101st would not be redeployed to the Far East as many individuals had expected with some trepidation.

Practice jumps for pay were made in September for those wishing to remain on jump status, with the extra money that went along with that status. A divisional jump school had been established at Reims, and volunteers from many of the traditionally glider-borne units were sent there to earn their jump wings. After an initial decision to retain the 101st Airborne as a postwar division, the army high command reversed its decision and designated the 82nd Airborne for that role instead. This was done in

VJ Day, August 8, 1945. 101st Airborne troopers on leave in London paraded in the street at Piccadilly (in front of the Red Cross Rainbow Corners center), knowing that they would soon sail home rather than sail to the Pacific theatre for more combat. *Signal Corps, Wierzbowski collection via Nadine Wierzbowski-Field*

A final obstacle before returning to the states was a practice parachute jump made in September 1945 at Joigny and Auxerre, France, to keep the parachutists entitled to jump pay. Some individuals opted out, feeling that they didn't want to risk getting killed so close to discharge after surviving combat in numerous campaigns. This photo shows a trooper of HQ 2/506 PIR awaiting the pay jump on a pile of chest pack reserve parachutes. *R. Lonnee Photo via Mike Bigalke*

Three battalion executive officers of the 506th PIR posed in 1945 after VE Day. Left to right: Maj. Knut Raudstein, former CO of C/506, Maj. R. D. Winters, former CO of E/506, and Maj. Fred "Andy" Anderson, former platoon leader of 3/506th. Andy Anderson always walked with his head cocked to the side. After returning to the states, he married the widow of his former battalion commander. *Anita Rex Martin*

The parachute maintenance company made this giant banner to be hung from the side of the *Queen Mary* when surviving members of the 101st Airborne sailed home. This was not to be, because the veterans came home in piecemeal lots according to the point system. This showing in Auxerre, France, was the last time the banner was seen until it was hung in front of a movie theatre in St. Louis, Missouri, for the premiere of the MGM film *Battleground* in 1950. After that, the banner again mysteriously disappeared into the woodwork and its current whereabouts are unknown. *Signal Corps, Wierzbowski collection via Nadine Wierzbowski-Field*

Survivors of the Battle of Bastogne, including Screaming Eagles and members of assorted infantry, armored, artillery, Air Corps, and combat engineer units, were selected to return to the United States before VJ Day to tour war production plants and stimulate production by telling of their combat experiences. This photo was taken at a Douglas aircraft plant in California. *Tuttle family*

Among those on the war production tour, was Cpl. Newman Tuttle from Minnesota, a veteran of the regimental S-2 section of the 502nd PIR. The lucky GIs who were selected for this tour had the opportunity to meet many starlets and celebrities, including George Burns and Gracie Allen, pictured with Tuttle. *Tuttle family*

recognition of the longer combat record of the 82nd, which had joined combat in 1943 in North Africa. As a result, the 82nd would get the honor of parading on Fifth Avenue in New York City in early 1946, while survivors of the 101st Airborne came back piecemeal over a period of many months, as various individuals reached the requisite eighty-five points.

The returning Screaming Eagles wore the patches of whatever units they sailed back with on their left shoulder, and now wore the eagle on their right shoulder as a former combat unit. The 101st Airborne Division was officially inactivated in France on November 30, 1945. A basic training unit at Camp Breckinridge, Kentucky, would wear the eagle head and black shield (minus the Airborne tab) from 1948 to 1952, supplying many replacements to various combat units in Korea. But the 101st was not reactivated as an airborne division until 1956. With subsequent combat in Vietnam, as well as Operation Desert Storm and Operation Iraqi Freedom, the 101st Airborne Division carries on in the new millennium as one of the most famous units in the U.S. Army.

APPENDIX

SCREAMING EAGLES WORLD WAR II ARTIFACTS

I began collecting 101st Airborne memorabilia in 1970, at a time when only a handful of serious collectors in North America were pursuing U.S. Airborne as a specialty. Even with a very finite supply of original items, the low demand kept prices affordable, with little significant fluctuation for almost three decades.

When the film *Saving Private Ryan* was released in 1997, it awakened the entire post–World War II populace to exploring Dad's or Grandpa's war and spawned a gigantic group of nouveau collectors and World War II reenactors with a newfound appreciation of elite units—particularly the World War II paratrooper. Following closely behind *SPR* was the HBO miniseries *Band of Brothers*, detailing the history of a single 101st Airborne parachute infantry company in World War II—just one of forty-five such companies in the Screaming Eagle Division.

The impact of these films and their resultant rennaissance of interest in World War II is many faceted, but in terms of collecting, the following consequences have been noted:

1. Prices for World War II U.S. Airborne memorabilia have multiplied since 1997. This includes uniforms, insignia, headgear, parachutes, gadgets and weapons.

Cpl. Glen A. Derber of the HQ 2/501 LMG platoon shows off his PRESTO M2 knife, made by *G. Schrade* in Bridgeport, Connecticut. This was the other type of M2 widely issued to 101st Airborne troopers in World War II. *Derber*

FORM B LOADING MANIFEST (PARACHUTE)

Exercise/Operation _____ Date __2 June 1944__

Details of Aircraft

Squadron: _____ A/C Type: C-47A Tail No. 42-_____ Chalk No. 30

Aircrew

Phillips, Oscar R., O-684747, 2nd Lt., Pilot
Ingle, Roy A., O-804670, 2nd Lt., Co-Pilot
Hagen, Orlien M., 1702558, T/Sgt., Crew Chief
Primmer, Richard M., 16136735, Sgt., Radio Operator

FORM B LOADING MANIFEST (PARACHUTE)

FORM B LOADING MANIFEST (PARACHUTE)

Exercise/Operation __Neptune__

AC No. (Tail No.) _____ Chalk No. __30__

PERSONNEL

Drop Order	Army Serial Number	Rank	Name and Initials	Remarks
1		1st Lt.	Parsons, Rodney T.	
2		2/Lt.	Lohn, William T.	
3		Pfc.	Lochbihler, Karl D.	Para.
4		Pvt.	Poley, Joseph R.	"
5		Pvt.	Mercer, Donald V.	"
6		Pvt.	Will, Francis F.	"
7		Pfc.	Innes, Aloysius J.	
8		Pfc.	Stephens, William H.	
9		Pvt.	Moran, Alvil J.	
10		Pvt.	Willson, Daniel	
11		Pvt.	Marcinkus, Stanley A.	
12		Pvt.	Prosser, James	
13		Pfc.	Scott, Oxley T.	
14		Pvt.	Nichols, Earl	
15		Pfc.	Sherry, Arthur L.	Mort. No.
16	34087403	Pfc.	Golden, Winfield	
17	17003513	Pvt.	Marsh, John J.	
18				
19				
20				

CONTAINERS

Rack No.	Type	Contents (general)	Gross Weight	Parachute Color/Light
A-1		.30 MG, Ammo.		
		Mortar Amm.		
		Mortar Amm.		
A-4				
A-5		LMG Reserve Ammo	175	6-4 Blue

Inspection completed: _____ Signed __Rodney T. Parsons__

FORM B LOADING MANIFEST (PARACHUTE) (Continued)

Here is an original Form B "loading manifest" for a stick of jumpers from Company D/502 PIR, for the D-Day jump. The jumpmaster was Lt. Rodney Parsons. As of this writing, no U.S. government archive has been found to contain these manifests, and the only surviving examples have been found in the possession of individual jumpmasters who retained a copy. *Author's collection via Rodney Parsons*

2. Profiteers and fraud artists have entered the picture, thus contaminating a field that was previously mostly immune to reproductions; fraudulent put-togethers (aka "hump jobs," derived from Humpty-Dumpty, who was "put together again") have proliferated, particularly with uniforms and helmets.

3. With sales on the Internet and thousands of novice buyers, a rather hideous situation has evolved, wherein unscrupulous profiteers continuously feed this insatiable market, by putting together "named" uniforms from generic components and fraudulently repainting steel helmets with unit stencils and other markings. Meanwhile, reproductions of insignia have continually improved, until some reproductions are so close to the originals that they occasionally deceive even long-time collectors.

There is still a way to avoid paying hundreds or even thousands of dollars for a reproduction insignia, which is actually worth about $5. This author has presented detailed images of known original eagle patch variants, regimental pocket patches, unit colored wing oval backgrounds, and distinctive insignia (DIs), which are small metal subunit pins worn on overseas caps, lapels, and officer epaulettes. Because these

Lt. Derwood Cann of G/506 was an ex-boxer who was a perfect officer in every way. His peers in the states referred to him as "Colonel Sink's fair-haired boy." While stationed at Ft. Bragg, North Carolina, after World War II, Cann was challenged by Capt. Ronald Speirs, who did not know that Cann was a trained boxer. After being knocked down repeatedly and bloodied, Speirs (who started the contest with a sucker punch), acknowledged defeat. In this studio portrait, Lieutenant Cann is clearly wearing a Type 8 eagle patch—these were made by a company in New York in 1943, just before the 101st Airborne Division sailed to the United Kingdom. Enough were made to provide every officer in the division with two patches, intended for wear on the dress uniforms. As with the later escape kits, only leftovers trickled down to the enlisted ranks, and no examples have been seen in the effects of 501st officers who did not sail to the United Kindgom in the initial voyage, instead joining the division in January 1944. Two variants of the basic Type 8 have been seen, both having aluminum thread highlights on the Airborne letters as well as on the feathers of the eagle. One highlighted type faces left and the other faces right, for wear on the former (combat) unit shoulder. In recent years, collectors have paid incredible sums for an original Type 8 shoulder patch. It has become the single most popular World War II–era variant of the Screaming Eagle SSI.
Kurt Barickman collection

insignia from the author's collection were obtained directly from World War II veterans, decades before the current insane prices took effect, one can simply compare a prospective purchase to the examples illustrated in this chapter, or those on the author's website: (www.101airborneww2.com). It is questionable if original World War II variants other than those shown do exist. Most of the documented variants have been illustrated in my various works, and the number of variants was few with the exception of eagle patches. If your planned purchase does not look exactly like the one illustrated, do not buy it. It is as simple as that.

When you buy a pocket patch or wing oval that looks different, you might be getting an obscure and ultra-rare variant, but the odds are against it being original.

If, however, you just want a similar-looking representative facsimile, go ahead and buy it—but be sure you pay an appropriate low amount for what you are getting and

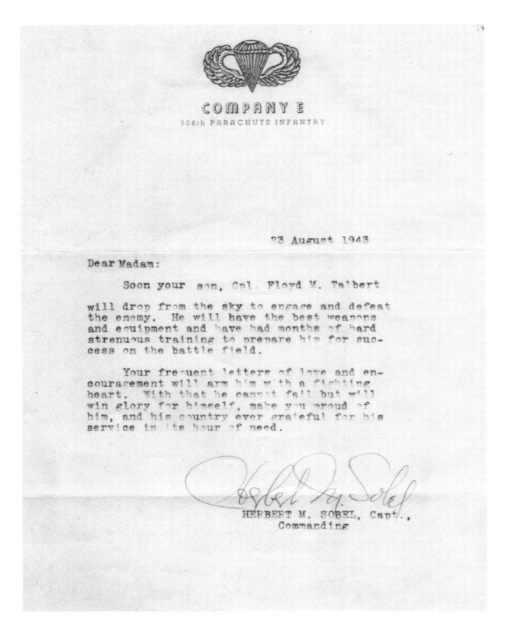

COMPANY E
506th PARACHUTE INFANTRY

23 August 1943

Dear Madam:

Soon your son, Cpl. Floyd M. Talbert will drop from the sky to engage and defeat the enemy. He will have the best weapons and equipment and have had months of hard strenuous training to prepare him for success on the battle field.

Your frequent letters of love and encouragement will arm him with a fighting heart. With that he cannot fail but will win glory for himself, make you proud of him, and his country ever grateful for his service in its hour of need.

HERBERT M. SOBEL, Capt.,
Commanding

This is the letter mailed to the mother of every paratrooper in E/506th PIR, by the famous commander, Capt. Herbert Sobel, shortly before the 506th departed for the United Kingdom to prepare for the D-Day Invasion. This example was sent to the mother of Floyd "Tab" Talbert. *Bob Talbert 11th ABD*

know that what you are getting is a reproduction. This fact needs to be made very clear: there is nothing wrong with dealers selling copies of rare items to fill a gap in a collection or to equip an army of reenactors. The problem comes when modern-made copies are misrepresented by the seller and sold for original or even near-original prices. Some dealers unwittingly pass on hump jobs or outright reproductions in good faith, not knowing that somebody in the chain of ownership before them has humped a uniform together or skillfully repainted a helmet. Sadly, the World War II Airborne collectibles market is already out of control and one can only imagine what will pass for original in another hundred years, when World War II is as distant as the American Civil War is now.

Many of the nouveau collectors want a quick fix and a bargain price, and they are simply not willing to believe what four decades of research in this field has told me. They become victims of their own wishful thinking in their haste and falsely predicated self-assurance that they know enough, after a few short years of investigating the market. Sadly, World War II U.S. Airborne collecting in the new millennium has become a veritable minefield and has gone the same way that Third Reich militaria started going back in the 1960s. As soon as public demand drove the prices up to levels comparable to the Nazi items, the demand soon outdistanced the finite supply and creatures of the deep, smelling blood in the waters, closed in to devour unsuspecting victims.

Here is some food for collector consideration:

First, when you consider buying a unit-painted helmet, assume it is fake. About 99 percent of the 101st World War II painted helmets offered for sale on eBay and by most militaria dealers were painted after World War II, usually within the past few years. Artistic craftsmen with some knowledge and a lot of skill can apply stencils, age them and the total paint job, and make the result look more than sixty years old and rather believable. Usually, however, the shape and size of the stencils is not correct when compared to vintage World War II photos. Never overlook comparisons to those

continued on page 247

506th Parachute Infantry
Airborne Command
United States Army
Camp Toccoa, Ga.

This is to Certify That:

1st Lieut. RICHARD D. WINTERS, O-1286582

has satisfactorily completed the prescribed course in Parachute Packing, Ground Training, and Jumping from a plane in flight. He is, therefore, entitled to be rated from this date, __9-30-42__, as a qualified Parachutist.

R+ Sink

Colonel, 506th Prcht. Inf.
Commanding

It seems that approximately fifteen different American insignia companies manufactured Screaming Eagle patches for the U.S. Army on government contracts during World War II. Each company had its own design style, with subtle differences in the details of eye, beak, tongue, and Airborne tab. The author has typed the basic manufacturer variants by numbers with number one being the most widely encountered type and higher numbers indicate increasing rarity. Illustrated are the nine most commonly seen World War II versions. *Author's collection*

Parachutist qualification certificate. This example was awarded to Lt. Richard D. Winters upon completion of five parachute jumps at Camp Toccoa, Georgia, in 1942. You will notice the date, the unit-specific heading, and the notation about Camp Toccoa. A single C-47 aircraft was commandeered to drop officers of the 506th for only a limited time, then the practice was discontinued and none of the 506th's enlisted personnel qualified at Toccoa. The remainder of Sink's regiment went to the Parachute School (TPS) at Ft. Benning, Georgia, to make their qualifying jumps in December 1942. Other variants of the jump school graduation certificate have been noted. Certificates for the earliest classes were printed horizontally on a similar-size paper, while the next version was done vertically, like this example, but with the heading "The Infantry School." The next and most common version reads "The Parachute School" on a vertical presentation. That version continued to be issued until the end of World War II. A vertical variation, with the title "101st Airborne Division Parachute Jumping School" at the top, was awarded to troopers who attended the jump school at Chilton Foliat, England. *Jake Powers collection*

Letterheads from regimental stationery of the 501st, 502nd, and 506th PIRs. Other variants of the 502nd and 506th designs exist without the regimental HQ designation. The 501st design shown was the only one used. It is interesting to note that none of the designs shown were officially approved by the office of heraldry in Washington, D.C., yet these nonapproved designs were actually widely displayed, worn, and used, due to their popularity with commanders and troops alike. *Author's collection*

501ST PARACHUTE INFANTRY

HEADQUARTERS 502D PARACHUTE INFANTRY
OFFICE OF THE REGIMENTAL COMMANDER

REGIMENTAL HEADQUARTERS
506th Parachute Infantry
UNITED STATES ARMY

At top, the 501st PIR pocket patch—except for some custom-made examples, there was no other mass-produced variant of this patch in World War II. Relatives of the real chief Geronimo had granted permission for use of his name in the unit insignia with pride. At lower left, is the fully embroidered bat wings and skull "widowmaker" patch of the 502nd PIR, known as the 5-0-Deuce. This is the most commonly seen version; two other main World War II vintage manufacturer variants of this are known. The 502nd regimental wing background, a powder blue wool disc with a darker blue cotton thread border, was seldom worn and is quite rare. Another version of the 502nd oval existed in World War II that is a twill oval, dark blue in the center, with a lighter blue cotton thread border around the outer edge. At lower right is the 506th PIR pocket patch (U.S. variant). The British version has a cotton embroidered design on a base of blue wool flannel. The U.S. version has a merrowed edge, rare among World War II patches. The fully embroidered wing background shown here had a very limited run made in late 1942. *Author's collection*

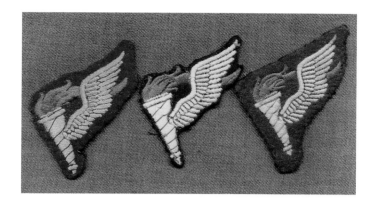

Three original examples of the Pathfinder wing, worn on the lower left sleeve. All original World War II vintage examples of this insignia, coming from 101st veterans, were Theatre-made. The examples shown above have the typical British wool felt base with the design embroidered onto the surface with cotton thread. The examples illustrated all have 101st veteran provenance; slight design and manufacturing variances suggest that a number of different British companies were making them. Although the examples at far left and far right look the same at first glance, the way the lines are configured on the stem of the torch suggests different lots, if not different makers. The reverse of the center example clearly suggests a different manufacturer. These "wings" were issued on a rectangular piece of felt, and the individual who sewed it on had to decide how to trim around the design. You can see that some individuals cropped the border quite close to the design, while others left a larger border. The right example even has a "corner" at the top left that was usually rounded off a lot closer to the flame. Other documented examples exist with a black background rather than the purplish-blue examples illustrated here. *Author's collection*

Four views of a rigger modified M42 jumpsuit with provenance to a lieutenant of 2/506 PIR. Note the canvas patches added to reinforce the lower jacket pockets, the trouser cargo pockets, the elbows, and the knees. Also notice the tie-downs attached to the inseam of each thigh to wrap around the leg cargo pockets to reduce load shifting while jumping or running. This suit was never impregnated with CC-2, an antigas chemical, so it is doubtful that it was worn in the Normandy Invasion. Our model, Vance McMorries, is a grandson of the legendary Melton "Tex" McMorries of G/501 PIR.

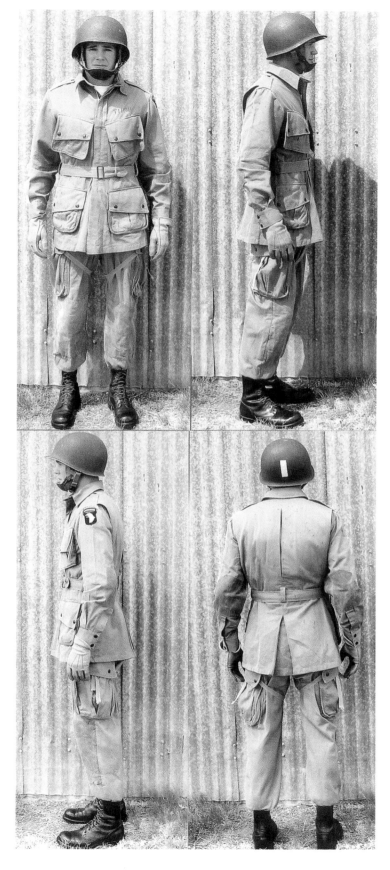

The Normandy M42 jumpsuit of Capt. Cecil L. Simmons, who at the time was CO of H/502 PIR. This example is rigger modified as well as impregnated with CC-2 against poison gas. Note the captain's rank bars sewn to each shoulder. The jacket lost some of its original color because Captain Simmons stirred it in a Calvados pot full of boiling water in an attempt to remove some of the foul-smelling impregnation chemical. When the author acquired this suit in 1989, it still smelled strongly of CC-2, but the odor has since diminished to almost nothing.

Like painted helmets, most Normandy-worn jumpsuits were turned in to endure an unknown fate. All but a few have simply vanished. As a result, documented and impregnated examples are so rare that they could be considered national treasures. *Author's collection*

A detail of the insignia on Simmons's Normandy jump jacket. Note the Type V white-tongued eagle patch (evidence that this was one of the types actually used in the invasion), the white name tape, and the rank bars, all hand-sewn to the jacket.

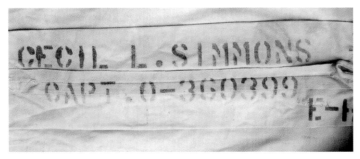

Stenciled along the vertical seam inside Simmons's jacket are his name, rank, and serial number. Similar markings have been noted on two other jackets in private collections, with Normandy-era provenance to 3/502.

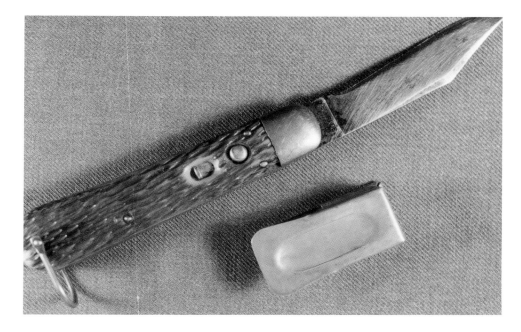

A detail of how the khaki web tape used to construct the leg ties was folded near the center and inserted into a spot at mid-thigh where the seam was opened and the crimped section tucked inside and sewn. Many troopers cut the leg ties off, considering them a nuisance more than a necessity. Original modified trousers have been observed with the crimped corner still sewn into the inseam and the rest of the ties clipped off.

The cricket and M2 jump knife issued to Pfc. Donald E. Zahn for the Normandy Invasion. The jump knife is marked *Schrade Cut. Co.*, and is one of the two commonly seen variants issued to 101st Airborne troopers in World War II. *Author's collection*

A grouping of World War II Airborne gadgets from Capt. Joseph Pangerl of IPW Team No. 1, 502nd PIR. Included is his jump wing with two stars for combat jumps in Normandy and Holland (note the vertical positioning), a compass of the type issued in the escape kits, a brass dog tag listing his home address and next of kin, a standard cricket signaling device, and a hacksaw blade with protective cardboard cover (also from an escape kit). *Author's collection via Pangerl*

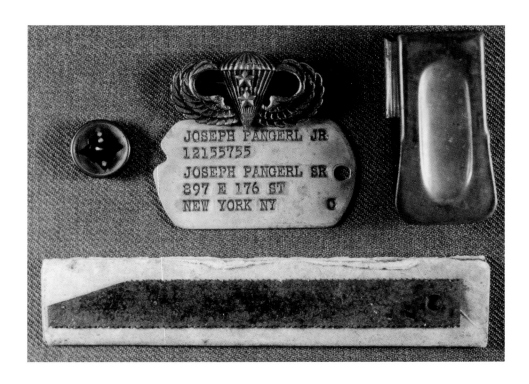

A miscellaneous grouping of airborne equipment. Included from top are a parachutist's first aid kit, a gas detection arm brassard, a corps of engineers black metal compass in creosote-treated canvas belt pouch, an M3 trench knife in M6 leather scabbard, a sound-powered field telephone (used on outposts where silence was crucial for survival), a pair of horsehide leather gloves, an M2 switchblade jump knife, a cricket, a French–English phrase book, an Acme "Thunderer" whistle, an Elgin wristwatch, dog tags on a plastic braided cord attached to a leather carrying pouch, and a pair of M36 suspenders, still adjusted to the original owner (Capt. Fred Hancock of C/502), with period-applied white medical tape. *Author's collection*

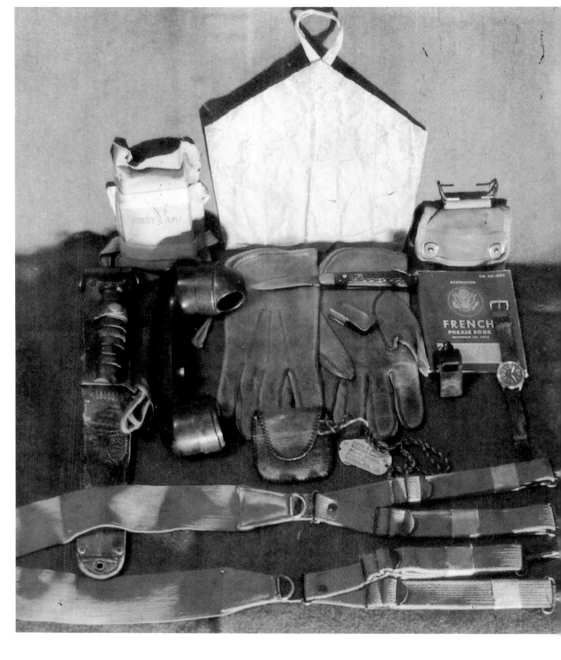

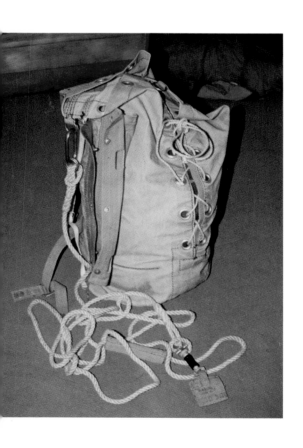

A British leg bag designed to carry heavy equipment such as mortars, light machine guns, bipods, tripods, base plates, large radio sets, and even bazookas. These were designed to be worn attached to the leg while jumping and, ideally, could be released to dangle below the jumper after the parachute opened so he wouldn't land with the weight attached to his leg. Little or no instruction was provided with these bags, nor did the 101st troopers get a chance to experiment with them on practice jumps. In addition, pilots were flying far faster than normal jump speeds and the vast majority of bags worn on the D-Day jump were ripped off the jumpers' legs in midair, never to be seen again. A newer, American-designed leg bag was developed by Master Sgt. Joseph Lanci of the 501st Riggers in time for the Holland jump. That design met with a much higher success rate. *Dennis Davies collection*

This is among the rarest accessories used by the World War II 101st Airborne Division—an Air Corps–style ammunition pouch, some of which were mass produced, which is evidenced by their presence in a quartermaster catalog. Parachute riggers also made cruder versions in various sizes, causing some collectors to refer to these as "rigger pouches." This is technically incorrect, as not all of them were made by riggers. Unit orders before D-Day refer to them as "Air Corps–style ammunition pouches," which is evidently the correct terminology. This specimen was found in the hayloft of a stone barn in Normandy in 2004, still loaded with several eight-round clips of M1 ammunition (all black-tipped AP). This is the only original example I've located in thirty-six years of collecting 101st memorabilia. Like painted helmets, these were worn and used only overseas, and most of the surviving examples have been found on Norman farms. After Normandy, these pouches were recalled, and they all but disappeared from use within the 101st division. The main complaint was that after one clip was removed, the remaining ones rattled around inside the pouch, as it does not contain dividers to hold the clips in place. To say these pouches are rare is an understatement. They have been widely reproduced with the copies varying greatly in quality of construction.

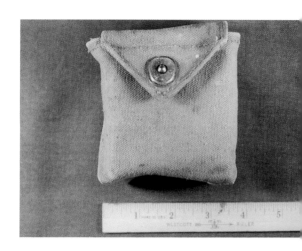

Continued from page 240

old photos, because they are the best guide there is. In general, the playing card symbols on real 101st painted helmets are a lot cruder and less elaborate in detail than most of the recent repaints. They are also a lot smaller in total size. What collectors don't realize is how rare original 101st painted helmets are. I have only obtained four of them directly from veterans after meeting and interviewing almost one thousand World War II 101st veterans over a thirty-eight-year time period. The reason the helmets are so rare is

that they were all collected after the war ended, while the unit was still in Europe, and they were either scrapped or given to a banana republic. Only a tiny percentage of individuals (mostly officers) were able to avoid turning in their helmet, with a few men bringing them back though the hospitals when wounded. Most of the originals in existence were picked up off battlefields by European farmers, and most of those examples reside in European collections. Very few painted helmets made it back to the United States in the hands of 101st Airborne vets—by my estimate, about one in two hundred vets managed to keep his.

Second, when buying a named uniform, with a World War II trooper's name attributed to it, beware. Again, assume it is not what it is represented to be. More than 90 percent of the "named" World War II 101st Airborne uniforms offered for sale by Internet dealers and

Cutting notches on equipment was a common practice, and parachute jumps were sometimes recorded by notching the edge of a leather chin cup. Examples of kills recorded with notches on firearms and trench knives have also been observed. This photo shows how Lt. Col. Benjamin Weisberg of the 377th PFAB recorded fifteen practice jumps and one combat jump Normandy on the rear edge of his jump helmet liner. *Author's collection*

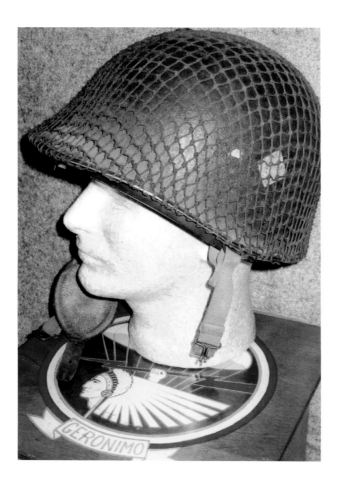

An original painted example of a 3/501 helmet brought out through the hospitals from Holland by a member of HQ 3/501. This D-bale helmet was issued to the trooper at Camp Toccoa in late 1942 and saw service in Normandy. The British-made small mesh net was applied to it for the Holland mission. The liner bears no unit stencils, suggesting that at least in this battalion, liner stencils were not added until later in the war. Note the relatively small size of the diamond stencil on the side of the steel pot. Most reenactors and repro helmet painters make the mistake of painting the stencils far too large. Although not all were this small, scrutiny of period photos indicates that stencils were seldom as large as most twenty-first-century helmet painters make them. *Author's collection*

other militaria dealers, are not what they are represented to be. Unprincipled dealers have obtained World War II unit rosters, and they can easily pluck the name of an individual from it (preferably a deceased individual), then attribute that name to a hump-job uniform. Think about it: take a generic Eisenhower jacket, worth maybe $100, add jump wings, a CIB, ribbons, shoulder patches, a presidential unit citation, overseas bars, maybe some rank chevrons, and top it off with a laundry number, consisting of the alleged owner's initial of last name and last four digits of his serial number. If the dealer is lucky enough to get a photo of this individual (usually a weak, fourth-generation copy), it adds to the credibility of the offering. Just because of this (fake and contrived) provenance, with an investment of about $300, the dealer sells the jacket for well over $1,000 because the unwary buyer has no way of disproving the seller's claim of who the jacket originally belonged to.

An experienced collector in this field might spot some technical errors in what is on such a uniform. Perhaps the eagle SSI is of a type that was not made until the 1950s or later. Perhaps there is an impossible number of campaign stars on the ETO ribbon or the number of overseas bars is wrong. Many of the fakers are knowledgeable but not quite smart enough. They might deceive the average buyer with a hump job that does not deceive me. Sadly, the only safe way to obtain a named uniform is directly from the veteran himself or from his immediate family. While some named uniforms have been in old-time collections for decades, even some of those have proven to be hump jobs. Also, as stated previously, even reputable dealers have been unknowingly guilty of passing along skillfully done hump jobs, because if all the components on the jacket are original, there is no way of determining if the jacket ever really belonged to the alleged original owner. If a humped-together jacket was done perfectly, with no mistakes and using all original components, it would be impossible for even a collector as experienced as myself to prove it was not authentic.

Bottom line: a jacket either really belonged to a World War II paratrooper or it did not. A generic hump job is only worth the sum of its parts and not a penny more.

Fake provenance is just a tool used by fraud artists to drive up the sale price. Efforts to make the sale convincing have even included poor-quality Xeroxes of the alleged original owner wearing an Airborne overseas cap and some exotic item of clothing, such as an A-2 jacket with a regimental pocket patch on the chest. A jacket that comes with such a weak photo should raise red flags immediately. If the jacket was really obtained from the veteran, why isn't it accompanied by something more compelling, such as an original, vintage wartime print of a studio portrait of the owner, or a copy of the vet's discharge, or a set of dog tags, or all of the above?

Also, if the alleged original owner has a common name such as Smith, Jones, Brown, or Johnson, another red flag should go up. With so many troopers having those last names, it effectively creates a smokescreen to camouflage the fact that no such person existed—or maybe it was this guy with a similar name? This element of

continued on page 253

The parachutist's first aid kit was introduced in 1944 in time for the Normandy Invasion and was contained in a tear-open cloth bag, with tie strings attached to facilitate carrying. The most common place to affix the strings was to tie them to the helmet net, but that practice caught on more after Normandy. The kit has also been seen attached to upper arms, belts, ankles, and even a trench knife scabbard—just about anywhere that space presented itself. Illustrated here is a complete, sealed kit along with some exposed contents from another kit, including a cloth tourniquet with metal clip, a Carlisle bandage in cardboard box, and a small lead tube with needle, containing a shot of morphine (in this case, the contents were squeezed out). As originally issued, the lead morphine tube came in a rectangular yellow cardboard box. *Author's collection*

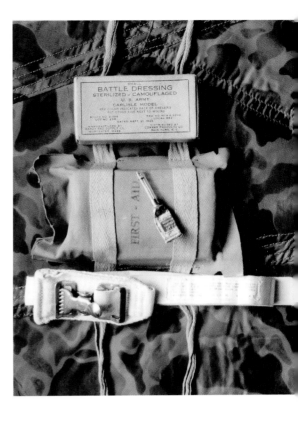

The assault-type gas mask was also new at the time of D-Day, replacing the previous type of gas mask that had a long hose connecting the face mask to a sizeable filter carried in a pouch on the user's side. This new mask had a smaller filter attached to the left cheek of the mask itself, providing size economy. The entire gadget fit in a rubberized bag with straps that could be affixed to the waist, the thigh, or even the ankle of a parachutist. Inside the bag was a paper shoulder brassard, chemically treated to turn red in the presence of poison gas— this was a warning to get the mask on. Some units made wearing the arm brassard mandatory, including elements of the 502nd PIR. Most of the 501st companies did not require wearing the gas detection brassard, and because many troopers threw their gas mask away after landing in enemy territory, many Geronimos never even looked in their gas mask bag prior to tossing it, brassard and all. Because of this many 501st veterans, when interviewed, stated they had never worn or even seen a gas brassard. *Author's collection*

The famous Eisenhower-style "Ike" jackets were issued to replace the former Class A four-pocket blouses in April 1945, while the 101st Airborne was moving through southern Germany toward Berchtesgaden. This example bears the typical insignia and decorations commonly worn by members of the 101st Division. Of interest are the green, horizontal bars under each rank chevron on the sleeves indicating "combat leadership." The original owner of this jacket, Staff Sgt. Walter Kawalek, was a platoon sergeant in D/502 PIR. *Author's collection*

Most paratrooper officers acquired a leather flight jacket via channels other than standard issue. The A2 jacket as shown here was a prized status symbol and could be worn with or without extra adornments such as divisional or regimental insignia, name tags, and so on. The example illustrated was worn by 1st Lt. Albert Hassenzahl, the CO of C/506 PIR and is adorned with a Type 1 eagle SSI, a nonapproved 506th "para dice" pocket patch, and a nametag printed in black paint on a leather strip. *Author's collection*

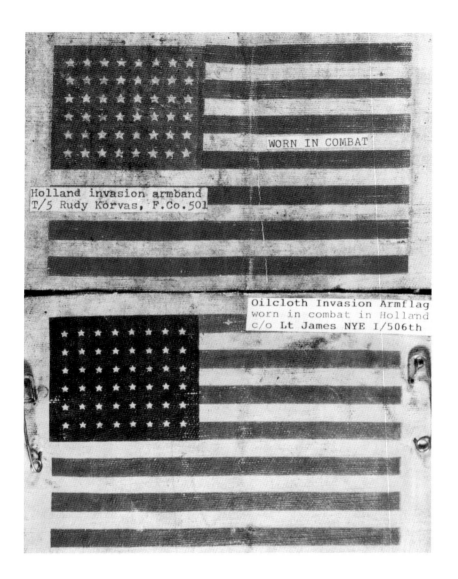

WORN IN COMBAT

Holland invasion armband
T/5 Rudy Korvas, F.Co.501

Oilcloth Invasion Armflag
worn in combat in Holland
c/o Lt James NYE I/506th

Although 101st Airborne troops did not wear arm flag brassards in Normandy (unlike those of the 82nd Airborne), all members of the 101st were required to wear large oilcloth flags into Holland for the Market-Garden campaign in September 1944. Two basic manufacturers' variations have been noted by the author in surviving examples acquired from 101st Airborne veterans. The more common type, illustrated at top, bore larger white stars on a medium blue background. The less common style, below, bore smaller stars on a dark blue field. The second type was evidently issued to the 506th PIR as well as the 321st GFAB, although both styles have been found in the effects of members of those units. Photo evidence suggests that infantry troopers removed these brassards within a few days after landing in enemy territory, probably because they made excellent and highly visible targets for enemy riflemen. *Author's collection*

This circular sleeve patch, designed for wear on the lower left sleeve was created for the regimental S-2 section of the 502nd PIR, by Capt. Cecil L. Simmons in summer 1944. After Normandy, Simmons briefly commanded regimental HQ/502 and of all the personnel in that company (including communications and demolitions specialists), he considered S-2 (intelligence) to have the most important job. Because of this sentiment, he felt they deserved a special insignia of their own, so he drew this design, incorporating the universal symbol for military intelligence (the sphinx), and the words *wisdom, power* and *silence.* Simmons contracted with a British insignia maker to produce about twenty-five of these patches, but he left RHQ after Lt. Col. Cole's death to become XO of 3rd Battalion. Simmons did return after VE Day, though, to pick up his batch of patches. He offered them for sale to members of the H&H S-2 section for thirty-five cents each in Austria in mid-1945, and he was trying to get approval at divisional level to allow all S-2 personnel in the 101st Airborne to wear the patch, including battalion S-2 sections in all subunits of the division. Before this approval could come about, the division was inactivated in 1945. Few original examples of this patch remain in existence. *Author's collection*

Souvenirs liberated from enemy forces in Normandy. The Luftwaffe officer peaked cap, BYF41 Luger pistol with holster, Fallschirmjager glove, and Luftwaffe-issue wristwatch were all taken from a single German supply officer of the 6th Parachute Regiment on the evening of June 7, 1944, about one mile north of Dead Man's Corner in a field east of the D913 road. Attacking elements of 1/506 were chasing retreating German troops south though the fields when two Germans passed a dirt mound, then doubled back to warn someone inside that their line had been overrun. Cut into the side of this dirt mound was a supply dump containing German rations and ammunition. Crates were piled high on either side of an aisle leading into the mound. Barney Becker (left, inset) followed the two Germans into the supply dump and eradicated both of them with a BAR he had found in a glider at Holdy on D-Day morning. Not realizing that any additional Germans were in the maze of crates, Richard Brinkley (right, inset), Becker's friend, strolled casually into the dump when, suddenly, 9mm bullets began cracking near his head. A German officer armed with a Luger pistol was taking shots at Brinkley from behind the crates, deeper inside the supply dump. Brink waited for the German to show himself again, then hit him with a burst from his Thompson submachine gun. In a hurry to catch up with the attack, Brink quickly stuffed the officer's cap into the cargo pocket of his jump pants, then removed his gloves, pistol, holster, and ring. He wore the ring and watch for years after World War II, but subsequently lost one of the gloves and the ring. The style of the glove confirms that the owner was a German parachutist—his name has not been established. Late that night, 1/506 was withdrawn to Beaumont, where they spent the night. Attacking the same area the next morning, Brinkley wandered into the supply dump and discovered that the ammunition crates had been removed during the hours of darkness, and all that remained were blue cans of mystery meat. The three dead German bodies had also been recovered. Barney Becker received a severe head wound in October 1944 at Opheusden, Holland, and died about fifteen years after World War II ended. *Author's collection via Richard Brinkley*

Continued from page 248

doubt will allow the buyer to remain uncertain as to whether he has been *had,* and the sale goes unchallenged. Even common names can be tracked on unit rosters; the Index of 101st Airborne General Orders contains the names of all members of the division who were ever awarded distinctions including the Combat Infantry Badge (CIB) the Combat Medic's Badge (CMB), Bronze or Silver Star medals, a Purple Heart, and so forth. Most hump-job uniforms come with assurance that the original owner participated in the Normandy Invasion. Although some rosters, such as the Piet Pulles roster from Holland, are mostly complete with few omissions, the names of almost every Normandy participant can be found in his rosters as well as in the divisional G.O. index (available at the National Archives II, College Park, Maryland).

Although some of the con artists will eventually avail themselves of those records to make ever more convincing hump jobs, remember that getting a uniform directly from a veteran or his family (or at least obtaining one that is directly traceable to same, via chain of custody/ownership) is the only reliable way to know your uniform is authentic and original. Be wary of any uniform offered that cannot be traced back through each previous owner directly to the vet—and if that vet is not listed on any rosters, it is cause for another red flag. About 75 percent of the World War II 101st veterans who survived the war have since passed on as I write this, and most hump jobs are attributed as belonging to men who have died since 1945.

The items illustrated in this chapter are all from the author's collection (unless otherwise noted) and can be used as comparisons for determining originality when considering a purchase to add to your collection. Lest anyone feel resentment or jealousy from this, please do not interpret this presentation as a message of "my stuff is real and yours is fake" because that is not my intention. Please remember that my collection results from devoting nearly four decades of my life to World War II 101st Airborne research. I'm sharing these

Souvenirs of the 17th SS Panzergrenadier Division, taken June 13, 1944, south of Carentan, France. The divisional cuff band, bearing the name of the patron saint of the 17th SS Division, was liberated along with the single collar tab from an officer at lower right by Sgt. Ed Benecke of A Battery of the 377th PFAB. The pair of *Untersturmfuehrer* (second lieutenant) collar tabs, still mounted on corners cut from a black Panzer uniform, were turned in to IPW Team No. 9 officer Lt. Werner Meier for unit identification purposes by an unknown 501st PIR paratrooper. The owner of the uniform, Lt. Siegfried Held, was blown from his Mk IV StuG by a shell fired by the 81st Airborne AA/AT Battalion, and a trickle of his dried blood can be seen running across the runic lightning flashes. Lieutenant Held was a member of the 17th SS Panzerjager *Abteilung* (tank hunting battalion) and was the only second lieutenant of the attacking force killed that day who could have been dressed in such a uniform. Other anomalies of the insignia are the extra thick aluminum braid around the collar edges and the different style of pip in the center of the rank collar tab. Evidently, Held was a *Standartenoberjunker* (officer candidate), wearing two pips, then after being promoted to a second lieutenant, he added a third pip, acquired from a different source, to upgrade the tab to the appropriate rank. *Author's collection*

Souvenirs from Panzer Battalion 100, which was stationed in the Cotentin on D-Day and was equipped with captured French Renault and Hotchkiss tanks. This unit had a tank park for maintenance and repair at the town of Baupte, which was liberated by Lieutenant Colonel Shanley's 2/508 PIR (82nd Airborne Division) in mid-June. Carl Beck and Robert Johnson, misdropped strays from H/501, joined Shanley's troops in the fighting at Baupte, where Beck liberated the Soldbuch of Walter Gartner, a member of Panzer Battalion 100. Like Lt. Siegfried Held, Gartner is buried in the German military cemetery at Orglandes, France, northwest of St. Mere Eglise. The German ID dog tag for a member of Panzer Battalion 100 was liberated by Capt. Joseph Pangerl of IPW Team No. 1, 502nd PIR, while Harry Plisevich of H/501 cut the blood-soaked front of a black Panzer M43 cap from a corpse that he passed daily, while dug in beyond Carentan in mid-June 1944. Harry noticed that the dead man's whiskers continued to grow for days after his death. *Author's collection*

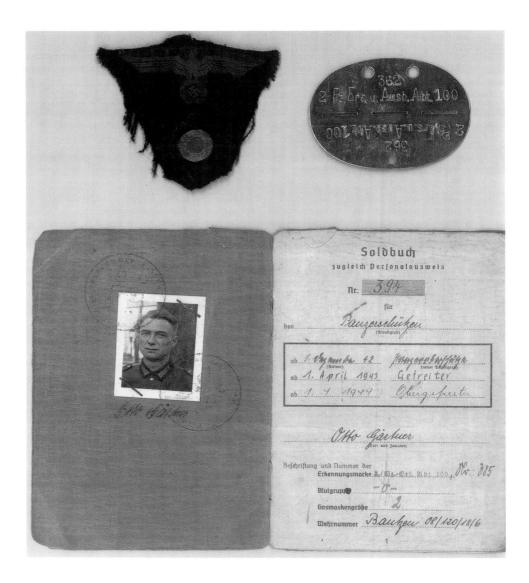

images of samples from that collection as a learning device, and nothing more.

I'm sorry that the introduction to this chapter had to be little more than a warning and cautionary message, but human greed and lack of scruples has created the current situation. I don't envision it getting any better with the passing of time. Do not contribute to it by falling prey to your own wishful thinking. Be wary of any item offered at a bargain price and remember that a high price is also no guarantee of originality or authenticity. I've seen some mighty high-priced trash change hands lately, so *buyer beware*. In this hobby, paranoia is a virtue.

If you are a collector, there is still some original material out there to find, but remember that only about 20 percent of the total being offered is real and that percentage is continually shrinking. Most of the good stuff that has come out of the woodwork is already in collections. Get to know the experienced collectors, keep an open mind, and learn through as much hands-on experience with original artifacts as possible. Good luck and preserve history to honor the troopers who wore and liberated the artifacts in question—that is the number one objective.

BIBLIOGRAPHY

Bando, Mark. *101st Airborne: The Screaming Eagles at Normandy.* St. Paul, Minn.: Zenith Press, 2001.

———. *Vanguard of the Crusade,* Bedford, Penn.: Aegis/Aberjona Press, 2003.

———. *Avenging Eagles-Forbidden Tales of the 101st Airborne in WWII,* Bando publishing, Detroit, Mich., 2006.

Burgett, Donald R. *Currahee.* New York: Houghton-Mifflin, 1967.

———. *The Road to Arnhem.* Novato, Calif.: Presidio Press, 1999.

———. *Seven Roads to Hell.* Novato, Calif.: Presidio Press, 1999.

———. *Beyond the Rhine.* Novato, Calif.: Presidio Press, 2001.

Isby, David. *Fighting in Normandy: The German Army from D-Day to Villers-Bocage.* Mechanicsburg, Penn.: Stackpole Books, 2001.

Koskimaki, George. *D-Day with the Screaming Eagles.* New York: Vantage Press, 1970.

———. *Hell's Highway.* Sweetwater, Tenn.: 101st Airborne Division Assn., 1989.

———. *The Battered Bastards of Bastogne.* Sweetwater, Tenn.: 101st Airborne Division Assn., 1994.

Mackenzie, Fred. *The Men of Bastogne.* Ace Books, 1968.

Marshall, Samuel, and Lyman Atwood. *Night Drop.* New York: Little, Brown, and Company, 1962.

———. *Battle at Best.* New York: William Morrow, 1964.

———. *Bastogne: The First Eight Days.* Infantry Journal Press, 1946.

Rapport, Leonard, and Arthur Northwood. *Rendezvous with Destiny.* Infantry Journal Press, 1948.

INDEX

3 6054 00136 4947

PUBLIC LIBRARY OF
SELMA & DALLAS CTY
1103 SELMA AVENUE
SELMA, AL 36701